T0070255

The Vedic Astrologer

The Spiritual Legacy of the Nakshatras

The Secret History of the Vedas, Volume IV

James Kalomiris

BALBOA.PRESS
A DIVISION OF HAY HOUSE

Copyright © 2019 James Kalomiris.

All rights reserved. No part of this book may be used or reproduced by any means, graphic, electronic, or mechanical, including photocopying, recording, taping or by any information storage retrieval system without the written permission of the author except in the case of brief quotations embodied in critical articles and reviews.

Balboa Press books may be ordered through booksellers or by contacting:

Balboa Press
A Division of Hay House
1663 Liberty Drive
Bloomington, IN 47403
www.balboapress.com
844-682-1282

Because of the dynamic nature of the Internet, any web addresses or links contained in this book may have changed since publication and may no longer be valid. The views expressed in this work are solely those of the author and do not necessarily reflect the views of the publisher, and the publisher hereby disclaims any responsibility for them.

The author of this book does not dispense medical advice or prescribe the use of any technique as a form of treatment for physical, emotional, or medical problems without the advice of a physician, either directly or indirectly. The intent of the author is only to offer information of a general nature to help you in your quest for emotional and spiritual well-being. In the event you use any of the information in this book for yourself, which is your constitutional right, the author and the publisher assume no responsibility for your actions.

Any people depicted in stock imagery provided by Getty Images are models, and such images are being used for illustrative purposes only.
Certain stock imagery © Getty Images.

Print information available on the last page.

ISBN: 978-1-9822-2637-4 (sc)
ISBN: 978-1-9822-2638-1 (e)

Balboa Press rev. date: 10/13/2020

DEDICATION

To my children, Kelley and Alex, my inspiration and my reason for being,

and

To Niki, my Flaming Star, my Love, my partner in crime.

TABLE OF CONTENTS

FOREWORD

This is a book of astrology unlike any other. This book presents an entirely new view of astrology — the astrology as conceived by the Vedic astrologer. It attempts to explain the numerous references to all things astronomical and astrological according to the Vedas and explain the true purpose of reading the stars. In the Vedas the purpose of the stellar population was not prognostication, to tell the future, but to guide the worshiper, to provide religious edification of the worshiper in the now and present. Accordingly, this book is not concerned with forecasting into the future. It is as astrology was intended to be — a vehicle of spiritual advancement.

This interpretation is entirely consistent with the Vedas taken as a whole. The Rg Veda is the "Book of Knowledge." The Vedas may be read on several levels and applied to different disciplines. Thus, the Rg Veda may be read as mythology, philosophy, a religious text, as history. As a true Book of Knowledge, the rcs (mantras) in the Rg Veda may be applied to science, physics, astronomy, mathematics, chemistry, alchemy, or, as in this book, astrology. The Vedic astrologer will explain, as far as is possible today given the great antiquity of the Vedas, what the stars, asterisms and planets have to offer the worshiper during the spiritual journey for salvation and liberation.

This book presents an astrological interpretation of the Vedas. In this presentation, the Vedic astrologer will interpret the Vedic forces and energies with reference to an astrological interpretation given in the Vedas, Brahmanas, Aranyakas and Upanishads, but only so much as it offers the spiritual information required for the edification of the worshiper during the spiritual journey. It will also introduce you to two individuals — the

1

Vedic astrologer and, of course, the worshiper. This book will give the Vedic astrologer a forum to explain the true astrology and its application to the worshiper seeking salvation and liberation. Thus, the Vedic astrologer is not so much concerned with the prognostication of future events, or the characteristics of newborns, or personality traits based on the time of birth, or with who is compatible with whom. The Vedic astrologer is concerned with what the Nakshatras (asterisms or lunar mansions) have to teach the worshiper and all sentient beings and how these lessons may be applied to the spiritual journey.

This book is the first part in this journey. The Vedic astrologer intends to release his companion volume, which concerns the Planets, the Zodiac and Equinoxes, and how they influence the worshiper on the spiritual journey.

INTRODUCTION

Dear Reader, you have no idea how brilliant the evening sky looks without the presence of city lights, pollution, evening overcast, or other obstructions, natural or man-made, blocking the view. The evening sky is absolutely dazzling. The stars do not look like little white specks in the sky — instead, they glisten and glow and sparkle. The moon looks so close you feel you can reach out and touch it. And most of all, the Milky Way, barely visible in an evening sky in an urban landscape, is not ill-defined or entirely absent from the celestial cover but has a warm glow. The Milky Way is brilliant, prominent, as if someone splashed a great amount of off-white paint in the firmament. It is therefore easy to understand the ancient Greek myth of how the Milky Way was created. According to Greek legend, the Milky Way was created when Hercules was suckling the breast of a mortal woman when Hera, Zeus' wife, pushed Hercules away, spilling the milk across the evening sky.

This is what the ancients observed when they looked above on the evening sky. Without any environmental impediments, that is exactly how the Milky Way looks, and this is the sky the Rishiis who revealed the rcs (mantras) of the Rg Veda saw. What particularly took the ancients' breath away was how the entire sky appeared to be full of light — stars, comets, the Milky Way, they were all there.

The ancients saw these stellar objects and more. They gazed above all to make sense out of this crowded, dazzling conglomeration of light. The ancients saw stars. From the stars, they saw patterns of stars. They noticed that some of the objects were stationary. They then saw that their positions moved relative to where they were observing. They noticed that the size of these bright spots of light were larger than others. At the same time, they noticed a coincidence between events on earth where they lived and the positions of the stellar objects. With these rudimentary observations, the ancients started to understand the stars, planets, constellations (Nakshatras), and zodiacal houses wherein these planets, Nakshatras and planets resided. The ancients understood that just as the Sun shines during the day, the stars and other astronomical phenomena are a reflection of the Sun's energy.

The marauding armies of Alexander the Great brought with them their learning of matters astronomical and astrological. As a result, Vedic astronomy and astrology was influenced — some would say infected — by outside learning. The Hellene tradition emphasized the micro-management of personal affairs and the ability to predict future conduct or behavioral personality traits. The Vedic tradition had been much different. The Vedic astrologer was concerned with the spiritual and religious guidance and learning that could be obtained from the stellar population. The Vedic astrologer believed that the members of the stellar population could guide that spiritual path. This was the great lesson the Vedic astrologer attempted to obtain from the planets, stars, Nakshatras, zodiacal houses, and the other astronomical and astrological influences. If the stars' lessons had any predictive, elective ability, the overall goal was to enhance the spiritual or religious experience. Thus, among other examples, Orion (Mrghashira) triggered the commencement of the year-long sacrificial rites.

At the same time, the Rishiis wanted to confine the knowledge which could be obtained from the stellar population on a need-to-know basis. For whatever reason, the lessons revealed to the Rishiis were couched in obtuse and obscure language and spoken in symbols. Any given rc of the Rg Veda may be interpreted on several levels. One of those levels is an astrological interpretation.

This work attempts to decipher rcs, stanzas and suktas of the Vedas, Brahmanas and Aranyakas, and find their astrological meaning. In some instances that meaning is readily apparent; in other instances, not. This book remains, then, one of doctrinal interpretation. This book is also intended to be one of spiritual guidance. Let's face it. There is no dearth of material on astrology, or even of Hindu astrology. While the authors are well-meaning, most books miss the point. The aim of astrology in its original sense was not to predict future events or find one's correct mate.

There is and has always been an astrological component to the Vedic dharma. In the post-Vedic periods, after the influence of Hellenism to the Indian sub-continent, Jyotis became associated with predictive astrology. To the worshiper and to the Vedic astrologer, there is indeed a wisdom to the stellar population. That wisdom is not associated with the prediction of modern events or happenings. There is indeed a measure of prognostication from the stellar population. But just as the efforts at achieving siddhis, or supernatural powers, to the yoga practitioner is possible but to be avoided, so is milking the stars to tell the future in present time is a waste of other valuable lessons that may be learned. The yogi masters advise that the achievement of the siddhis are to avoided because they are an unnecessary distraction. In the same way the Vedic astrologer cautions that attempting to tell the future is vulnerable to all manner of quackery and ignores the real lessons that can be obtained from the stellar population.

It is clear from the earliest writings that astrological signs were consulted for spiritual edification. Relevant portions of the Atharva Veda and Tattiriya Brahmana immediately come to mind. However, in order to understand one's spiritual path, one needs to know answers to the most basic questions — How did the Universe Start? How did the Stars come to be? What am I? To what extent, if any, am I "stuff of the Stars"? What if anything do the Stars have for me? What a is there to learn, if anything, from the Stars? These and other questions have been around since humans left their caves and looked around the world and looked up in the sky. Articulated in another way, if the purpose of the transcendent, spiritual life is to transcend the bounds of space and time, those boundaries must first be understood.

This is an astrology manual like no other. It strives to stay true to the earliest writings contained in the Vedas and the emphasis is on the spiritual teachings explained by the stellar population according to the Vedas. It strives not to fall into the trap of predictive astrology. Thus, to the Vedic astrologer, the lessons of the stars resemble nothing of what is now considered "astrology." To understand those lessons we must have a handle on how the stellar population came to be in the first place as understood by the Vedic astrologer.

Creation

The Veda is the "Book of Knowledge." That knowledge includes both spiritual edification, philosophical insights — and knowledge of the universe around us. The Veda tells us the Vedic dharma established the asterisms and placed those asterisms in their respective zodiacal houses. It also describes the stellar paths of the critical asterisms take, their basis, what propels them, and the effect they have on the Vedic astrologer.

In order for the worshiper to receive the wisdom of the stellar population, it must first be understood how and when they came to be. In Vedic literature and scripture there is no dearth of versions of how the universe was created. There are no less than four versions of creation in the Vedas, not considering the well-known Purusa or *Hiranyagarbha* Suktas. These seemingly different versions do not reflect internal inconsistencies. While these versions differ in the specific details, the Vedic Astrologer knows that these are not different, inconsistent versions of the story of creation, but that combined these differing accounts of creation represent different stages in the creation of the universe. They are not different versions of how the Vedic dharma was created. Instead, they are accounts of creation based on specific stages of creation. Taken together, they present a coherent, linear, picture of the evolution of creation is not to be found in any one Sukta, or even in any one portion of a Mandala. Most pieces of this puzzle are found in the Tenth Mandala, albeit in different places. Instead, the Vedic astrologer must piece together a coherent story of the linear evolution of creation in a manner akin to completing a jig-saw puzzle.

Step One: Creation of the Purusa

The Vedic astrologer has identified many steps from the beginning of creation to the Nakshatras and the rest of the Vedic dharma. Granted, creation begins from the presence of the undermined mass of indiscriminate matter. The Vedic astrologer believes all subsequent steps from this mass of indiscriminate matter spring from and depend on the application and influence of three elements, Viraj, Virat, and Purusa:

- From Viraj, the Masculine Principle (RV 10.90.5; BU 4.2.3), the Purusa was born. (RV 10.90.5; TA 3.12.5.)
- From Purusa, Virat, the Feminine Principle (RV 10.90.5; AV 9.10.24), was born. (RV 10.90.5; TA 3.12.5.)
- Having seen Viraj, Purusa created the Past and the Future. (TS, 3.3.5.3.)

This is the "stellar stuff" of the cosmos, the phrase Carl Sagan was so fond of saying. The evolutionary process begins with an absolute mutual self-identification of the Viraj, the Masculine Principle, and ends with the emergence of the Purusa. Purusa will be instrumental to the formulation of the Nakshatras, because in Purusa the Nakshatras derive their discriminative powers and strengths. The Purusa contains the elements which make the Nakshatras so important to the worshiper:

- Consciousness.
- Creation. Virat, the Feminine Principle, is the omnipresent intelligence which manifests itself in and which causes the appearance of diversity in the Vedic dharma. *(https://en.wikipedia. org/wiki/Purusha_Sukta.)* The Veda expresses these creational powers in symbols. That symbol is the Purusa in its representative capacity as the Bull, the principle of Regeneration. (RV 10.5.7.)
- Sacrifice, *yajna.* There are some words which do not convey their full meaning in English and must be described in the original wording. Sacrifice, *yajna,* is one such word. The English word conveys the image of ritualistic offerings of animal or human flesh to the greater deity or deities, but yajna is so much more than that. Yajna is properly a principle that runs throughout the Vedic dharma. On a very general level it is exemplified by a give-and-take process. In this process, one object is given (sacrificed) so that another object may continue in existence. On the individual level, it is where the worshiper offers the body, mind and spirit, to receive a spiritual endowment in aid of the spiritual journey. From the standpoint of the Nakshatras, it is where a spiritual endowment is given so that the worshiper may receive it in the spiritual journey. The common denominator throughout is that there is two-prong,

complementary movement constituting a unitary whole. This is *yajna*, and its elements will be seen herein in the movements of Saman, the Life Force (prana), and finally the Nakshatras.

These are the most elemental building blocks to the creation of the Nakshatras. They are indeed instrumental in the operation of the Vedic dharma. Classically, they can be considered the "first principles." Purusa, the epitome of these first principles, eventually became established in the asterisms, the Nakshatras, as manifested in the Vedic forces and energies. ...

But the Vedic astrologer is getting ahead of the story. The process begin at the very beginning. It is well-known that before the appearance of the cosmos there was the great mass of indiscriminate darkness, not existence and not non-existence. (RV 10.129.1) The Vedic astrologer, piecing together this great cosmic jigsaw puzzle, with a little from here and a little from there, believes the material universe, including, of course, the stellar population, evolved in a very linear, straightforward, manner.

Even before this period of indiscriminate darkness, however, there was Viraj. Viraj is the recurring cycles of indiscriminate darkness. (AV 8.9.7; 8.10.11; 19.6.9.) You will notice, Dear Reader, that the Vedic astrologer states that Viraj is the *"cycles"* of indiscriminate darkness. There were actually many periods of this indiscriminate darkness. The Vedas do not tell us, or does the Vedic astrologer dare guess, for how long, or how many periods of this darkness occurred, or whether there were one or many cycles of this indiscriminate darkness, because it is impossible to accurately say. That there was in reality more than one cycle of indiscriminate darkness is almost certain, as a close reading of the Viraj reveals. Indeed, the very starting point of the current cycle of indiscriminate darkness is open to interpretation. It can be described as a straightforward period of darkness upon darkness enveloped by more darkness.

It can also be described as the envelopment of darkness engineered by Vrtra. So central is the struggle between Indra and Vrtra is to the story of creation in the Veda, that it can also be stated with certainty that this very initial period of darkness differs essentially from the period of darkness described in RV 10.129.1. That period of darkness intermixed existence with non-existence. When this secret was revealed to the Rishiis, they could have revealed this condition with *sat* and *asat*. But they did not, because indiscriminate cycles of indiscriminate darkness represented by Viraj, prior to the period described in RV 10.129.1, were more dark and more indiscriminate. The Rishiis thus revealed this very early condition of the cosmos with different words. RV 6.24.5 speaks of a period when "What is" (*adya/*) was undifferentiated from "What is not." (*anya/d*). Monier Williams defines "*yad*" as "What is" but also as the Purusa. In this prior, very primitive, stage of evolution, consistent with RV 6.24.5, Indra transformed *anya/d*, What is not, to *adya/*, what is, setting the stage for the current period of indiscriminate darkness between *sat* and *asat*. The creation of the Purusa, the Vedic astrologer concludes, is what is meant by Indra recovering the "light" when Vrtra is subdued. This, through the Vedic force of Indra, was performed at a critical point in the evolution of the universe. The Vedic powers of Indra executed this conversion to "what was" perpetually and continually, and it continues to this very day. Indra converted this dead mass of matter (*anayad*) into existence (*adya/*)(RV 6.24.5) through the intense heat of *Tapas*. (RV 10.190.1.)

You've probably noticed, Dear Reader, the juxtaposition of *adya – yad* and *sat – asat*. From the very beginning the Two-Dimensional Universe existed in this manner of juxtaposition. (JUB 1.53.1.) Further development was needed. In a bit later the Vedic astrologer will introduce you to Saman and how it played its part in the development. For the moment, however, the Purusa will step back. There really is no need for the Purusa to act on its own, since the wheels have been set in motion. The Purusa, however, will appear again.

Step Two: Existence and Non-Existence is Separated

For our purposes now, however, the period of existence and non-existence begins the current cycle of evolution, and it likes this:

- In this current cycle of indiscriminate darkness, as in the others, there was neither existence nor non-existence, nor was there movement, yet Waters covered everything and was an umbrella to a fathomless abyss. (RV 10.129.1.)

- There was neither Life nor Death, nor the division of Day and Night, yet during this period the One began its first breath due to its own inherent power (*svadha*). (RV 10.129.2.)
- In this period, darkness enveloped an inner darkness. The Waters which were present were without mental awareness. (RV 10.129.3.)
- In this ocean without mental awareness Desire (*kama*) arose. (RV 1.129.4.)
- Then the seed (*retas*) of mind (*Manas*) arose. (RV 1.129.4.)
- From the Seed of Mind sprung the Purusa, who assumed the Vedic powers of Agni. (RV 10.5.7.)
- From the Forces of Wisdom, the purposeful impulsion (*pratishya*) and the connection of the heart and mind (*manisha*) produced existence which sprang (*bandhum*) from the mass of non-existence. (RV 10.72.3; 10.129.4.)
- The existential bases of the Vedic dharma (*Satya*) was born from non-existence (*asat*). (RV 10.5.7; 10.72.2.)

While these existential bases had been created, they had not taken shape into the Two-, Three-, Five-, and Seven-Dimensional Universes we now know. The Vedic force of Agni thereupon was transformed into the "Bull," the Purusa, the principle of regeneration which guaranteed further existence of these universes:

- At that point, the Vedic force of Agni transforms that which "was not" (*a/sac*) and converts it to "what was (*sac*)." (RV 10.5.7.)
- The Vedic force of Agni, through the Purusa, assumed the qualities of existence (*sac*). (RV 10.7.5.)

At this point, matter is brought into being, but this is inert matter, lacked the breath of life or vitality which could permit this newly formed matter to flourish. The evolutionary process was still at a very elemental basis.

Step Three: Appearance of the Golden Seed, *Hiranyagarbha* and the Reappearance of the Purusa

At this primitive level, there emerged an Overseer, and that Overseer was the Golden Seed, *hiranyagarbha*.

- The Golden Seed was born from the undefined, shapeless, and jelly-like material of the indiscriminate mass existing at the beginning of creation. (AU, 1.3.)
- The death of Vrtra allowed the emergence of the Cosmic Egg, the Seed containing the potentiality of what will become the Vedic dharma. Indra with the weapon created by Tvastr releases of the waters which give birth to the *hiranyabarbha*, the cosmic egg. (RV 10.121.7, 8.)
- From the Golden Seed *Rta,* the Natural Oder of the Vedic dharma, and *Satya*, night were born. (RV 10.190.1.)
- The movements of the primordial ocean were thereupon born. (RV 10.190.1.)
- From the movements of that ocean the time divisions were born, giving rise to the occurrence of days and nights, which presided over their procession. (RV 10.190.2)
- The Golden Seed (*hiranyagarbha*), which was carried by the great Ocean, upheld the earth and heaven. (RV 10.121.1.)
- The Golden Seed (*hiranyagarbha*) supplied the dynamism behind the Universal Soul (*Atman*) and the powers behind the Vedic dynamic forces and astral powers. (RV 10.121.2.)
- The Golden Seed (*hiranyagarbha*) gave birth to Agni, then Prajapati, then gave the breath of life to the dynamic Vedic forces and energies. (RV 10.121.4.)
- The Creator, the *hiranyagarbha*, made heaven and earth, the Sun and the Moon, the midworld and the Svar (world of light). (RV 10.190.3. RV 10.190.3.)
- The Golden Seed (*hiranyagarbha*), became the sole lord of every creature. (RV 1.121.1.)
- The Golden Seed (*hiranyagarbha*) presided over the Life Force of cosmos and became the lord of the Two-Dimensional Universe,

the material universe, and indeed is lorded over the four existential levels of the Two-, Three-, Five-, and Seven-Dimension Universes. (RV 10.121.3.)

The Golden Seed, the *hiranyagarbha*, is so called for a good reason. As the Seed, it contains the potentiality and potential forms of everything in creation. That specific form, however, is subtle, and the material basis for everything in creation must evolve according to its own internal design, or *svadha*. The *hiranyagarbha*, then, provides the subtle outline for everything in creation, and from there the Purusa continues that work.

- Purusa came to consist in both the gross and subtle aspects of the natural order. The Two-Dimensional material universe represented one-quarter of the Purusa, and the Three-, Five-, and Seven-Dimension Universes represented the subtle aspects of the natural order (Vedic dharma). (RV 10.90.3.)
- Purusa then became the sacrifice (*yajna*), placed on grass (*barhi*) and consecrated, sprinkled, with water. (RV 10.90.7; VS 31.9; TA 3.12.8.)

Purusa contemplated the energies and forces in the Vedic dharma. These energies and forces coalesced to establish the powers of the Vedic forces and Nakshatras. (SA, 10.1.) Purusa thereupon installed the powers inherent in the asterisms:

- Purusa empowers the asterism of Krittika and the zodiacal houses of Mesa (Aries) and Vrsabha (Taurus). This enables the Lunar Mansion of Agni to dispense the spiritual endowments of the inner secrets and essence of yajna, Sacrifice, and divine response. Thereby, Purusa articulated Speech and Speech articulated the Fire of Agni, which delighted the earth, which delights everything that covers the earth, and everything which was, is and will be so delighted. (SA, 10.2.) The fire of Agni thus became Purusa's speech. (SA 10.2.) Indeed, the fire of Agni became the Bull, the regenerative principle of Purusa. (RV 10.5.7.)

- Purusa empowers the asterism of Rohini in conjunction with the zodiacal house of Vrsabha (Taurus). This power would later in the evolution of the Vedic dharma to enable the Vedic force of Prajapati to dispense the spiritual endowments of the inner secrets and essence of *yajna*, Sacrifice, and divine response.

- Purusa establishes the energy empowering the asterism of Mrgashirsha to dispense the spiritual endowment of Bliss to the worshiper. The mind is Soma, the Moon. Soma is empowered by the Nakshatra Mrgashirsha with the zodiacal houses of Mesa (Aries) and Vrsabha (Taurus). Purusa delights Mind (Soma) and the Mind (Soma) delights the Moon, which delights in turn, the Naksastra (Stellar constellations), and in tandem, the months, half-months, days and nights, the seasons, the year, and everything which is under the Year, and everything which was, is and will be so delighted. (SA, 10.5.)

- Purusa empowers the asterism of Ardra in conjunction with the zodiacal house of Mithuna (Gemini). This power would later in the evolution of the Vedic dharma enable the Vedic force of Rudra to dispense the spiritual endowment of *Sam,* union, conjunction.

- Purusa empowers Punavasu in conjunction with the zodiacal houses of Mithuna (Gemini) and Karkata (Cancer). This power would later in the evolution of the Vedic dharma enable the Vedic force of Aditi to dispense the spiritual endowment of *Sunrta,* "true speech," which are any words, speech or articulation which furthers any Words of the understanding of *Rta,* the Vedic dharma.

- Purusa empowers the asterism of Pushya and the zodiacal house of Karkata (Cancer). This power would later in the evolution of the Vedic dharma enable the Vedic force of Brhaspati to dispense the spiritual endowment of Beauty.

- Purusa empowers the power of the asterism of Ashlasha and the zodiacal house Karkata (Cancer). This power would later in the evolution of the Vedic dharma enable the Vedic force of the Nagas to dispense the spiritual endowment of *Bhanu,* the shining rays of Light. Purusa so configured this asterism that would emit this ray of light containing the individual wisdom and inspiration of each of the asterisms.

- Purusa empowers the asterism of Magha to work in conjunction with the power of and the zodiacal house of Simha (Leo). This power would later in the evolution of the Vedic dharma enable the Vedic force of the ptrs, or forefathers or ancestors, to dispense the spiritual endowment of *Ayana*, guide for the worshiper to follow the right conduct during the spiritual journey.
- Purusa empowers the asterism of Purva Phalguni to work in conjunction with the power of and the zodiacal house of Simha (Leo). This power would later in the evolution of the Vedic dharma enable the Vedic force of Bhaga to dispense the spiritual endowment of Good Works.
- Purusa empowers the asterism of Uttara Phalguni to work in conjunction with the power of and the zodiacal houses of Kanya (Virgo). This power would later in the evolution of the Vedic dharma enable the Vedic force of Aryaman to dispense the spiritual endowment of dispense the spiritual endowment of Good Works.
- Purusa empowers its Eye, Savitr, the Sun. Purusa delights eye and eye delights Savitr, the Sun, which is empowers Savitr through the asterism of Hasta and the zodiacal house of Kanya (Virgo) to dispense the spiritual endowment of Bliss. They, in turn, delight the sky, everything covered by the sky, and everything which was, is and will be so delighted. (SA, 10.4.)
- Purusa establishes the energy empowering the breath of the Lunar house of Indra. (SA, 10.3.) This is manifested in all the Nakshatras in which Indra participates. Purusa establishes in the Nakshatra of Chitra and zodiacal houses of Kanya (Virgo) and Tula (Libra), the spiritual endowment of Bliss. Purusa establishes in the Nakshatra of Vasakra (Scorpio), again in the zodiacal house of Mithuna (Gemini), the spiritual endowment of *radha*, spiritual Increase. Purusa establishes in the Nakshatra of Jyestra, zodiacal house of Vasakra (Scorpio), the spiritual endowment of Happiness. Purusa provides the Breath and the breath sustains the Lunar house of Indra, which conveys this breath to the akasha (ether), which delights everything that consists in akasha (ether), and everything which was, is and will be so delighted. (SA, 10.3.)

- Purusa empowers the asterism of Svasti (Srati) to work in conjunction with the power of and the zodiacal house of Tula (Libra). This power would later in the evolution of the Vedic dharma to enable the Vedic force of Vayu to dispense the spiritual endowment of *Sukha*, which is the sense of profound spiritual fulfillment and happiness

- Purusa empowers the asterism of Anuradha to work in conjunction with the power of and the zodiacal house of Tula (Libra). This power would later in the evolution of the Vedic dharma to enable the Vedic force of Mitra to dispense the spiritual endowment of Response.

- Purusa empowers the asterism of Mula to work in conjunction with the power of and the zodiacal house of Dhanus (Saggitarius). This power would later in the evolution of the Vedic dharma enable the Vedic force of Nirrti to dispense the spiritual endowment of *Amrtra*, which is the Eternal, Undying Principle.

- Purusa empowers the asterism of Purva Ashada to work in conjunction with the power of and the zodiacal house of Dhanus (Saggitarius). This power would later in the evolution of the Vedic dharma enable the Vedic force of Apas to dispense the spiritual endowment of Food, *Anna*.

- Purusa empowers the asterism of Uttara Ashada to work in conjunction with the power of and the zodiacal house of Dhanus (Saggitarius). This power would later in the evolution of the Vedic dharma enable the Vedic force of the Visvedevas, the collective Vedic forces, to dispense the spiritual endowment of Strength.

- Purusa empowers the asterism of Abhijit to work in conjunction with the power of and the zodiacal house of Makara (Capricorn). This power would later in the evolution of the Vedic dharma enable the Vedic force of Brahma to dispense the spiritual endowment of *Punya*, the offering at the Sacrifice.

- Purusa empowers the asterism of Sravna to work in conjunction with the power of and the zodiacal house of Makara (Capricorn). This power would later in the evolution of the Vedic dharma enable the Vedic force of Visnu to dispense the spiritual endowment of Nourishment.

- Purusa empowers the asterism of Dhanishta to work in conjunction with the power of and the zodiacal houses of Makara (Capricorn) and Kumba (Aquarius). This power would later in the evolution of the Vedic dharma to enable the Vedic force of the Vasus to dispense the spiritual endowment of Nourishment.

- Purusa establishes the energy empowering Varuna, the Lord Protector of the very inner essence of the Vedic dharma, the Waters. (SA, 10.7.) The Waters is the Purusa's seed. (SA, 10.1.) Purusa delights in its seed and the seed delights the waters and Varuna, Lord Protector of the Vedic dharma. Varuna is empowered by the asterism of Shatabhisha and the zodiacal house of Kumba (Aquarius), which delight the rivers (the symbol of Consciousness), which delight the ocean (the symbol of the absolute Self, the Atman), which delights whatever is covered by the ocean, and everything which was, is and will be so delighted. (SA, 10.7.)

- Purusa empowers the asterism of Purva Bhadrapada to work in conjunction with the power of and the zodiacal houses of Mina (Pisces) and Kumba (Aquarius). This power would later in the evolution of the Vedic dharma enable the Vedic force of Ajikapada to dispense the spiritual endowment of Protection.

- Purusa empowers the asterism of Uttara Bhadrapada to work in conjunction with the power of and the zodiacal house of Mina (Pisces). This power would later in the evolution of the Vedic dharma enable the Vedic force of Ahir Budhyana to dispense the spiritual endowment of *susarma*, Protection.

- Purusa empowers the asterism of Asvini to work in conjunction with the power of and the zodiacal house of Mesa (Aries). This power would later in the evolution of the Vedic dharma enable the Vedic force of the Asvins to dispense the spiritual endowment of *Bhaga*, enjoyment.

- Purusa empowers the asterism of Bharani to work in conjunction with the power of and the zodiacal house of Mina (Pisces). This power would later in the evolution of the Vedic dharma enable the Vedic force of Yama to dispense the spiritual endowment of spiritual riches.

Purusa also contributes to the inner fabric of the Vedic dharma. Purusa establishes the energy empowering the *disha*, the subtle networks of laser energy beams permeating the Vedic dharma, about which the Vedic astrologer will explain later. Purusa delights the ears and the ears delight the quarters (disha), which delight the intermediate quarters, and everything which was, is and will be so delighted. (SA, 10.6.)

Mostly, Purusa establishes these powers in the Vedic forces and energies. The actual integration of those powers will follow soon in the evolution of the Vedic dharma. At this point the Rishiis revealed the basis of all Samkhya philosophy to describe the Purusa making contact with Prakrti to describe the moment when the breath of life was infused to inert matter to create the Vital Life force in the Vedic dharma. From the upward movement of Pure Consciousness inert matter acquired the spark of life and the material world was born. (RV 10.72.4.) This journey of Consciousness begins from the top down.

Step Four: A Fork in the Creational Road

From this moment creation takes two potential trajectories and travels in two directions. One is the individual direction, where the subtle basis of the microcosm is described. The other, two, the subtle basis of the macrocosm. At some point these trajectories will converge, meeting to create the material world. We are concerned with and the Vedic astrologer will describe how the microcosm came to be. While it concerns the microcosm life in the material world, if you will it has bearing on the formation of the macrocosm wherein reside the stellar population.

Step Five: Creation, Subtly and Individually

The individual trajectory according to Samkhya applies to this evolutionary task:

- Purusa, pure consciousness makes contact with the gunas, the subtle basis for matter. It is at that point that when it makes contact with Purusa, the universal consciousness, and makes this contact, or is "conjoined," that Prakrti, primordial, inert, matter, is transformed into living, breathing, organic, matter. (SK, 20.)

17

- From *Prakrti* arises *Mahat* (intellect, *Buddhi*), and from *Mahat* arises *Ahamkara* (ego, self-identification). (SK, 22.) *Ahamkara* contains sattvic, tamasic, and rajasic aspects.
- From the sattvic aspect of *Ahamkara* arises these eleven categories: The senses of cognition: Mind; Cognition, Hearing, Touching, Seeing, Tasting, Smelling; and the senses of action: Speaking, Gasping, Moving, Excreting, and Procreating. (SK 24, 25.)
- From the tamasic aspect of Ahamkara arises the subtle elements: Sound, Touch, Form, Taste, and Smell. (SK 26.)

From the ego, Manas, the mind, and the attributes and qualities of contained in the sense objects, arise. (S.K., 22, 24.) One of the millions of these sense objects include the Nakshatras and the other members of the stellar population. There will be more on the stages subsequent to this step of evolution later.

The ego presides over the sattvic mental operations of the *Indriyas*. It is at this stage that the mind of the Vedic astrologer is able to perceive all that around it in the world through the ten *Indriyas*: the Five Sense organs (*Jnanendriyas*) and Five Organs of action. (*Karmendriyas*.) Prana drives the ten *Indriyas*: Prana is the source of energy that operates the ten *Indriyas*. (*http://www.awaken.com/2018/09/process-of-kundalini-awakening-part-i-2/*.) There are five *Karmendriyas* or instruments of actions, which are elimination, procreation, motion, grasping and speaking. There are five *Jnanendriyas* or cognitive senses, which are smelling, tasting, seeing, touching, and hearing. These ten operate through the chakras and receive their power from the Prana.

This is admittedly a truncated version of the evolution of prana in the Samkhya system. We want to know only as much as will permit us to understand how the asterisms, Nakshatras and other members of the stellar population came to be in the beginning. What the Nakshatras do in conjunction with the gunas will be explained later in this book. We still, however, do not know how or by what process the stars were formed. At this point, Samkhya explains how prana arose and how it operates in the Vedic dharma. To understand how the asterisms, Nakshatras and other members of the stellar population arose, we need to start from an unlikely place, only to return back to the prana in the Vedic astrologer.

Step Five: Creation of the Nakshatras (Asterisms)

First came the establishment of the powers of the Nakshatras and then came the creation of the Nakshatras themselves. Curiously, the process of star creation began with the act of giving found in the sacrificial process. The Nakshatras were created from the combined elements of breath, prana, and time. Time, indeed, created the sky, the earth, and all that is contained therein. (AV 19.53.5.) So as with all the other objects in creation, and so is with Space. The level of creation is still on a very subtle level. The only thing which has been established is a temporal sequence of events, and even that establishment is at a fine, very subtle level. How do we arrive at the presence of heavenly bodies from here? This process begins with sacrificial giving, then proceeds to the presence of prana in the human organism and ends in the stars.

- Purusa consists of both the gross and subtle aspects of *Rta*, the Vedic dharma, and created the sacrificial act of giving, which is so important to the Sacrificial Process. (RV 10.90.8; VS 31.6; TA 3.12.9.)
- These acts of sacrificial giving occasioned by the chanting of the rcs (mantras of the Rg Veda), samans (mantras of the Sama Veda), and chhandas (mantras of the Yajur Veda) of the Vedas gave rise to the creation. (RV 10.90.9.)
- In particular, *sat*, the existence found at the beginning stages of the universe, was the chants of the Sama Veda, the Saman, and Non-existence, *asat*, was the rcs, the chants of the Rg Veda. (JUB, 1.53.1, 2.)
- The saman chant was Mind and breath, and the rc chant was Speech and Exhalation. (JUB, 1.53.2.)
- The rc chant desired sexual union with the saman chant, and when it did so, created the fabric of Time-Space in the Vedic dharma. (JUB, 1.53.2.)
- Further, the acts of sacrificial giving by the recitation of the rcs (mantras of the Rg Veda), samans (mantras of the Sama Veda), and chhandas (mantras of the Yajur Veda) of the Vedas during the sacrifice (*yajna*) give rise to acts of worship which weave out

to the fabric of the universe and weave back. By virtue of these acts of worship, the chanting and recitation of the rcs (mantras of the Rg Veda), samans (mantras of the Sama Veda), and chhandas (mantras of the Yajur Veda) of the Vedas during the sacrifice (*yajna*) cause a constant vibration which literally, physically bends the fabric of the universe by weaving it back and forth across its surface. (RV 10.130.1.)

• In other words, from the subtle element of Sound emitted from the chanting of the rcs (mantras of the Rg Veda), samans (mantras of the Sama Veda), and chhandas (mantras of the Yajur Veda) the gross element of Space-Time is created. The very material substance of the universe is born.

Notice the dynamics in RV 10.130.1. The sounds of the chanting rcs (mantras of the Rg Veda), samans (mantras of the Sama Veda), and chhandas (mantras of the Yajur Veda) of the Vedas during the sacrifice (*yajna*) literally mold the fabric of space-time. The alterations work on a gross, material, level and on a subtle, intangible level. Materially space-time is altered by the very vibration of the sound waves themselves acting on the fabric of the universe. On an intangible level space-time is altered by the profound power of the revelations of the Rishiis on the Vedic astrologer's mind and soul. The power of the mind on the world around it is great. The siddhis, or supernatural powers in the Yoga Sutras, are predicated on the ability of the focused, concentrated mind to bend the physical laws of physics. All this, of course, had been revealed in the Vedas and is known to the Vedic astrologer:

• The recitation of the rcs (mantras of the Rg Veda), samans (mantras of the Sama Veda), and chhandas (mantras of the Yajur Veda) of the Vedas vibrate the very fabric of the Vedic dharma. From the vibration of these acts of worship the realm of worship was born, as well as the two aspects of Time, the Past and the Future. 10.90.10.)

• In this way the Purusa became this entire universe and everything in it, all of what has been, and what is to be. (RV 10.90.1; TA, 3.12.2.)

There is an essential and very profound symbiosis with breath, sacrifice and the act of physical creation. The Nakshatras are undeniably a major element in the Stellar population, and they are also a function of and originate from the function of Time and Prana, the vital life force permeating all matters in creation. This is demonstrated here:

- In the human organism, a life force is exhibited in the movement of one's life breath from one's heart and going to a spot at thirty-six finger breaths away, in both the out-going and in-going breaths. (T.S., 6.)
- Time is divided by days and nights, months, years, and are measured by the time span that is absorbed within that same thirty-six finger measure. (T.S., 6.)
- On a purely chronometric level, this time span consists of pranas, is measured with one prana equaling four seconds. (SS 1.12; *Surya Siddhanta*, cited in *https: //en.wikipedia.org/wiki/Nakshatra*.)
- According to this measure of prana, fifteen pranas produce one minute. (SS 1.12; *Surya Siddhanta*, cited in *https://en.wikipedia. org/ wiki/ Nakshatra*.)
- 900 pranas make up one hour. (SS 1.12; *Surya Siddhanta*, cited in *https://en. wikipedia.org/wiki/Nakshatra*.)
- There are 21,000 pranas in one day. (900 pranas make up one hour. (SS 1.12; *Surya Siddhanta*, cited in *https://en.wikipedia. org/ wiki/ Nakshatra*.) This is the origin of a teaching mentioned in too many Vedic and Hindu yoga texts that there are 21,000 breaths, or some close approximation thereof, in one day. The Tantraloka, for example, states the number of breaths as 21,600. (T.L., 6.132-234.)
- On a subtle level, prana, the vital breath, is measured in finger lengths. A finger length is measured by the distance between the heart and the nose during the practice of pranayama. (T.L., 6.114.)

Each finger length contains sixty days (*tithis*) or two dates (*sankrantis*), yielding the following measurements (T.S., 6).

sixty days (tithis)	two months
thirty days	one month (*sankranti*)
360 days	one year

Lunar and celestial dates are measured the same way. The Stellar Population is measured in units and subunits of prana.

- Lunar dates are measured by their own standard of finger length, where the lunar days is considered as the in-breath and the lunar night is considered as the out-breath. (T.S., 6.)
- These two-week periods are divided into dark and shining fortnights, the first represented by the moon and considered in the form of apana, the out-breath, which informs the second fortnight, represented by the sun and considered in the form of prana, the in-breath. (T.S., 6.)
- There is an oscillating in-and-out movement in prana. The sun takes over the actions of prana (the in-breath) is in the form of consciousness and thereupon fills the moon with apana, the out-breath. (T.S., 6.)
- The month, again, is measured by finger length, where the in-breath is considered as the first two-week period and the out-breath is considered as the second. (T.S., 6.)

Given that these lunar and celestial dates are measured by prana, there must exist self-contained mechanism, like a clock or timepiece, which regulates that prana. This is where Saman comes in the picture

Saman

It is apparent that there is a relationship between this formulation of time and the stellar population. A direct line exists from prana to the Nakshatras and planets to the living organisms below. Now what can possibly be the common denominator between these diverse elements, the Nakshatras (lunar mansions), Time, and prana the Vital Breath?

That answer is Saman.

Saman means many things and implicates several areas of the Vedic universe. The reference to Saman predominates the Chandogya Upanishad, but a precise definition is tantalizingly fleeting. Officially, on the surface level, saman is a type of Vedic chanting. This type of chanting is reserved especially for the Soma sacrifice, and one of the Vedas, the Sama

Veda, consists almost exclusively on the Sama chant. A saman is a chant of a mantra from the Sama Veda. A principal portion of an important Upanishad, the Chandogya, is devoted to the nature of Saman.

Most of all, Saman is balance. (JB, 1.166.) Saman is the state of equipoise, that state where the three gunas, Tamas, Sattva, and Rajas, are in a state of balance. We will shortly see that the actual chanting of the mantras of the Rg Veda, SamaVeda, and Yajur Veda, play a substantial part in bending and transforming the very fabric of time-space in the Vedic dharma to create the shapes and forms of the objects therein. Significantly, Saman, this chanting, creates the Left-and Right-Handed movements which energize this transformation. All of this chanting and movement is made in balance. In Saman all movements and gyrations are made in balance. The chaos in the Two-Dimensional Universe, the material world, is due to its imbalance.

The precise progression from Saman, to prana and to the Nakshatras, and the universe in general, is the result of a gradual arrival towards materiality. Saman begins as a predominately subtle substance, and proceeds to prana, which shares a subtle and material component, which is ultimately reflected in the Nakshatras, and the general universe, which is wholly material. Therefore, Saman has two aspects:

- The gross meaning of the word is associated with the practice of *yajna*.
- The esoteric meaning of saman, developed more fully in later Vedas, is "vital force" a forerunner to "prana," and the cause of creation itself.
- On a deeper level, the esoteric meaning of saman is the correspondence of the expanding and contracting movements of the universe, on the microcosmic and macrocosmic levels, to greater and greater levels of materiality.

The Vedic astrologer understands the mystical significance of Saman and its relationship with prana and the Nakshatras. The Vedic astrologer surmises that the following can be said of Saman:

- Saman serves as the inspiration for the Nakshatras, which are its end product, the sacrificial representation of the Vital Breath, prana, and of all things. At the same time, at one time, given the amazing regularity of observation the Nakshatras did serve as a sort of time piece. Thus stargazing served to keep track of the days and months to properly celebrate sacrifices and observe various rites. (RVJ, 7.)

- On a deeper level the rhythmic cadences of the chanting recited at the sacrifices symbolize the pulse of the cosmos as much as it represents and relies on the upward and downward movements of breath. The entire phenomenon is crystalized by the frequent discussion of Sama.

- On an esoteric level, the sacrifice, is the representation of the universe, with its own movement and sequence of events. *Rta*, the dynamic energy of cosmic order, is sacrifice. *Rta* is reflected in the saman, the hymns and chanting recited during the sacrifice. (RV 1.147.1.) There is a reflexive equivalence between *Rta*, which is in the nature of sacrifice, *yajna*, and saman. (RV 8.25.4.)

Vibration of Saman is the subtle aspect of energy which permeates into and through everything in the world. On a sub-atomic level this vibration is reflected in the movement of atoms, and it is present in the saman, chanting, in the sacrifice. On a divine level, this back-and-forth movement is reflected in the Divine Duality (the Asvins), who assist the power and energy of Divine grace and Knowledge, embodied in Indra, to give rise to the Right-and Left-Handed movements of the universe, which sama is the sacrificial representation. In this way, Sama is responsible for making all objects in the universe visible. (TB, 2.2.8.7.) These Left-and Right-Handed movements are reflected in longitudinal sound waves, the very vibrations of which alter the fabric of the space-time in the universe.

- Saman is the Word. (CU, 1.1.5.) In this sense the Word is the articulation of the universe. This Word is represented by the divine sound, nada, and is grounded from the beginning of the universe's creation. With articulation the indiscriminate mass which existed before the beginning is given form. The evolution from the divine sound to creation is represented by Om, the divine sound, to Saman, the articulation and manifestation of form, the Word.

- Speech, the Word, is the light of prana. (TS, 5.3.2.3.) The movements of sama undulate with the outward and inward breathes of prana while the hymns are chanted or otherwise; sama also travels inward and outward, rhythmically, as the chanter performs the sama song or mantra. The physical manifestation of these expansion/contraction movements are reflected in the physical effects of the sound vibrations of musical notes traveling through the air. In the same way, the upward and downward aspirations of the Sama chant affect the vibration of the air around and about the chanter. We saw how these upward and downward aspirations affected both the inner prana of the chanter and the air around him. Thus the Sama chant creates the environment for both the microcosm, represented by the Saman Chanter, and the macrocosm, the air around him and beyond. That the Tattiriya Samhita would use the phrase "light of prana" is significant here, because it makes the express connection between prana and light, the Nakshatras.

- The interplay between these Right-Handed and Left-Handed movements of sama is esoteric, occult, and unknown to most. (RV 2.27.11.) The esoteric essence of sama is that it represents the expanding and contracting vibrations of the dynamic energies of the universe. The Vedic astrologer considers the Left-Handed movement to be holy and auspicious. The movement from the auspicious to the profane right-handed movement of the material world, and back again, is reflected in the very vibration that permeates to the pith of every substance in the material world.

- On a physical level the vibration in the universe is made in the articulation of the original sacred syllable, OM. At the very creation of each kalpa, the cycle beginning the appearance of the universe, the sacred syllable makes its appearance.

At that moment, the Divine Sound, OM, resonates, and from that sound the Vedas, specifically the teachings of the Rg Veda, is articulated. At that point, the operational mechanism of Sama is born. Sama is the vocal reflection of nada, articulated in the chant recited at the sacrifice, and represents the divine vibration of the universe after its creation and is reflected in all the aspects of that creation. The intricacies of Sama consist of the principle portion of perhaps the most occult and obscure of all Upanishads, the Chandogya Upanishad, where the many manifestations of Sama were thoroughly discussed and explored. Sama, then, is not just the chant at the sacrifice. It is its external reflection. Internally, esoterically, Saman represents the very oscillating vibrations of the universe in its macrocosmic and microcosmic aspects.

These oscillating vibrations are reflected in the worshiper and all other sentient beings as the inward and outward movements of prana, breathing. The Vedic astrologer moreover understands that the Nakshatras and all the other members of the Stellar Population, indeed, the entire Vedic dharma, is a result and a function of these outward (expanding) and inward (contracting) movements of prana. For one, it is evident from these stanzas that the vibrating movements of prana effect alterations in the space-time of the universe. The very fabric is altered, changed by the stanzas. It stands to reason that if the fabric of the universe is changed, so too must the compartments of that universe. The Vedic astrologer understands that these compartments consist of the subtle paths undertaken by the soul in their travels in the sky after death. This is present in the Southern and Northern Paths, as well as the year, and is considered as one movement of prana, the in-breath, prana, considered as the Southern Path, the path of the forefathers, and the Northern Path is considered as the out-breath, apana. (T.S., 6.)

The most notable alteration in the space-time fabric of the universe is the creation of the lunar houses in the Zodiac. The Vedic astrologer understands that the lunar houses are basically the creation of the sound waves produced by the rcs (mantras of the Rg Veda), samans (mantras of the Sama Veda), and chhandas (mantras of the Yajur Veda) of the Vedas during the sacrifice. (*yajna*). The progression from the simple act of breathing to the stars above and life below is surprisingly linear and, no pun intended, breath-taking. Remember what we saw earlier on how the effect of chanting the rcs (mantras of the Rg Veda), samans (mantras of the Sama Veda), and chhandas (mantras of the Yajur Veda) of the Vedas vibrated the very fabric of the Vedic dharma and from the vibration of these acts of worship the realm of worship was born, as well as the two aspects of Time, the Past and the Future? (RV 10.90.10.)

The Nakshatras are the practical results of prana, the Vital Life Force. The Nakshatras are measured by units called prana. This is the same prana which is the principle of the vital life force. Vedic wisdom confirms the system of movement of breathing, the in-breadth and out-breadth, the human organism, the dates, months, and years, and the Nakshatras which follow therefrom, are all one and the same. (T.L., 6.63.) In other words, as above, so is below. The common denominator is prana, the life-giving source of life. The Nakshatras then are no different than the Vedic Astrologer or any other object or organism in the cosmos.

The Nakshatras are the end result of the operation of Vital Life Force, prana, making contact with Time. They, like the Vedic Astrologer, are subject to the strictures of time and space. Indeed, the Nakshatras are the product of Real Time. (SS, 1.11, 12.) Real Time is measured by praana, the Vital Breath or the Vital Life Force, the most basic constituent of the stellar population. (SS 1.11.) Real Time is measured in the following manner:

- Sixty vinaaris produce one naari;
- Sixty naaris make one *ahoratra* (day and night), which is one sidereal day, the measure of time between two sun rises. (Krishna Ramadas, *Ancient Skies and Astronomy Now*, (2013), p. 30.)

The Nakshatras are the physical embodiment of the sidereal day. (Goswami, *Surya Siddanta and Siddanta Siromani* (2007), p. 759.)

- Each of the six finger lengths between the heart and the nose represents the movement of the Sun from one constellation, asterism, to another, beginning at Magha, Virgo, and ending at the Path of the Gods, *uttarayana*, the Vernal Equinox. (T.L., 6.114.)
- The inward movement of breath is considered to begin at the zodiacal house of Makara (Capricorn), and to end at the zodiacal house of Mithuna (Gemini). (T.S., 6.)
- The days and nights generate the zodiacal houses, with the night houses consisting of Aries, Taurus, Gemini, Cancer, Saggitarius

and Capricorn, and the day houses consisting of Leo, Virgo, Libra, Scorpio, Aquarius, and Pisces. (BJ, 1.10, 11.)

- By implication, the outward movement of breath is considered to begin at the zodiacal house of Kumbha (Aquarius), and ends at the house in Karkata (Cancer). (T.S., 6.)
- The in-breath (Sun) is considered as the lunar day and out-breath (Moon) is considered as the lunar night. The meeting of these two movements is called *Sandhya*. (T.L., 6.66.) In this manner the Moon came into being with its respective Nakshatra. (AV 19.19.4.)

The Vedic astrologer knows that creation is a function of Time. Thirty sidereal days make one sidereal month. Because sidereal time is a time scale that is based on the Earth's rate of rotation measured relative to the fixed stars rather than the Sun (*https: //en.wikipedia.org/wiki-/Sidereal_time#*), there are 27 months to a sidereal year. (*https://en.wikipedia.org/wiki /Lunar_month#*.) This is precisely the number of Nakshatras in the stellar sky. Therefore there is an essential bond between the Nakshatras and the very pith and marrow of breath, prana, in the material universe. Of course, these alterations caused by sound waves are not limited to the lunar houses but to the asterisms and planets as well:

- The Nakshatras, as well as Ketu and Rahu, the lunar nodes, are the participants to these days and nights. (T.L., 6.66.)
- 583,200 pranas make up one Nakshatra, or lunar mansion. (*Surya Siddhanta*, cited in *https://en.wikipedia.org/wiki/Nakshatra*.)

The Nakshatras are thus the vessels into which the prana is poured. Saman is the subtle basis for alternating movements, of which the Breath is just one example. The breaths are reflected in vibratory actions, left and right. The vibratory actions go into the creation of the Nakshatras.

Saman, the Expanding and Contracting Movements of the Universe

Saman provides the underpinnings for the mechanics of prana. Prana, in turn, is a reflection of the rhythmic movements of the greater creation. This reflection then bounces back to Sama in the Sacrificial chant. In reality, Saman is the subtle aspect of prana. Prana consists of the mechanical aspect of breathing, and Saman is the subtle foundation of that breathing. The esoteric aspect of Saman, prana and the entire universe is translated into the rhythms of expansion and contraction which pervade the Vedic dharma. These movements are representative of the most basic functions of the universe. As a pragmatic matter, we know from modern astrophysics that the greater cosmos expands and contracts, and we know now that these expansion/contraction movements which occur from the creation and movements of the Stellar population all the way down to the sub-atomic level. To the Vedic astrologer, this was always a known fact.

The interplay between the Right-and Left-Handed movements of saman is esoteric, occult, and unknown to most. (RV 2.27.11.) The esoteric essence of sama is that it represents the expanding and contracting vibrations of the dynamic energies of the universe, through the powers of Conjunction and Unity (Indra) and the active interplay of the worshiper. The Right-and Left-Handed motions of the universe are a reflection of these very same powers in the Vedic forces and energies (divinities).

- The contracting, uniting and conjoining powers of Indra protects all humans from the perils of evil. (RV 8.24.6.)
- The Left-Handed powers of Conjunction and Unity (Indra) brings spiritual blessings. (RV 8.81.6.)
- The contracting powers of Conjunction and Unity (Indra) protect all with the powers of purification (Soma). (RV 8.4.8.)
- The contracting powers of Conjunction and Unity (Indra) bestows spiritual riches after receiving the same. (RV 5.36.4.)
- The Left-Handed powers of the blessing is based on the action of giving. (RV 1.4.22; TS 1.4.22; VYS 8.2.)
- Consciousness, mind and thought are established by the right-handed movement of discernment and is reflected in and a product of the sacrifice itself, which it establishes. (VYV 4.19; 4.23; TS 1.2.5.6-8.)

According to the Pancavimsa Brahmana, there are two movements to the saman chant: Aarohanam, the upward movement of air, and Avarhanam, the downward movement of air. Himkara, Prastava, Adi,

Udgitha, Pratihara, Upadrava, and Nidhana all represent stages of the in-breath and out-breath in the sama chant as explained in the Chandogya Upanishad, which consists of the last seven chapters of the Chandogya Brahmana.

The vibration of Saman is reflected in the Vedic dharma (*Rta*), and that movement is also made in two movements. Those movements are Aarohanam (the upward movement of air) and Avaroham (the downward movement of air). These movements permeate every creature and object in creation. These movements provide the subtle and material energy supplying the Vital Force (prana) of creatures and objects in the Vedic dharma. They are also vibrations from the recitations of the rcs (mantras of the Rg Veda), samans (mantras of the Sama Veda), and chhandas (mantras of the Yajur Veda) of the Vedas which alter and modify the very fabric of the Vedic dharma. The correspondences of these movements to the sama chant are the following: (CU, 2.9.)

Aarohanam-Upward Movement of Air

Saman	Breathing Mechanism
Himkara	Inward Contraction and Stretching of Abdomen
Prastava	Inhalation of Air
Adi	Expansion of Stomach
Uthgita	Last Portion of Inhalation

Avaroham-Downward Movement of Air

Saman	Material Mechanism
Pratihara	First Exhalation of Air
Upadrava	Profuse Exhalation of Air
Nidhana	Last Stage of Exhalation

The downward movement of air is reflected in transverse sound waves which move up and down, as opposed to longitudinal sound waves which move left and right, the vibrations of both movements. This principle of air movement was further developed in the Brahmanas with a concept called Dhur. Dhur is related to Saman and prana and is a measure of the movement of air. The Brahmanas explain the physical, material changes on the material world are produced by the sound waves of these movements of air. It is reflected in the numerous correspondences found in the Rg Veda and the Brahmanas. The equiposition of air not only is intended to signify the equality of the breath while chanting the hymns sung but is a subtle representation of the gunas in equiposition.

This equinity in the movement of air is applied not only to the physical environment but is applied to the worshiper in the movement of breathing when practicing pranayama. This is reflected in the following correspondence with prana as found in the Sadvimsa Brahmana. (SB, 2.2.20 – 25.)

Sama	Dhur	Prana
Himkara	First Dhur	Prana (Down)
Prastava	Second Dhur	Apana
Adi	Third Dhur	Prana (Up)
Udgitha	Fourth Dhur	Vyana
Pratihara	Fifth Dhur	
Upadrava	Sixth Dhur	Udana
Nidhana		

Dhur has been called the "chant of the yoke," the yokes being the breath and retaining of breath. (PB, 14.9.18.) As the yoke it guides and gives direction to the chant, allowing the formational properties of the chant to create the subtle basis of the Vedic dharma.

Dhur is the active element of spoken words, prana, but prana as applied to the saman chant and the operation of Saman. This correspondence is significant, however, because it not only equates the sama chant with the pattern of inhaling and retaining breath, but in further corresponding this air movement to the different stages of prana. The intertwining of prana and sama is intimate and inextricable. Taken to its further implication of prana representing the life energy or vital energy of life, sama is equated with life itself.

Prana corresponds to the ministers administering the Vedic rituals. The following chart, SB, 2.6.5-7.2, assigns the pranas to the following ministrants:

Sacrificer	Apana
Hotr	Prana
Adhvaryu	Apana
Brahman	Vyana
Udgitr	Samana

One such correspondence unites the upward and downward movements of air with the human body and the offerings presented during the sacrifice: (SPB 11.5.2.4.)

Deity, Sacrifice	Body Part	Breath
Prajapati	Mouth	Upward Breath
Samtapaniya Pap	Chest	Kumbaka (retention)
Grhamedhiya Pap	Belly	Foundation
Kraidma Pap	Male Organ	
Offering (puja) to Aditi		Downward Breath

With the proper breathing performed during the sacrifice the worshiper is in tune with the divine forces in the cosmic order. By performing this opening sacrifice to Aditi, the divine force presiding over the Adityas (astrological houses), the worshiper becomes Aditi. (SPB 12.1.3.2.) This is a religious austerity mastered by the Vedic astrologer to which the worshiper aspires.

The Udgitr is the chanter who sings the samans of the Sama Veda. Samana is that position in equipoise which balances the prana and the apana. The samans themselves are sung in different meters. There are four principle meters, Gayatri, containing three padas and eight syllables; Tristubh, containing four padas, and eleven syllables; Jagati, containing four 4 padas, and twelve syllables; and Anustabh, containing four padas, and eight syllables. The significance in this correspondence is that samana serves a regulatory and governing function of prana, and thus occupies a higher position, just as the Sama Veda occupies a higher position among the Vedas in containing the distillation of the Rg Veda's slotras.

The combined operation of Dhur, Saman, and prana, combine to result in the appearance of the physical world. On an individual level this combined action enable the worshiper to perceive the material world. The correspondences show how the meters of saman enable the worshiper to use the senses to perceive the sensible world. (SB, 2.3.7):

Head	Smell	Gayatri
Chest	Sight	Tristubh
Waist	Hearing	Jagati
Feet	Voice	Anustabh

The Vedic chant, Saman, the constituent parts of Saman and other ingredients of chanting all operate together to create the subtle and gross foundation of the Vedic dharma, from the Stellar population, to the worshiper, the sub-atomic particles from which they all comprise. The third column refers to the different meters in which the Rg Vedic hymns are chanted. Gayatri is three padas, or lines of Vedic verse, consisting of eight syllables; tristubh is four padas of eleven syllables; Jagati is four padas of twelve syllables; and anustup, four padas of eight syllables, typical shloka of classical Sanskrit poetry. The anthropomorphic correspondence in this chart refer first the outer surface and then to the sense organs of the microcosmic Purusa. Esoterically, these correspondences provide the explanation of how the sensible universe originated. Prana may be considered the life energy of all subtle and gross objects. The third column referring to the Vedic meters demonstrate the interplay between Saman and prana. It is through the interplay of prana and sama that objects become sensible in the world. (TB, 2.2.8.7.) Sama emits prana at the *yajna*. (SB, 1.3.21.) Sama emits prana with the upward and downward movements of the Sama chant. At the *yajna*, the Udgitr "connects the eye" to the outer world by making two syllables brilliant and connecting them with prana. (Sad. Br., 2.1.45.) Whoever meditates on the Udgitha becomes the possessor of food and the enjoyer of food. (Ch.Up., 3.7.) "Enjoying food" is a coded reference to the sensible and invisible world which is presented before the conscious perceiver as a great feast. This is the explanation given in the Maitrayaniya Upanishad, 4.10:

> "The conscious person exists in the midst of matter. He is the enjoyer because he enjoys the food of matter (Prakriti). Even this individual soul is food for him; its producer is matter. Hence, what is to be enjoyed has three attributes (Gunas). The enjoyer is the person who exists in the midst of matter.
>
> Matter is that which is to be enjoyed. Pleasure, pain, delusion, everything is food. There is no knowledge of the essence (i.e., quality) of the source (matter), when it is not manifest. The manifest is food, and the unmanliest also is food."

In this way, then, through the Sama chant, all objects thereby become sensible. Time was when instead of chanting from memory without a written manuscript of the Vedas in front of the chanter, the Samanya chanted from a written record. There was a need to attribute the written Vedas to divine origin, and so the Rishis developed correspondences to explain their origin. The Satapatha Brahman recites the following correspondences of the syllable count for stanzas found in Vedas. (SPB, 10.3.1.1.) The divine origin of the mantras were then explained, based on the number of syllables found in the stanza.

Metre in Stanza	Syllables in Metres	Divine Source
Gayatri	24	Breath of Prajapati
Ushnih	28	Juice of Prajapati
Anustubh	32	Eye of Prajapati
Brhati	36	Mind of Prajapati
Pankti	40	Ear of Prajapati
Tristubh	44	Generative Breath of Prajapati
Gagati	48	Downward Breath of Prajapati

Note that as the number of syllables increase, so does the quality of bodily function. The correspondence commences with Gayatri (prana) at twenty-four syllables and ends with Gagati, with forty-eight, having at its source the downward breath of Prajapati, or, *Avaroham*, the downward movement of air in Saman. This explains much how the understanding of the metre progressions achieves liberation and salvation. These metre progressions apply to the Vedic dharma, but does it apply to the worshiper in the Vedic path to liberation and salvation? The following chart attempts to answer this question.

Metre	Presiding Deity	Corresponding Body Part
Gayatri	Agni	Head
Ushnih	Savitr	Neck
Brhati	Brhaspati	Spine
Brihat	Ranthantara	Arms
Tristubh	Indra	Waist
Jagati	Aditya	Hips
Atikhandas	Prajapati	Upward Prana (Prana)
Yagnayagniya	Visvanara	Downward Prana(Apana)
Anustubh	Visvedevas	Thighs
Pankti	Maruts	Knees
Dvipada	Vayu	Vital Airs

The metre progression is a reflection of the worshiper. The Satapatha Brahmana (SPB 10.3.2.1 – 12) demonstrates, in detail, that the progression of the metre and rhythm of the sacrificial chant corresponds to the worshiper, and that this progression is presided by the various dynamic Vedic forces. The evolution of this progression applies not only to the worshiper, but of course to the Vedic astrologer, and to the Vedic forces and energies themselves. The sounds represented in these metres articulated not only in the chanting, but in the subtle vibration of the most essential sound. That sound, AUM, is discussed next.

The Movement of Saman is Represented in AUM

AUM is the subtle evolution of the universe, and Saman is the culmination of AUM.

Saman is identified with the uncreated source of energy of the universe and is a vehicle to deification. The Brahmanas explain this esoteric meaning:

- Saman is the truth and saman is born of the gods. (SPB 2.4.2.16.)
- By uttering that sacred syllable of the universe, AUM, the sacrificer becomes saman. (SPB, 1.4.1.1.)
- For this reason Saman is the vital airs, prana, and the vital airs are immortality. (SPB 9.1.2.32.)

The Brhad Brahmana emphasizes the soma-nature of saman. (B.B., 1.3.22.) Most authorities, however, emphasize the rc nature of sama.

- Atharva Veda 14.2.71 states that "sama" is derived from "sa," meaning "rc," "praise," "verse," or "thou" and "ama," "I."
- The Chandogya Upanishad 1.6.7 states that sama is based on rc.
- The Jaiminiya Brahmana states that sama is derived from *sameta*, meaning "combination," in other words, the combination of rc and yajus.
- The Papasutra states that sama is the musical rendering of the rc.
- The Samavidhana Brahmana is derived from samata, meaning "equality."
- The Aitareya Brahmana 12.12 presents a compromise between the two traditions in stating that "sama" is a derivation of "sa," meaning "rc" and "ama," meaning "soma," which has also been held to mean "food."

There are many references to saman (RV 1.62.2; 1.164.24; 1.173.1; 2.23.16, 17; 2.43.2; 4.5.3; 8.29.10; 8.81.5; 8.98.1; 9.96.22; 9.111.2; 10.93.8; 10.99.2; 10.130.2; 1.96.5; 1.102.2; 1.121.11; 1.140.13; 3.8.7; 4.2.16; 6.31.2; 10.12.1; 10.36.1; 10.45.4; 10.176.1) or saman (RV 1.147.1;8.89.7; 10/59.2; 6.15.5; 10.130.2) in the Rg Veda. The majority of the references is to the exoteric, sacrificial, sense of the sama chant. The esoteric meaning however is not lost in the Rg Veda. In a couplet of mantras, the esoteric and exoteric meanings coincide. In the first, Sayana interpreted sama as the "power to dispel evil spirits." (RV 2.23.16.) In the following mantra sama is used in the conventional meaning of the Soma chant. (RV 2.23.17.) Similarly, RV 9.96.22 speaks of Soma as the Udgatr as the driving force of invoking the gods at the sacrifice:

> His copious streams flow forth; blended with the milk and curds he enters the pitchers; uttering chants the skillful chanter (Soma) hasten invoking (the gods) towards (the cups) like (libertine) to the wife of a friend.

There is indeed an equivalence, identity, homogeneity, and equiposition at work here. That equiposition is between the microcosm and macrocosm. According to the ethos in the Rg Veda, there is a non-distinction between the microcosm and macrocosm. The non-distinction between the micro- and macrocosm implies a general equivalence between these two plains of existence. This equivalence is a principle function of the Purusa sukta, as we previously saw, equating the individual and cosmic person. This becomes the primary function as well for saman, only this time with the unifying power of saman.

As far as the Vedic astrologer is concerned, it is here that we get to the heart of the matter. The up and down movements of Sama is reflected in the repetitive processes of dissolution and evolution in the creation of the whole universe. These processes are manifested in the appearance of Name and Word in the articulation of the objects in the universe.

Name is foundational to the worshiper's understanding of the world and is related to the Word (vak). Name and the Word are inextricably related to the creation of the cyclic evolution and dissolution of the universe. Name and the Word are born from OM. Whenever the universe is dissolved and subsequently evolves, the Divine Sound, OM, resonated. (JUB 1.7.1; 1.9.1; 1.10.1.)

OM is the eternal truth from which the entire universe and on which the entire universe is established and understood. (JUB 1.2.3; 2.3.) The worshiper's understanding of the word is completed with Name and the Word to make intelligible the manifest universe, which is certainly the thought behind the following correspondence (JUB, 1.2.1):

- OM is Agni, the Sun, speech is Earth;
- OM is Vayu (Wind), speech is atmosphere;
- OM is Aditya (Sun), speech is sky.

That both name and the Word are a result of OM indicates the divine origins of the world. There is a direct line leading from OM to the manifest universe:

- The essence of all beings is the earth.
- The essence of the earth is water.
- The essence of water is the plants.
- The essence of plants is man.
- The essence of man is speech.
- The essence of speech is the Rig Veda.
- The essence of the Rg Veda is the Samaveda.
- The essence of Samaveda is Udgitha.
- Udgitha is OM. (CU, 1.1.2, 1.1.3.)

In the entire Vedic corpus the Gopatha Brahmana engaged in the first and perhaps most comprehensive discussion of the pervasive influence of OM. (GB, 1.17-21.) There, OM is described as consisting of two letters and four vocalic instants. From these elements the stages in the creation of the universe corresponded to the letters and vocalic instants of OM. These stages are articulated in the progression of the alphabet and in the language of music:

- From its first letter was produced heaven; and from it, the second letter created vigor and the luminaries,
- From its first vocalic instant were produced the earth, fire, herbs, trees, the Rig Veda, the mystic syllable him, the Gayatri metre, the threefold stoma, the eastern side, the spring season, the instrument of speech tongue, and the power of taste.
- From its second vocalic instant were produced ether, air, the Yajur Veda, the mystic syllable bhuva, the tristubha metre, the fifteen-fold stoma, the western side, the summer season, the organs of breath the nostrils, and the power of smelling.

- From its third vocalic instant were produced the heaven, the sun, the Sama Veda, the mystic syllable svah, the jagati metre, the seventeen-fold stoma, the northern side, the rainy season, the seats of light, eyes, and the power of vision.

- From its consonantal instant "b" were produced the water, the moon, the Atharva Veda, the stars, the circumflex, the Angirasas, the anustubh metre, the twenty-one-fold stoma, the southern side, the autumn season, the seat of knowledge mind, and the power of knowing.

- From its consonantal instant "m" were produced the Itiliasa Parana, speech, metrical language, Indrasansi, the Upanishads, the commanding syllables Vridkat, Karat, Guhan, Makat, Tat, and Sam, the great Vyahriti Om, harmony of many corded instruments, voice, dancing, singing, music, the Devas, lightning, light, the vrihati metre, the thirty-three-fold stoma, the upper and lower sides, the cold and lowly seasons, the organs of hearing ears, and the power of audition.

A correspondence is established by these passages. Whereas the Chandogya Upanishad emphasized the divine origin of Name and the objects name refers to in the world, the Gopatha Brahmana stresses Om as the origin of all objects, physical and nonphysical. The scheme of OM in the Gopatha Brahmana contemplates an ordered progression from the transcendental to the material. Just as physically the process of evolution springs from an indeterminate mass of matter (RV 10.129.1), so the conceptual basis of that matter begins from the land of Being where name and word and thought do not exist, but where that whole simply exist in a unitary state of Pure Being.

The progressions of OM in the creation and dissolution of the universe mimic the upward and downward movements of Saman in the articulation of the chants during the sacrifice. In one movement there is a downward path from Subject to Object, and in the other there is a correspondingly converse upward path from Object to Subject, each path one of progressive corporealization or rarefication. Name and Word take on a progressive more material mantle, until Name and word take on the arbitrary assignment of meaning for the multitude of becoming in its many forms as this process of evolution proceeds to its downward descent to the sensible world. Classical Vedanta reflected this downward progression in categorizing the four stages of Vak: Beginning first with *Vak*, the physical manifestation of sound; second with paravak, third with *para*, and fourth with *turiya*.

There is a progression of articulation from the most subtle to the material, as this progression traverses upward in the converse manner. It is the divine dynamic power of Bala (Indra) which governs this progression back and forth. (RV 1.10.1.) As an adjunct of this divine, dynamic power, Bala (Indra) is responsible for giving form to the subtle world. (RV 1.10.11.)

The classical categories of Name and Word are present in the Vedas. Turiya, the most subtle state of Pure Being, is found to be the transcendent word, from which the conceptualization of the world is contemplated:

- The divine dynamic energy of Bala, as the maker of forms (RV 1.6.3; 3.53.8; 3.54.17; 6.47.8) assumes the mantel of creator through its transcendental name. (RV 8.3.24; 8.80.9.)
- Soma also assumes the transcendental name (RV 9.96.10) and gives shape to forms according to the knowledge obtained therefrom. (RV 9.14.5.)
- It is the role of the Rishis to reveal this transcendental knowledge. (RV 10.67.1.)

While Turiya the transcendental name is the highest form of name and word, it is reposed in the conceptual world above the sensible world of form. The articulation and assignment of name and word begins to be more material as they descend to the sensible.

From Turiya, Name and Word assumes its Divine Name in Mahat. The unitary conceptualization of name and word is first introduced to duality, a function carried out by the principle of duality inherent in the Asvins, the divine twins:

- Through the divine action of the Asvins traverse and create the four corners of the universe. (RV 1.80.10.)
- The divine name of Bala (Indra) is responsible for the articulation of all forms in the sensible universe. (RV 3.38.4; 3.54.17.)

- The Asvins, the divine embodiment of duality, and Rhbus, the semi-divine fashioner, articulate that level of reality beyond the senses ("without horses") and beyond discernment ("without reins").
- The processes of Agni, the Sun, the Fire of Change, articulate the many forms which envelop the waters (i.e., "the pervasion).

This is the ultimate esoteric meaning of sama. It is the inner meaning understood by the Hindu texts of the day. One scripture tells of Wise Men knowing that prana moves with the oscillations between the two nadis, ida and susumna, in accordance with movements of the time during the year, and particularly whether the Sun is in the Northern or Southern Paths, the daksinayana and uttarayma. (SST, 7.205.)

The Vedic astrologer knows this as well. The Vedic astrologer understands that the Nakshatras represent Time and consist of the measure of time. The Vedic astrologer understands that Speech is Word, and Word is Breath, and is regulated by the rhythms of expansion and contraction. The Vedic astrologer understands that the movements of Time, prana and Saman are representative of the most basic functions of the universe. The Vedic astrologer knows that these movements power every function in the universe. The Vedic astrologer knows that vibratory expansion/contraction movements occur on the subtle sub-atomic level, and on every physical level above. This, indeed, is how the Nakshatras are created:

- The Vedic astrologer understands that the sequential aspects of *Rta*, the Vedic dharma, establish the vibration in the cosmos which regulates the motion and movement of all things.
- More importantly the Vedic astrologer knows the sequential aspects of sama translates that vibration into the rhythms and cadences of the hymns at the sacrifice.
- The rhythms and cadences of the hymns at the sacrifice, accordingly, provide the oscillating vibrations between the Right-and Left-Handed powers. The Vedic astrologer knows the sequential aspects of both are reflected in the oscillations between the Left-Handed powers.

- The Vedic astrologer understands that the expansion/contraction movements of sama represent the Left-Handed powers of the cosmic order, and that the Left-Handed powers of the cosmic order are correspondingly reflected in the Nakshatras as they progress between the southern and northern hemispheres of the sky.

These progressions are as regular as the movement of the hand as it travels around a clock. It is no mistake that the Chandogya Upanishad, which was so concerned with the Saman chant, is considered one of the most esoteric of all the Upanishads. This is the little-understood or appreciated meaning of the Saman Chant.

The sum total of the actions of Saman, Dhur, and Prana results in the creation of the Nakshatras and the other members of the Stellar Population. That which is measured is the vibration and rhythm of the universe, which is symbolically represented part and parcel in the Sama chant. The oscillating movements of saman are interpreted in the creation of the elements of the stellar population. Specifically, with the Sun and the Moon the great Kashmiri thinker Abinavagupta in Chapter Six of the *Tantrasara* explained how the inward and outward movements of prana and saman lead to the creation of the Sun and the Moon:

In-Breath	Out-Breath
Prana, the Sun, Consciousness	Apana, the Moon
Lunar Day, the Sun	Lunar Night, the Moon
In a month, the second two-weeks, the Sun	In a month, the first two-weeks, the Moon
Prana, the Southern Path	Apana, the Moon
Makara, Capricorn	Mithuna, Gemini
Karkata, Cancer	Kumbha, Aquarius

While on a macrocosmic level, the Saman and prana give rise to the Sun and the Moon, on a microcosmic level the worshiper uses this paradigm as a meditative tool to get in touch with the greater Vedic dharma. As Abinavagupta would note in the Tantra Loka, 6.66, the meeting of the Sun and the Moon, used to represent the union of these great cosmic powers, is called "Sandhya."

The Vedic astrologer knows that these vibrations, oscillations and movements originate from and return to be incorporated in the inner life of the worshiper. In this way the aspiration of the Vedic astrologer's and worshiper's life is to live in accordance with the rhythms of the universe. Given that the sound waves of religious chanting alters the physical fabric of space-time, those changes must occur within its subtle foundation. That subtle foundation is the Vedic Field.

The Vedic Field

We are still in the land of subtle existence. The Nakshatras and other members of the stellar population, the planets and lunar houses, have been created, but only on a subtle level. Even at this level there must be a common glue holding this subtle basis of existence. There is indeed a glue that holds the cosmos — and the stellar population within that cosmos — together. This is the purpose of the Vedic field. As with the Nakshatras, Time is a necessary element in the formation of the Vedic field.

The Vedic astrologer knows the material universe, all things contained in it, the time divisions, and the stellar population, collectively and individually, is just like a human organism. They, as the Vedic astrologer, live and function in the material level, and yet operate in a subtle, causal and transcendent level. These levels communicate with each other and are interwoven and work together to sustain the entire organism. Each level is self-impelled by its own power and yet are powered by the forces of mutual attraction. They operate over the discreet areas of space and time in which they exert their influence which facilitate the functioning of the cosmos. In science and for the Vedic astrologer, they are called "Fields." Pervasion, the capacity to fill their respective discreet region of influence, and the tendency to attract and be attracted by other fields, are the essential characteristics of Vedic (and scientific) fields.

From the perspective of the Vedic astrologer, fields are represented by *dishah*, waves of ethereal space, belonging to akasha, the fifth element. The *dishah* are waves, waves emanating from the mind as it perceives the world around it.

Those waves undulate as it perceives the world and are excited by the movements of rajas, tamas, and sattva, the three gunas (J.C. Chatterji,

The Wisdom of the Vedas (1980, 1992), pp. 63 – 66). Monier Williams, the Sanskrit authoritative dictionary, defines "guna," as "string, thread, or strand," or "virtue, merit, excellence," or "quality, peculiarity, attribute, property." All these meanings are used in Samkhya philosophy to signify the original materials that weave together and are woven together a process which will result in the appearance of reality, both in the macrocosmic universe to the microcosmic individual. (*https://en.wikipedia.org/wiki/Guna.*) The state of this material world depends on the level of balance within the gunas: Serenity is found when the gunas are in balance; when the gunas are not in balance, there is conflict in the world and the worshiper's mind is in turmoil. The following process is present when the gunas are applied to the waves of the Vedic field:

- Rajas, working with Manas, the mind, runs out everywhere, imaging that perceived sounds and other information obtained from the sense perceptions, come in from all directions. This seemingly haphazard, unorganized scattering of waves is depicted in the following manner:
- Tamas, in conjunction with the soul, the Atman, and by virtue of its centripetal pull, reach out and pull back the mental waves of rajas.
- Sattva competes the return of these waves of mental energy back to the Atman, if through a curved, coiled path. The result is a complicated, complex network of mental energy. This network represent lines of pulsating energy residing in the realm of ethereal space (*Akasha*) influencing, maintaining, and pervading the objects of the physical material universe.
- In Sattva, there are innumerable rigid straight lines going out in all directions, originating from the soul, the Atman, the radiating agent. These lines turn back after reaching a certain point from its point of radiation. Each of these lines return, coiling around the straight lines, back to the Atman. These lines, coiled and straight, constitute the fabric of the ethereal space, Akasha. This network provides the physical frame of reference for all physical objects experienced by the Atman. The Vedas spoke of *dishah*, although in

a context the Vedic astrologer could appreciate and any Vedantin could understand.

- When Indra, in his Vedic capacity to act in conjunction with the planet Mars, as assisted by the zodiacal house of Vrscika (Scorpio), counter-act and defeat the enemies, the end result is the dishah field networks open up. (RV 3.1.21; 1.132.2.)

These rcs (mantas) make clear that the *dishah* exists thanks to the actions of the dynamic Lunar house of Indra and gross (Mars) and subtle (Scorpio) astrological members. The *dishah* field networks direct the worshiper towards the light regions. (RV 10.110.7.) According to Monier-Williams, the "light regions" in this rc refer to the light emitted from the moon, Sun and other astronomical bodies. This aspect of the *dishah* no doubt refer to the recoiling of the energy fields influenced by the guna Sattwa. The Maruts impel the motion of the *dishah*, thereby supplying the Gotama River with water. (RV 1.85.11.) This is a significant rc (mantra). The Maruts are dynamic Vedic energies under the sphere of Indra's influence. At the same time they are a manifestation of the Fire of Agni in the firmament. In this capacity the Maruts act like a conduit between the Vedic astrologer and the greater stellar population, supplying the lessons they have to offer to the worshiper. The reference to Water is significant. This rc associates the *dishah* with Water because like water, the *dishah* are flows of energy. This association is carried to many different levels, because Water is a Vedic field with an almost ubiquitous presence in the Vedas. The reference to the Gotama River is significant. By acting upon the dishah, the Maruts contribute to the gross and subtle levels of the Vedic dharma. On a gross level, they actually supply the water to feed into the Gotama River. (RV 1.85.11.) On a subtle level it is important to remember that the River is symbolic for the flow of consciousness. The brilliant and adamantine character of the Maruts supply the impulsion firing mental activity.

Water is the great Vedic field pervading the stellar population in the cosmos. The Waters is *ratna*, the essence of the Vedic dharma. (RV 3.21.11.) All "this," the greater stellar population and the cosmic underpinning therefrom, is Water. (AA, 8.1.) This "Water" should not be considered what we know as H^2O. What is the material manifestation of Water in the subtle basis is considered more as "fluidity." Water was that essential characteristic in the very beginning of creation (RV 1.129.3), and creation never lost its nature. While water is the essential nature of the creation, it has various permutations, fields within fields, as it were. Not only should "Water" be considered as "fluidity," but "the Waters" is coded language for that element of the natural order (the Vedic dharma) whose essential nature is a flowing field.

The Vedic fields which are interwoven in the pervasion of matter and space can be found in the various permutations of the Water. The Waters, the very essence of the Vedic dharma, were created by the mechanisms of Time. (AV 19.54.1.) The Waters consist of many different types and permutations. The first permutation is the physical water found in the visible, material world of the Two-Dimensional Universe: The Vedic Field of Physical Water, *alpaasa*. (RV 154.8; 4.2.14.) These characteristics thereupon are followed in the Three-Dimensional Universe:

- The Vedic Field of Matter and Space. These aspects of the Waters under this field correspond to the three levels of material existence. For example, there is *apa/* (TA, 1.1.6; 1.36.8; 5.2.11; 5.30.6; 6.32.4; 6.39.5; 8.6.16; 9.85.4; 10.36.1), most commonly associated with heaven and earth or the heavens. (RV 1.36.8; 5.2.12; 6.32.5; 8.6.16; 10.36.1.)
- *Alpas* (RV 1.110.1; 6.23.5) is the watery pervasion in the air, or mid-world.
- *Apa/h* (RV 1.10.8; 1.51.11; 1.52.7, 12; 1.57.6; 1.10.18; 1.80.5; 1.103.2; 1.131.4; 1.1.131.4; 1.151.5; 1.161.11; 1.174.9; 1.180.5; 2.22.4; 2.27.13; 3.9.2; 5.14.4; 5.46.3; 6.20.12; 6.28.7; 6.60.2, 11; 6.73.3; 7.44.1; 8.6.13; 86.13; 8.7.22, 28; 8.15.2; 8.32.2; 8.76.3; 9.61.22; 9.63.7; 9.68.7; 9.90.4; 9.91.6; 9.109.22; 10.36.1; 10.43.7; 10.65.11; 10.89.4; 10.124.7; 10.138.1; 10.147.1) and *amuu/r* (RV 1.23.7) are associated with the Svar. This association is clearly made when *apa/h* is said to shine from the "Sun," the Svar (RV 1.10.8), and is so defined for the remainder of the Vedas.

The upwards ascent to the three levels of the material universe (the Three-Dimensional) serves a double purpose. Not only is the ascent to higher levels of the subtle levels of the material universe, but that final arrival to the Svar transitions the watery field to the next level of subtleness. That next higher level is the Five-Dimensional Universe. The Svar fulfils this purpose as the vortex or portal to the Five Dimension Universe. The Vedic field which pervades this universe is the Vedic Field of Consciousness and Energy.

There are several Vedic Fields of Consciousness and Energy. These fields belong to the Five-Dimensional Universe and share a common relationship with Time. The Rishiis discovered so long ago what modern science has only recently found out: Time is both the constituent element of Energy (AV 19.53.8) and a function of Consciousness. (AV 19.53.7.)

- *Apaa/m* (RV 1.22.6; 1.23.9, 11; 1.46.4; 1.51.4 10; 1.56.5; 1.57.1; 1.61.12; 1.70.3; 1.85.9; 1.100.11; 1.122.3, 4; 1.134.5; 1.143.1; 1.144.2; 1.149.4; 1.158.6; 1.164.52; 1.168.2; 1.186.5; 1.187.8; 2.4.2; 2.12.7; 2.17.5; 2.19.9; 2.23.8; 2.30.1; 2.35.1, 3, 7, 9, 10; 3.1.3.; 3.9.1.; 3.25.5; 3.5.2; 4.21.8; 4,5,111 5.45.7; 6.8.4; 6.44.18; 6.47.27; 6.52.15;6.41.1; 8.14.10, 13; 8.16.2; 8.19.4; 8.25.14; 8.44.16; 8.93.22; 9.76.5; 9.86.25; 9.95.3; 9.96.19; 9.97.57; 9.108.5, 10; 10.8.1, 5; 10.17.14) is that aspect of the Waters which represent the Vedic field of consciousness and energy found in the material world, the Two-Dimensional Universe.
- *Apo* (RV 1.23.15; 1.52.6; 1.56.6; 1.64.1, 6; 1.80.3, 4; 1.91.22; 1.105.11; 1.122.9; 1.131.4; 1.156.4; 1.164.47; 1.174.2; 1.180.4; 1.190.6; 2.11.5; 2.14.2; 2.31.6; 2.36.1; 3.6.7; 3.32.5, 6; 4.16.6, 7, 8; 4.26.2; 4.28.1; 4.42.4; 4.45.2; 5.29.2; 5.30.5; 5.31.6, 8; 5.48.21; 5.83.6; 6.20.2; 6.30.4, 5; 6.47.14; 6.50.13; 6.57.4; 6.60.2; 6.68.8; 7.9.3; 7.32.27; 7.47.2; 7.56.24; 7.65.3; 7.68.8; 7.95.1; 8.12.3; 8.15.6; 8.26.25; 8.40.5, 10, 11; 8.83.3; 9.86.8; 9.96.18; 9.97.15; 9.2.3; 9.3.6; 9.7.2; 9.33.1; 9.42.1; 9.49.1; 9.62.26; 9.70.2; 9.78.1; 9.72.7; 9.86.40; 9.99.7; 9.107.18, 26; 9.108.4; 9.109.21; 10.8.5; 10.16.3; 10.1, 4, 5, 10; 10.58.7; 10.30.14; 10.64.8; 10.76.3; 10.30.14; 10.92.13; 10.95.10; 10.98.5, 12; 10.104.9) is that aspect of the Waters which represent one form of the Vedic field of consciousness and energy found in the Three-Dimensional Universe.
- *Apsu* (RV 1.23.19; 1.104.6; 10.105.1; 1.135.6; 10.135.6; 1.182.6; 2.11.5; 2.35.7, 8; 3.1.3; 3.13.4; 3.22.2; 4.13.4; 5.85.2; 7.18.12; 8.43.9; 9.96.24; 9.107.1; 10.10.4; 10.27.17; 10.30.4; 10.45.3;

10.51.3; 10.125.7) is that aspect of the Waters which represent the another form of the Vedic field of consciousness and energy found in the Five-Dimensional Universe.

• *Aasu* (RV 1.95.4; 6.72.4; 8.41.8; 9.86.43; 9.99.7; 10.27.8; 10.49.10; 10.95.8, 9) is that aspect of the Waters which represent yet another form of the Vedic field of consciousness and energy emanating from the Seven-Dimensional Universe.

It should be remembered that the pervasion of water preceded all things in the evolutionary chain, even the creation of the dynamic Vedic forces that sustain the cosmos. Thus, it is appropriate that these dynamic Vedic forces, immense in their strength and power they may be, are properly considered the offspring of the Waters. The aspects of this Vedic field are responsible for energizing and bestowing consciousness to not only the dynamic Vedic forces, but to all life, material or subtle. Considered in connection with these aspects of the Vedic field of consciousness, the following nomenclatures of these Vedic forces are more properly easily understood:

• The lunar house of Agni, the Sun, the Fire of Change as the Child of the Waters. (*apam*) (RV 1.70.3; 1.122.1.143.1; 1.186.5; 2.35.1, 2, 3, 7, 9, 10, 13; 3.1.3; 3.9.1; 5.41.10; 7.34.15; 7.35.13; 10.30.3)
• The lunar house of Indra, as the Child of the Waters (*apam*). (RV 1.164.52.)
• The lunar house of Savitr, as the Child of the Waters (*apam*). (RV 1.22.6.)

The imagery extends to the dynamic Vedic forces "sitting on the lap" of the Waters. In the symbolic language of the Vedas, being "seated" means resting at the very heart of the Waters. The Waters, as we should know by now, is the inner essence of the Vedic dharma. The following Vedic forces therefore rest at the inner essence of the Vedic dharma.

• The lunar house of Agni, the Sun, the Fire of Change (RV 1.144.2; 6.8.4; 10.8.1; 10.45.3; 10..46.1), seated on the lap of the Waters (*apam*).
• The lunar house of Soma (RV 9.76.5; 9.86.25) is seated on the lap of the Waters (*apam*).

The passage of Time is like a driver of a horse with seven reins. What this means is that the passage of Time is spread over every existential level. Therefore, there is a Field of Vedic Transcendent Consciousness, which moves beyond the four other existential levels in a place beyond space and time:

- *alpah* (TA, 1.1.6; RV 2.32.4) and *aalpah*. (TA, 1.1.6; RV 1.23.21; 1.32.11; 1.65.4; 3.35.8; 4.18.8; 5.34.9; 5.41.12; 6.34.4; 8.15.8; 9.82.5; 10.9.7; 10.65.13; 10.137.6.)

These fields ascend upwards through the various dimensions of space until reaching the top of the chain. The boundaries of these fields are sometimes hazy and ill-defined. One dimension at times intermix with another.

These fields run through different dimensions or levels of reality. At a rudimentary level, the analysis begins with the visible, material, gross world we all live and breathe in, the Two-Dimensional Universe, to the Seven-Dimension Universe. The progression to higher stages brings the worshiper to levels of existence which are ever more and more subtle and abstract. In the current parlance this existential scheme can be considered parallel universes. The only difference is that the different existential levels in the Vedic dharma pertain to the same set of phenomena, not mirror images. Viewed from the bottom up, the progression can be summarized as follows:

- The Two-Dimensional Universe consists of the material world itself, roughly corresponding to *Prakrti*, the inert matter of the everyday world, and the larger macrocosm, corresponding to Purusa, Consciousness. In this world, the worshiper lives in a confused, chaotic world. It is the world we all wake up to and confront every day.
- The Three-Dimensional Universe introduces the first intervention of the Mind, consciousness. Samkhya, one of the branches of the Vedas, describes this moment as that instant when Purusa makes contact with inert matter, Prakrti, energizing the evolution of the world. In this Vedic dharma, because Prakrti is inert and essentially cannot act on its own accord at this point, that contact is made through the Mind. Mind, Consciousness, therefore, acts as the bridge between Prakrti and Purusa. That this means to the

worshiper is that these are the beginning "baby steps" made in the spiritual search.

- The Five-Dimensional Universe continues the process begun in the Three Dimensional Universe. Here, the Mind, Consciousness, is more fully developed, becomes meditative, exhibits the first indicators of enlightenment. At this stage the worshiper begins and proceeds in earnest to restrain and control the mind in yoga or engaged in any of the other paths to liberation or salvation.

- The highest level, at the Seven-Dimensional Universe, is the most subtle, and goes by different names, such as Heaven, svar, rocane, and others. It represents the liberation of the worshiper and the culmination of the spiritual journey.

These fields lay dormant and inert until they are activated. In the terminology of the Vedas this period of dormancy exits when they are

Field	Water Element	Dimension
Physical Water	*alpaasa*	Two-Dimensional Universe
Matter and Space	*apal, alpas, apalh (amuurl)*	Three-Dimensional Universe
Consciousness and Energy	*apaalm, apo, apsu, aasu*	Five-Dimensional Universe
Transcendent Consciousness	*alpah* and *aalpah*	Seven-Dimensional Universe

"concealed" or "restrained." The Vedas are cloaked in this condition due to the actions of Vrtra, the serpent. This action is described in the Veda as Vrtra "restraining the waters." (RV 1.55.5; 1.57.6; 5.32.2; 5.33.1.) Vrtra affects every aspect of these watery fields: Vrtra affects the material aspect associated with heaven and earth or the heavens located in the first level of the Three-Dimension Universe. (RV 1.36.8.)

- Vrtra affects the material aspect associated with heaven and earth or the heavens located in the second level of the Three-Dimension Universe. (RV 2.20.7.)
- Vrtra affects the material aspect associated with heaven and earth or the heavens located in the third level of the Three-Dimension Universe, the Svar. (RV 1.52.8; 1.80.5; 6.72.3; 8.6.13; 8.76.3.)
- Vrtra affects the field of consciousness *apam* located in the Five-Dimension Universe. (RV 1.51.4; 1.85.9; 3.45.2; 8.96.18.)
- Vrtra affects the field of consciousness *apo* located in the Five-Dimension Universe. (RV 1.32.10; 1.52.6; 1.56.6; 1.80.3; 1.174.2; 2.4.2; 3.32.6; 6.20.6; 8.33.1; 8.89.4, 5, 17; 10.66.8.)
- Vrtra affects the transcendent fields of *alpah* and *aalpah* in the Seven-Dimension Universe. (RV 1.528; 1.80.5; 8.76.3; 10.124.8.)

The Lunar house of Indra activates inert matter. Once energized, the fields operate to sustain all dimensions in the cosmos. Indra, in conjunction with Brhaspati (Jupiter), in the zodiacal houses of Vrscika slays Vrtra to release the Vedic fields in time-space. (RV 1.33.13; 1.51.11; 1.80.10; 2.28.4; 3.31.11, 16; 4.18.7; 4.19.8; 5.30.10.) This action is articulated in various ways:

- Indra released the streams after slaying Vrtra, releasing the waters. (RV 6.20.2.)
- The waters are set free. (RV 1.32.4.) The waters is that aspect of the divine Vedic dharma symbolizing the forces of creation, purification and life. hold especial significance to the divine Vedic dharma (*Rta*). The seven rivers represent the seven-dimensional, transcendent, world.
- Indra becomes *apsuji*, the beloved conqueror of the waters. (RV 8.13.2; 8.36.1-6; 8.43.28; 9.106.3.)
- Indra releases the seven rivers. (RV 1.32.12; 2.12.3; 10.67.12.)
- The releasing of the waters gives birth to the *hiranyabarbha*, the cosmic egg. (RV 10.121.7, 8.)

- *Asat* (non-being, non-existence, anti-matter) is converted into sat (being, existence, matter). (RV 6.24.5.) In other words by conquering Vrtra Indra gives the spark of existence to dead, inert matter. This is not surprising because that very essence of life is symbolized by the Waters, which Indra also set free.

We will hear more about Vrtra later. For now, these Watery Fields and dimensions of reality are then expressed in astronomical objects:

- In Bhumi (RV 1.52.12; 1.64.5; 1.164.51; 2.30.9; 4.26.2; 4.57.8; 5.59.4; 5.84.1; 5.85.4; 6.67.6; 8.14.5; 10.18.10; 10.27.13; 10.58.3; 10.59.3; 10.90.1; 10.90.5; 10.14.2), the material manifestation of the planet, the earth element.
- In Prthvi, the world and its surrounding atmosphere.
- In Candra, the moon. (SPB 4.12.25.)
- In Surya, the sun.
- In Rodasi (RV 1.52.10; 1.105.1-18; 1.167.4 5; 1.185.3; 3.26.9; 3.54.3, 4, 10; 4.55.6; 4.56.4, 8; 6.50.5; 6.62.8; 6.66.6; 6.70.2, 3; 9.7.9; 9.98.9; 10.12.4; 10.67.11; 10.79.4; 10.88.5, 10; 10.92.11), the first manifestation of heaven and earth conjoined.
- In Krandasi (RV 2.12.8; 6.25.4; 10.121.6), the second manifestation of heaven and earth conjoined.
- In Paramesthi, that spatial area beyond heaven and earth. It is that spatial region wherein resides the highest personage in the universe. (SPB 3.10.9.) Later traditions indicate that paramesthi is the region where Brahma (SPB 3.13.6), the creator of the universe (SPB 2.8.25) resides.
- In Samyati (RV 2.12.8; 5.37.5; 9.68.3; 9.69.3), the region beyond the spatial and temporal expanses of heaven and earth, that place of Pure Being.

There is also a second evolutionary track. This is the establishment of the macrocosm. The macrocosm is also expressed in astrological terms, corresponding these members of the stellar population to the worshiper and Vedic astrologer. These correspondences are set out in the following chart.

Macrocosmic Level	Microcosmic Level	Level of Being	Psychic Correlate	Astrological House	Astronomical Entity
Bhuh	Bhur	Matter	Growth	Vrushabh (Taurus)	Bhumi (Earth)
Bhuvah	Bhuvah	Prana	Decay, Change	Kanya (Virgo)	Prthvi (World) Candra (Moon)
Svah	Manah	Mind	First Birth	Kumbha (Aquarius)	Surya (Sun) Rodasi (Heaven and Earth)
Janah Mahah	Mahas	Supermind	First Existence	Mithuna (Gemini)	Krandasi (Heaven and Earth) Paramesthi (Beyond Heaven)
Satya/m *Tapas*	Jana Maya	Bliss	Pure Being		Samyati

We will be seeing these existential categories intermittently in this book. We will also be seeing the Vedic forces with which they are associated:

- Bhuh, Agni, the Sun, the Fire of Change.
- Candra, Religious Ecstasy and Purification (Soma).
- Surya, Agni, the Sun, the Fire of Change.
- Parameshthi, Religious Ecstasy and Purification (Soma).
- Svyambhu, Agni, the Sun, the Fire of Change.

The correspondence is raised to an additional level. Once the sensible world is established the three levels of the world are ruled by different divine dynamic forces:

- The Earth, ruled by Agni, the Fire of Change and Transformation.
- The Atmosphere, ruled by Vayu, the personification of Prana, the Vital Breath.
- The Sky, by Surya, the personification of the Sun.

All Creatures Great and Small
"We are stardust, we are golden."

The Vedic astrologer had noted earlier that once the Purusa and Prakrti made contact, the evolutionary track branched into two paths. In the first trajectory the subtle basis of the Vedic dharma was created, with this subtle, fundamental basis of the Vedic dharma established in Water, the Vedic field, the dimensions of reality, Saman, and prana, leading to the establishment of the Nakshatras. In the second trajectory, the Vedic forces appeared and became aligned with the gunas, proceeding on their own evolutionary path. The stages of this evolutionary process ended with the Nakshatras falling into groups based on their alignment with the Lunar houses. This second trajectory is the one examined in this chapter. At some point these trajectories will converge in creating the raw material for the physical world.

The Vedic dynamic forces and astral powers were born early, very early, in this evolutionary process, from the indiscriminate, undifferentiated mass of the primordial ocean pervading the Vedic dharma before there was a Vedic dharma. (RV 10.72.2.) It is at this point that these energies and forces take form into the personifications that we all know now and take different names and manifestations. Wise men know the Vedic forces by different names, and the Vedic astrologer is no exception. The Vedic forces carry very specific properties. A short list of the principal Vedic deities, and the forces they represent, and the specific meaning given by the Vedic astrologer, are the following:

Vedic force	Meaning in the Vedic dharma	Meaning given by Vedic astrologer
Agni	Principle of Transformation	The Sun. Agni, with Indra, dispenses the spiritual endowment of radha (Spiritual Increase, Great Achievements). Agni dispenses these endowments through the agencies of the Sun, the zodiacal houses of Mesa (Aries) and Vrsabha (Taurus), and through the lunar house or asterisms of Krittika.
Indra	Principle of Increase	Indra gives the spark of existence to dead, inert matter. Once enlivened, the fields operate to sustain all dimensions in the cosmos. Indra, in conjunction with Brhaspati (Jupiter), in the zodiacal houses of Vrscika (Scorpio) and the lunar house of asterism of Jyestra, slays Vrtra to release the Vedic fields from time-space. The release of these Vedic fields is accomplished by Indra as an incarnation of Agni.

Asvins	Principle of Duality	The Asvins are ruled by Indrani, the consort of Indra. The Asvins dispense *Bhaga*, mistakenly thought of as "enjoyment." The Visnu Purana defines *Bhaga* as having six elements: dominion, might, glory, splendor, wisdom, and dispassion. The dispensation of dominion, might, glory, splendor, wisdom, and dispassion are conveyed to the worshiper through the zodiacal house of Mesa (Aries) and the lunar house or asterism of Ashvini.
Pusan	Principle of Direction and Pathways, *dishah*	Pusan also dispenses Bhaga, dominion, might, glory, splendor, wisdom, and dispassion. Pusan is ruled by Rudra, who is a manifestation of the Fire of Agni in the firmament. Pusan dispenses Bhaga through the asterism of Revati in conjunction with the zodiacal house of Mina (Pisces).
Soma	Principle of Bliss, Purification, and Spiritual Ecstasy	Soma rules the Moon. Soma dispenses Bliss and religious ecstacy though the asterism of Mrgashirsha.

Savitr	Principle of the Perpetuality of Creation	Savitr is ruled by Indrani, the consort of Indra. Savitr dispenses Bliss. Savitr's dispensations are made through the zodiacal house of Kanya (Virgo) and the lunar house or asterism of Hasta.
Surya	Principle of *Satya*, Truth	Surya according to the Vedic astrologer is treated as the alter ego for the Fire of Agni.
Vayu	Principle of the Vital Life Force	Vayu is ruled by Rudra, who is a manifestation of the Fire of Agni in the firmament. Vayu dispenses *sukha*, which is deep Spiritual Fulfillment, Happiness. Vayu dispenses Sukha through the zodiacal house of Tula (Libra), and the lunar house of Svasti (Srati).
Varuna	Principle of *Rta*, the Vedic dharma	Varuna is ruled by the planet Jupiter which itself is ruled by Indra. Varuna dispenses Greatness to the worshiper through the lunar house or asterism Shatabhisha and the zodiacal house of Kumba (Aquarius).

These are the principal Vedic forces and energies. There are other minor, but important, Vedic forces. At this early stage in which they appeared, gunas attached to the Vedic forces and energies. Since the Purusa had not arrived, these gunas were at a dormant stage, yet they had become attracted to and joined to their respective Vedic force. The gunas (See, *http://www. academia. edu/6437050 /Introduction_to_Vedic_Astrology*) accordingly aligned themselves with the principal Lunar houses (BPHS, 1.22) in the following manner:

Vedic force	Predominate Guna
Saraswati	Rajas
Soma	Sattva
Agni	Sattva
Durga	(Sattva)
Indrani	Rajas
Rudra	Tamas
Indra	Sattva
Yama	Tamas

These Vedic forces and energies work in conjunction with the gunas to create gross, material objects in the Vedic dharma, the Nakshatras and other members of the stellar population being just a few. The nature and composition of the gunas are well-known and established.

- "Sattva manifests itself as purity, knowledge and harmony. It is the quality of goodness, joy, satisfaction, nobility and contentment. It is free of fear, wrath and malice. Sattvic quality is pure and forgiving. It is the guna that people want to increase in order to reach the state of Samadhi or Liberation." (*https:// www.arhantayogaindia. com/sattva-rajas-tamas-gunas/*.)
- "Rajas represents itself by passion, action, energy and motion. Rajas is characterized by a feeling of attachment, a longing for satisfaction and desire." (*https://www.arhantayogaindia.com/ sattva-rajas-tamas-gu-nas/*.)

- "Tamas manifests itself as impurity, laziness and darkness. It is the consequence of ignorance and it prevents all beings from seeing the reality." (*https://www. arhantayogaindia.com/sattva-rajas-tamas-gunas/.*)

The gunas attached to the Lunar Houses, the Asterisms.

- Sattva attaches to Krittika, Ardra, Ashlesha, Uttara Phalguna, Svati, Jyestha, Uttara Ashada, Satahisja, and Revati.
- Rajas attaches to Rohini Purnavasu, Maghah, Hesta, Visakha, Mula, Srava, Purnabhadha, and Asvini.
- Tamas attaches to Mrghashira, Pushya, Purva Phalguni, Citra, Anuradha, Purva Ashada, Dhanishta, Uttara Bharada, and Bharani.

The gunas act in conjunction with the Vedic forces and energies to create the Nakshatras, Lunar Houses (asterisms), and zodiacal houses. On their creation the Nakshatras (Asterism) sought the Vedic forces and energies present in the Vedic dharma which matched their dynamic energy and joined with these Vedic forces to form individual units. (See, *http:// www. academia. edu/6437050 /Introduction_to_Vedic_Astrology*) Thus, the Nakshatras thereby paired up with the following Vedic forces and energies:

Vedic Asterism	Presiding Vedic Force (Asterism)
Krittika	Agni
Rohini	Prajapati
Mrgashirsha	Soma
Ardra	Rudra
Punavasu	Aditi
Pushya	Brhaspati
Ashlasha	Nagas
Magha	Pitrs
Purva Phalguni	Bhaga
Uttara Phalguni	Aryaman
Hasta	Savitr
Chitra	Indra (Tvastr)
Svasti (Srati)	Vayu
Vasakra	Indra/Agni

Anuradha	Mitra
Jyestra	Indra
Mula	Nirrti
Purva Ashada	Apas
Uttara Ashada	Visvedevas
Abhijit	Brahma
Sravana	Visnu
Dhanishta	Vasus
Shatabhisha	Varuna
Purva Bhadrapada	Ajikapada
Uttara Bhadrapada	Ahir Budhyana
Revati	Pusan
Ashvini	Asvins
Bharani	Yama

These Vedic forces and energies were already possessed in their individual *svadha* which contained certain spiritual qualities. (See, *http://www. academia.edu /6437050/ Introduction_to_Vedic_Astrology)*These spiritual qualities intermingled in congress with their respective asterism, and the two, Vedic force and asterism, became one.

Presiding Vedic Force	Spiritual Endowment From Asterism
Agni	*Yajna*, Divine Response
Prajapati	*Yajna*, Divine Response
Soma	Bliss
Rudra	*sam* (Conjunction, union)
Aditi	*sunrta* ("true speech," understanding of the Vedic dharma (*Rta*))
Brhaspati	Beauty
Nagas	*Bhanu* (Shining rays of Light)
Pitrs	*ayana* (Guide to right conduct during the spiritual journey)
Bhaga	Good Works
Aryaman	Good Works
Savitr	Bliss

Indra (Tvastr)	Bliss
Vayu	*sukha* (Deep Spiritual Fulfillment, Happiness)
Indra/Agni	*radha* (Spiritual Increase, Great Achievements)
Mitra	Response
Indra	Happiness
Nirrti	*amrtra* (the Eternal,
Apas	Undying Principle)
	Anna (Food)
Visvedevas	Strength
Brahma	*punya* (Offering to Divine)
Visnu	Nourishment
Vasus	Nourishment
Varuna	Greatness
Ajikapada	Protection
Ahir Budhyana	*susarma* (Protection)
Pusan	*Bhaga* (Enjoyment)
Asvins	*Bhaga* (Enjoyment)
Yama	Spiritual Riches

The Vedic forces and energies had at that point sought to distribute the new qualities present in their asterisms in groups with other Vedic forces and energies based on their mutual compatibility with other Vedic forces and associate themselves in zodiacal houses. (See, http://www. *academia. edu/6437050 /Introduction_to_Vedic_Astrology*):

Vedic Force	Zodiacal House(s)
Agni	Mesa (Aries)
	Vrsabha (Taurus)
Prajapati	Vrsabha (Taurus)
Soma	Vrsabha (Taurus)
	Mithuna (Gemini)
Rudra	Mithuna (Gemini)
Aditi	Mithuna (Gemini)
	Karkata (Cancer)

Brhaspati	Karkata (Cancer)
Nagas	Karkata (Cancer)
Pitrs	Simha (Leo)
Bhaga	Simha (Leo)
Aryaman	Simha (Leo) Kanya (Virgo)
Savitr	Kanya (Virgo)
Indra (Tvastr)	Kanya (Virgo) Tula (Libra)
Vayu	Tula (Libra)
Indra/Agni	Tula (Libra)
Mitra	Vrscika (Scorpio)
Indra	Vrscika (Scorpio)
Nirrti	Dhanus (Saggitarius)
Apas	Dhanus (Saggitarius)
Visvedevas	Dhanus (Saggitarius)
Brahma	Makara (Capricorn)
Visnu	Makara (Capricorn)
Vasus	Makara (Capricorn) Kumba (Aquarius)
Varuna	Kumba (Aquarius)
Ajikapada	Kumba (Aquarius) Mina (Pisces)
Ahir Budhyana	Mina (Pisces)
Pusan	Mina (Pisces)
Asvins	Mesa (Aries)
Yama	Mesa (Aries)

The Purusa then creates a broad, general framework for these Nakshatras to reside. For instance (RV 10.90.13 – 14), Purusa creates:

- The Moon, from Purusa's mind.
- The Sun, from Purusa's Eye.
- Indra and Agni, from Purusa's Mouth.

- Vayu, from Purusa's Breath.
- The Firmament, from Purusa's Navel.
- Earth, from Purusa's Feet.
- The Region, directions, from Purusa's car.

Some, but not all, Lunar houses exerted their dominion over the Vedic planetary system.

- Saraswati became the presiding deity over Mercury.
- Soma ruled the Moon.
- Agni presided over the Sun.
- Durga, a warrior Goddess, ruled Rahu, Rahu represents the ascend of the moon in its processional orbit around the earth.
- Indrani, Indra's consort, ruled over Venus.
- Rudra, a terrestrial manifestation of Agni, presided over Mars.
- Yama, the Lunar house having dominion over death, ruled Saturn.
- Indra ruled over Jupiter.

The energies and forces of the Vedic forces were created by Purusa. The further evolution of the cosmos proceeded when Purusa touched Prakrti. These movements created by Purusa created the Nakshatras (asterisms). Together these energies and forces in the Vedic dharma became associated together to form of what the Vedic astrologer calls the Stellar Population:

Guna	Presiding Vedic Energies (Zodiac)	Planet Ruling Zodiacal House (Ruling Deity)	Vedic Asterism	Zodiacal House
Sattva Rajas Tamas	Agni Prajapati Soma	Mercury (Saraswati)	Krittika Rohini Mrgashirsha	Mithuna (Gemini)
Sattva Rajas	Rudra Aditi	Moon (Soma)	Ardra Punavasu	Karkata (Cancer)
Tamas Sattva	Brhaspati Nagas	Sun (Agni)	Pushya Ashlasha	Simha (Leo)
Rajas Tamas	Pitrs Bhaga	Rahu (Durga)	Magha P. Phalguni	Kanya (Virgo)
Sattva Rajas	Aryaman Savitr	Venus (Indrani)	U. Phalguni Hasta	Tula (Libra)
Tamas Sattva Rajas	Indra (Tvastr) Vayu Indra/Agni	Mars (Rudra)	Chitra Svasti (Srati) Vasakra	Vrscika (Scorpio)
Tamas	Mitra Indra	Jupiter (Indra)	Anuradha Jyestra	Dhanus (Saggitarius)
Sattva Rajas	Nirrti Apas	Saturn (Yama)	Mula Purva Ashada	Makara (Capricorn)
Tamas Sattva Rajas	Visvedevas Brahma Visnu	Saturn (Yama)	Uttara Ashada Abhijit Sravana	Kumba (Aquarius)
Tamas Sattva Rajas	Vasus Varuna Ajikapada	Jupiter (Indra)	Dhanishta Shatabhisha Purva Bhadrapada	Mina (Pisces)

Tamas Sattva	Ahir Budhyana Pusan	Mars (Rudra)	U. Bhadrapada Revati	Mesa (Aries)
Rajas Tamas	Asvins Yama	Venus (Indrani)	Ashvini Bharani	Vrsabha (Tarius)

After the intervention of the gunas, however, the names and natures of the Vedic forces are transformed according to the schema contemplated by the Atharva Veda. In the Vedas, a Name is not something to be trifled. A Name has meaning and power. It has an inherent power to effect transformation and change of that person or thing it seeks to define. The Name is foundational to the worshiper's understanding of the world and is related to the Word (*Vak*). Articulation, Name and the Word, are born from OM, the most auspicious of names. Articulation is Name and Word bound together, and they are inextricably related to the creation of the cyclic evolution and dissolution of the universe. There is *Mahat*, the "great name" that permits a divine force to assume the role of other forces. It is ultimately a secret name, as in RV 3.38.1 and 3.38.4, which state that by this great secret name creatures were born in the past and will continue to be created in the future. The Vedic astrologer thus henceforth and as required addresses the Vedic forces by their new names, their *Mahat*, or Great Names. The gunas with the assistance of the Purusa then associates these names with their representational powers and assigns Lunar houses for these Vedic forces. You will notice in what follows that it is the asterisms (Nakshatras) which empower the spiritual endowments supplied by their respective Vedic energies and forces. This feature of the Vedic dharma is founded on science and Vedic wisdom. Just as every star we see in the evening star is in actuality a Sun much like the same which is in our solar system which supplies the source of all life on Earth, the group of stars consisting of the respective asterism (Nakshatras) are the power sources of the divine constitution (svadha) of the Vedic forces and energies over which they preside. Receiving these spiritual endowments from their respective asterisms, these Vedic forces and energies dispense the same to the worshiper.

- Agni is the Vedic force representing Change and Transformation. The Vedic Astrologer knows Agni differently. Agni is the Lunar house whose powers are conducted in his representation as the Sun. Agni is the presiding deity of the asterism of Krittika, and, in conjunction with the zodiacal houses of Mesa (Aries)and Vrsabha (Taurus), dispenses the spiritual endowments of *yajna*, the essential meaning of Sacrifice, and Divine Response.

- Prajapati is the Vedic force representing creation and protection. (*https://en.wikipedia.org/wiki/Prajapati*.) In the Vedic cosmos Prajapati dispenses the inner secrets of the yajna, the Sacrifice, and divine response. These spiritual gifts are given through the asterism of Rohini, in conjunction with the zodiacal house of Vrsabha (Taurus).

- Soma is the Vedic force representing religious ecstacy and liberation. These spiritual gifts are given through Soma's representation as the Moon, and Soma's dispensation of Bliss is made through the asterism of Mrgashirsha, in conjunction with the zodiacal houses of Vrsabha (Taurus) and Mithuna (Gemini).

- The lunar house of Rudra is a manifestation of Agni present in the firmament, the Mid-World, and a supplicant to Agni. (BD, 1.103.) Rudra rulers through the Ardra asterism and in conjunction with the zodiacal house of Mithuna (Gemini).

- The lunar house of Aditi is the leader of the Adityas, a group of Vedic forces and energies traditionally called "storm gods." The Vedic astrologer knows them as the representations and incorporations of the zodiacal houses. Aditi is the presiding deity of the houses of the zodiac. Aditi is the incarnation of Agni. (RV 2.1.11.) Aditi conducts those functions through the Punavasu asterism and through the zodiacal offices of Mithuna (Gemini) and Karkata, Cancer. Through these agencies, Aditi dispenses *Sunrta*, which is "true speech," or that which speaks in the language of, or gives, offers, or fosters an understanding of the Vedic dharma (*Rta*).

- *Brhad*, is the Sanskrit for "Vast." Brhaspati is a Lunar house in the dharma and represents *Brhad*, the Vastness of the Vedic dharma, from whence his name is derived. Brhaspati dispenses Beauty to the worshiper and is responsible for creating the Beauty which is present in the universe. Brhaspati dispenses this beauty through the Pushya asterism and in conjunction with the zodiacal house of Karkata, Cancer.

- The lunar house of Nagas is a Vedic energy which dispenses its spiritual endowment, *Bhanu*, the effulgent light of all asterisms. Nagas is a supplicant of Agni. Therefore, Nagas dispenses its light of *Bhanu* from the astral capabilities of Kritika and the Sun. The Vedic astrologer also knows Naga to dispense these spiritual endowments through its own astral offices of the asterism of Ashlasha and zodiacal house of Karkata, Cancer.

- Pitrs are neither Vedic forces nor energies, but are the spirits of the departed ancestors in Hindu culture. (*https://en.wikipedia. org/ wiki /Pitrs.*) Still, these spirits dispense their own spiritual endowments of *ayana* and serve as a guide for the worshiper to right conduct during the spiritual journey. This valuable spiritual endowment is made through the asterism of Magha and the zodiacal house of Simha (Leo).

- Bhaga is a mixture of divine and mortal manifestations. On the one hand, Bhaga is the Lunar house of Enjoyment — but the full spectrum of enjoyment. Bhaga is the divine Vedic force which consists of six distinct qualities. According to the Mahabharata, those qualities are (1) Lordship, (2) Righteousness, (3) Glory, (4) Wealth, (5) Wisdom, and (6) Detachment. The Vedic astrologer summarizes these attributes as Good Works. These spiritual endowments are dispensed through the asterism of Purva Phalguni and the zodiacal house of Simha (Leo), and this is how Bhaga is known to the Vedic astrologer, as the dispenser of Good Works.

- The lunar house of Aryaman is described as the protector of mares, and the Milky Way, which is called in the Rg Veda the *aryamnaḥ panthaḥ* and is said to be his path. (*https: //en. wikipedia. org /wiki /Aryaman#cite_refReferenceA-_1-1.*) Aryaman dispenses the spiritual endowment of Good Works. That the spiritual endowments of Aryaman shine through the brightness of the Milky Way justifies special mention. The Vedic astrologer also knows Aryaman as the dispenser of the spiritual endowment of

Good Works, through the asterism of Uttara Phalguni and the zodiacal houses of Simha (Leo) and Kanya (Virgo).

- Savitr is the Principle of Immortality. He bestows the benefit of immortality to other dynamic Vedic forces and to mortal humans. The lunar house of Savitr is the dispenser of the spiritual endowment of Bliss through the asterism of Hasta and the zodiacal house of Kanya (Virgo).

- The lunar house of Indra (Tvastr). The Vedic force of Indra is a complex collection of properties. When The presence of Tvastr complicates the overall complexion of this Vedic force. For the purposes of our Vedic astrologer, Indra and Tvastr are supplicants of Agni, for Tvastr fashioned Vayra, the weapon which killed Vrtr, the concealer of the inner truth and essence of the Vedic dharma (RV 1.31.2), and while slaying Vrtra Indra acts as an incarnation of Agni. (RV 1.59.6.) The Vedic astrologer knows this side of Indra and Tvastr as the dispenser of Bliss, through the asterism of Chitra and the zodiacal house of Kanya (Virgo) and Tula (Libra). Indra alone presides over another asterism, Jyestra, and administers his Vedic spiritual dispensations in conjunction with other members of the stellar population. The capacity of Indra and Tvastr which are displayed here represents a specialized capacity of this Vedic force. Indra and Tvastr act as supplicants of Agni because they both participate in the struggle with Vrtr, and in this capacity they act as incarnations of Agni. Indra who presides over the Jyestra asterism is the general function of this complex Vedic force, and Indra and Tvastr act as specialized, individual functions.

- Vayu is traditionally known in the Vedic dharma as the deity of prana, breath, life force. The lunar house of Vayu is ruled by Rudra, who is a manifestation of the Fire of Agni in the firmament. The Vedic astrologer knows Vayu as the dispenser of *sukha*, which is profound Spiritual Fulfillment, Happiness. Vayu dispenses *Sukha* through the zodiacal house of Tula (Libra), and the lunar house of Svasti (Srati).

- The lunar house of Indra/Agni is the combination of formidable and complex Vedic powers. Agni is presiding force of the Principle of Transformation, and Indra is Vedic force powering the Principle of Increase. The Vedic astrologer knows these Vedic forces better. The Sun. Agni, with Indra, dispenses the spiritual endowment of *radha* (Spiritual Increase, Great Achievements). Agni dispenses these endowments through the agencies of the Sun, the zodiacal houses of Mesa (Aries) and Vrsabha (Taurus), and through the lunar houses or asterisms of Krittika and Vasakra. Indra gives the spark of existence to dead, inert matter. Once enlivened, the fields operate to sustain all dimensions in the cosmos. Indra, in his capacity as the presiding deity of the planet Jupiter, the zodiacal house of Vrscika (Scorpio), and the lunar house of asterism of Jyestra, slays Vrtra to release the Vedic fields from time-space. The release of these Vedic fields is accomplished by Indra as an incarnation of Agni. Together, they are the dispensers of *radha* (Spiritual Increase, Great Achievements) in conjunction with the zodiacal house of Tula (Libra).

- The lunar house of Mitra has essentially the same attributes as his counterpart, Varuna, alone, as the principal guardian of the inner essence of the Vedic dharma, *Rta*, the breaches of which are punished. (*https://en. wikipedia. org/wiki /Mitra_(Vedic).*) The Vedic astrologer knows Mitra as the dispenser of Divine Response, through the asterism of Anuradha and in conjunction with the zodiacal house of Vrscika (Scorpio). Mitra dispenses this spiritual endowment additionally with the assistance of Indra in his capacity as the presiding deity of the planet Jupiter.

- Indra, a prominent Vedic deity, gives the spark of existence to dead, inert matter. Once enlivened, the fields operate to sustain all dimensions in the cosmos. Once enlivened, the fields operate to sustain all dimensions in the cosmos. Indra, in Vrscika (Scorpio) and the lunar house of asterism of Jyestra, slays Vrtra to release the Vedic fields from time-space. The release of these Vedic fields is accomplished by Indra as an incarnation of Agni. The Vedic astrologer knows his capacity as the presiding deity of the planet Jupiter, in the zodiacal house of Indra as the dispenser of Happiness. The lunar house of Indra dispenses this spiritual endowment additionally in his capacity as the presiding deity of the planet Jupiter.

- Nirrti is a nebulous Vedic force, one of the many from which the worshiper seeks protection. The nature of Nirrti's protection is in the form of its spiritual endowment, *amrtra*, which is "the Eternal, Undying Principle." *Amrta* is made up of two components, *am* ("to go towards") + *Rta* ("the essence of the inner truth of the Vedic dharma"). *Amrtra* thus connotes anything that encourages or supports action towards the inner essence of the Vedic dharma. It becomes the assurance the worshiper has in the spiritual journey; namely, a journey properly and successfully done yields the discovery of the inner essence of the Vedic dharma. (the Eternal, Undying Principle). It constitutes protection on the salvation and liberation of the worshiper's soul. It is, of sorts, a form of insurance policy. The Vedic astrologer knows that this protection is endowed to the worshiper from the power emitted from the Mula asterism and conveyed in conjunction with the zodiacal house of Dhanus (Saggitarius) and with the additional assistance of Yama as the presiding deity of Saturn.

- Apas is the deification of the essence of the Vedic dharma, the Waters. The Waters make a frequent appearance in this book and constitute the very nature of the Vedic dharma, which is fluidity and flow. The spiritual endowment dispensed by Apas is *anna*, food. Anna, food, carries with it a highly symbolic meaning. Water or the waters are considered food. (RV 1.30.1, 1.33.11, 1.52.2, 1.63.8, 1.100.5, 2.34.5, 2.35.1, 11, 2.41.18, 3.4.7, SPB 2.1.1.3, 13.8.1.4, 13.) The "Eater" can mean anything from the dissolving entity of the Vedic dharma, to the Vedic force which superimposes the material universe, to obtaining knowledge, enlightenment, or consciousness. In effect, this is coded language of the Subject or the Absolute Self. That the Waters — the inner essence of the Vedic dharma — is the food itself implies a self-sacrifice presenting an instance of the give-and-take of the Vedic sacrifice ritual. The Vedic astrologer knows that this protection is endowed to the worshiper from the power emitted from the asterism of Purva Ashada and conveyed in conjunction with the zodiacal house of Dhanus (Saggitarius) and with the additional assistance of Yama as the presiding deity of Saturn.

- Visvedevas are the collective Vedic gods taken together as a whole. (*https:// en.wikipedia.org/wiki/Visvedevas.*) The spiritual endowment dispensed by the Visvedevas is Strength, an appropriate endowment given that these Vedic forces taken together are indeed a formidable force to be reckoned. The Vedic astrologer know the Visvedevas as dispensing this spiritual gift through the power emitted from the asterism of Uttara Ashada, the zodiacal house of Dhanus (Saggitarius) and the additional assistance of Yama as the presiding deity of Saturn.

- The lunar house of Brahma dispenses the *punya*, offerings made to the Divine. *Punya* is an essential element of the give-and-take of the sacrificial process. *Punya* is the representation of the "give" element of the give-and-take exchange. While modernly *punya* became reduced to offerings of material objects, in the times of the Vedic astrologer *punya* was originally intended to be something more substantial. In those times, the worshiper offered the body, heart and soul at the sacrifice in the hopes of becoming born again. Brahma provides the framework for this exchange. This exchange is conducted through the power provided by the asterism Abhijit, in conjunction with the zodiacal house of Makara (Capricorn) with the additional assistance of Yama as the presiding deity of Saturn.

- The lunar house of Visnu provides nourishment. This spiritual endowment is conveyed to the worshiper through the power provided by the asterism Sravana, in conjunction with the zodiacal house of Makara (Capricorn) with the additional assistance of Yama as the presiding deity of Saturn.

- The lunar house of Vasus are attendant deities of Indra, and they were later associated with Visnu. (*https://en.wikipedia.org/ wiki / Vasu.*) The Vasus will have a greater importance in the history of the formation of the zodiacal houses. For now, the Vedic astrologer knows them as the dispenser of Nourishment, with Visnu. This spiritual endowment is conveyed to the worshiper through the power provided by the asterism Dhanishta, in conjunction with the zodiacal houses of Makara (Capricorn) and Kumbha (Aquarius) with the additional assistance of Yama as the presiding deity of Saturn.

- Varuna is the Lunar house administering of *Rta*, the over-arching principle of the Vedic dharma. The Vedic astrologer knows Varuna to be the dispenser of the spiritual endowment of Greatness, for once understood the worshiper indeed becomes "great." Varuna dispenses this spiritual endowment with the assistance of the planet Jupiter which itself is ruled by Indra. Varuna also dispenses Greatness to the worshiper through the lunar house or asterism Shatabhisha and the zodiacal house of Kumbha (Aquarius).

- Ajikapada is an ancient fire dragon. It stands for purification and penance. (*https://www.hindutsav.com/nakshatras/*.) It also is viewed as a form of Shiva, and a vehicle for the transport of Agni, the Sun, representing the cleansing spiritual power of fire. (*http://www.bhavans.info/jyotisha/nakshatra_purvabhadra-pada.pdf*.) Purification, thus, figures high in Ajikapada's estimation. The Vedic astrologer knows Ajikapada as the dispenser of Protection, through the astral offices of the asterism Purva Bhadrapada and zodiacal houses of Kumba (Aquarius) and Mina (Pisces).

- Ahir Budhyana is a serpent God, belonging to the depths of the sea and one of Rudras. (*https://en.wikipedia.org/wiki/ List_of_Nakshatras*.) Ahir Budhyana dispenses *susarma* or providing refuge or protection. The Lunar house of Rudra, the presiding deity of the planet Mars, provides assistance in this dispensation. Rudra is a terrestrial manifestation of the fire of Agni. The Vedic astrologer knows Ahir Budhyana as the dispenser of Protection, through the astral offices of the asterism Uttara Bhadrapada and zodiacal house of Mina (Pisces).

- The lunar house of Pusan administers the Vedic Principle of Direction and Pathways, *dishah*. The Vedic astrologer knows Pusan as dispensing Bhaga, or Enjoyment. We encountered Bhaga once before as a Vedic force. As an operating principle Bhaga carries the same meaning. Bhaga thus is not just having a good time but includes a cluster of qualities, all of which apply here as well. Pusan thus dispenses *Bhaga* (dominion, might, glory, splendor, wisdom, and dispassion) as a manifestation of the Fire of Agni in the firmament, and also through the asterism of Revati in conjunction with the zodiacal house of Mina (Pisces).

- The Asvins. The Twins represent the duality present in the Vedic dharma and are frequently associates for Indra. They too dispense the qualities of Bhaga, but though the asterism of Asvini, and through the zodiacal house of Mesa (Aries) in conjunction with assistance from Indriani, Indra's consort, the presiding deity of Venus.

- Yama is a god of death, the south direction, and the underworld. (*https://en. wikipedia.org/wiki/Yama*.) The Vedic astrologer however knows Yama as the provider of spiritual riches. This is what the Vedic astrologer means when he says, "spiritual riches." It is also the often-misunderstood phraseology in the Veda, those references to "property, riches, treasures," and the like. A frequent Code-Word for these spiritual riches are translated from the Sanskrit root, *vrs/*, which is translates as the Bull. Thus, Yama dispenses these gifts through the zodiacal house of Mesa (Aries). This spiritual endowment is also made through the power of the asterism Bharani and through the Lunar house of Indriani, Indra's consort, the presiding deity of Venus. It seems oddly fitting that the worshiper would be endowed with these gifts on death, many times the real end of the spiritual journey.

A few of the Vedic forces created thereby had to decide where the Nakshatras would ultimately rest.

- The Fore-Fathers, the *ptrs*, through their lunar mansion of Magha, placed the Nakshatras — specifically, "decorated" the sky — above the evening sky. (RV 10.68.11.)
- Varuna, as the Lord Protector of the Vedic dharma (Rta), through the powers given to him by the lunar mansion of Shatabhisha, created vehicle by which the Nakshatras appear in the evening sky — the Lunar Mansions. Varuna established the present system whereby the Nakshatras appear at night, do not appear during daylight, and congregate with the progressions of the Moon. (RV 1.24.10.)

What is interesting about this framework is its larger cosmological-religious context. The Fore-Fathers, the *ptrs*, those who "decorated" the sky with the Nakshatras, who preside over the Southern Path, are not concerned with the liberation or salvation of the worshiper or any aspect of the spiritual journey. This is the nature of the Southern Path. The Vedic astrologer will shortly explain that the Southern Path is the world of transmigration, that place where the soul goes if liberation has not been achieved in this lifetime. The Northern Path is that path belonging to Varuna and other Vedic forces and energies, and this is where the worshiper's soul goes when liberation has been achieved in this life. It is appropriately proper than mere placement of the Nakshatras should be undertaken by those Vedic forces associated with the Southern Path. The Southern Path is most closely associated with the Two-Dimensional Universe, the viable, material world in which we live and breathe. However, when Varuna assigns the movements and positions of the Nakshatras in conjunction with their respective lunar houses, well, this is a subtle world that is not tangible, one grounded solely on organization and function and which pertain to subtle functions in the Vedic dharma. As such, it is a path a step or two above the Two-Dimensional Universe, one which indeed exists, but which must be experienced and recognized to be fully exploited for the purposes of the spiritual journey.

This is the macrocosm for the cosmic portion of the Vedic dharma. Once establishing the macrocosm, the gunas, the Nakshatras and the planets work to create the microcosm. Following this tradition, the Vedic Astrologer assigns the five elements to the following planets. In the next part, the gunas act to establish the microcosm.

The Gunas Create the Material World

At this point, all evolutionary branches and trajectories converge to create the material world. The planets establish the gross elements of the material world (BPHS, 1.18,1.20). The Vedic astrologer presents the following chart to set forth the planet, ruling deity with the elements which operated in the Vedic dharma:

Planet	Ruling Deity	Element
Mars	Rudra	Fire
Mercury	Saraswati	Earth
Jupiter	Indra	Akasha (Ether, Sky)
Venus	Indrani	Water
Saturn	Tama	Air

From these stellar elements, the remaining creation living below is created. Vedic texts would established correspondences between the zodiacal houses, through the Nakshatras, and the human organisms which lived below (BJ, 1.11):

Zodiacal House	Sign	Part Of Human Body
Aries	Mesha	Head
Vrishabha	Taurus	Face
Mithuna	Gemini	Breast
Karkata	Cancer	Heart
Simha	Leo	Belly
Kanya	Virgo	Navel
Tula	Libra	Abdomen
Vrischka	Scorpio	Genitals
Dhanus	Saggitarius	Thighs
Makara	Capricorn	Knees
Kumbha	Aquarius	Ankles
Meena	Pisces	Feet

Once the physical organism is established, the mental and psychological characteristics coalesce. The same forces which created the physical body are responsible for the mental states that inhabit those bodies. Those forces include not only the zodiacal houses, and by implication their Nakshatras, but the planets and the Vedic astral forces which impel these phenomena. Now that the worshiper and Vedic astrologer have a body the gunas and the Vedic forces and energies act in conjunction with and through the zodiacal houses and planets to provide the psychic components for their body, mind and soul (PBHS, 12, 13, 19, 22.):

Planet	Ruler	Zodiacal House	Characteristic	Gender	Gunas
Sun (Surya)	Agni	Mesa (Aries) Vrsabha (Taurus)	The Soul of All	Masculine	Sattva
Moon (Candra)	Soma	Vrsabha (Taurus)	The Mind of All	Feminine	Sattva
Mercury (Budha)	Sarawati		Giver of Speech	Neutral	Rajas
Venus (Sukra)	Indrani (Indra's consort)		Governs semen (potency)	Feminine	Rajas
Mars (Kuja)	Rudra	Mithuna (Gemini)	Strength	Masculine	Tamas
Jupiter (Brhaspati)	Indra	Vrscika (Scorpio)	Confers Happiness and Knowledge	Masculine	Sattva
Saturn (Sani)	Yama	Mesa (Aries)	Indicates Grief	Neutral	Tamas
Rahu	Durga		The Mind of All	Feminine	
Ketu	Rudra		The Mind of All	Feminine	

The Vedic astrologer understands there is a different rule for the animal world. In the case of quadrupeds the following correspondences exist (BJ, 3.3):

Zodiacal House	Sign	Part Of Animal Body
Aries	Mesha	Head
Vrishabha	Taurus	Face, Neck
Mithuna	Gemini	Forelegs and shoulders
Karkata	Cancer	The Back
Simha	Leo	Breast
Kanyn	Virgo	The Flanks
Tula	Libra	Belly
Vrischka	Scorpio	Anus
Dhanus	Saggitarius	Hind Legs
Makara	Capricorn	Genitals
Kumbha	Aquarius	Buttocks
Meena	Pisces	Tail

Changing perspective, the gunas have all they need to establish the Nakshatras with their respective zodiacal houses. Once established by the gunas, the Nakshatras acquire a name, (Kak, *The Astronomical Code of the RgVeda*, (2011), pp. 173 – 174), find a location, conjoin with a zodiacal house, and are presided over by a Vedic force or energy:

Asterism	Name	Location	Zodiacal House	Presiding Deity
Krittika	From the root, krt, "to cut."	Pleiades, η Tauri	Mesa (Aries) Vrsabha (Taurus)	Agni
Rohini	"ruddy"	α Tauri	Vrsabha (Taurus)	Prajapati

Mrgashirsha	"deer's head"	β Tauri	Vrsabha (Taurus) Mithuna (Gemini)	Soma
Ardra	"moist"	γ Geminorum	Mithuna (Gemini)	Rudra
Punavasu	"who gives wealth again"	Pollux, or β Geminorum	Mithuna (Gemini) Karkata (Cancer)	Aditi
Pushya	"flowered"	δ Cancri	Karkata (Cancer)	Brhaspati
Ashlasha	The "embracer"	δ, ε, ζ Hydrae	Karkata (Cancer)	Nagas
Magha	"the bounties"	The group of stars near Regulus, or α, η, γ, ζ, μ, ν, Leonis	Simha (Leo)	Pitrs
Purva Phalguni	"Bright"	δ and θ Leonis	Simha (Leo)	Bhaga
U. Phalguni	"Bright"	β and 93 Leonis	Simha (Leo) Kanya (Virgo)	Aryaman
Hasta	"Hand"	γ Virginis	Kanya (Virgo)	Savitr
Chitra	"Bright"	Spica or α Virginis	Kanya (Virgo) Tula (Libra)	Indra (Tvastr)
Svasti (Srati)	"Self-Bound"	π Hydrae	Tula (Libra)	Vayu
Vasakra	"Without Branches"	α2, β, σ Librae	Tula (Libra)	Indra/Agni

Anuradha	"Propitious"	β, δ, π Scorpii	Vrscika (Scorpio)	Mitra
Jyestra	The "Eldest"	α Scorpii	Vrscika (Scorpio)	Indra
Mula	The "Root"	ε-λ, ν Scorpii	Dhanus (Saggitarius)	Nirrti
Purva Ashada	"unconquered"	δ, ε Sagittarii	Dhanus (Saggitarius)	Apas
Uttara Ashada	"unconquered"	σ, ζ Sagittarii	Dhanus (Saggitarius)	Visvedevas
Abhijit	"reaching victory."	Vega, the brilliant α Lyrae	Makara (Capricorn)	Brahma
Sravana	"Ear"	β Capricornus	Makara (Capricorn)	Visnu
Dhanishta	"Most wealthy"	δ Capricornus	Makara (Capricorn) Kumba (Aquarius)	Vasus
Shatabhisha	"having a hundred physicians"	λ Aquarii	Kumba (Aquarius)	Varuna
Purva Bhadrapada	"auspicious feet"	α Pegasi	Kumba (Aquarius) Mina (Pisces)	Ajikapada
U. Bhadrapada	"auspicious feet"	γ Pegasi	Mina (Pisces)	Ahir Budhyana
Revati	"Wealthy"	η Piscium	Mina (Pisces)	Pusan
Ashvini	"The two horse-harnessers"	β and α Arietis	Mesa (Aries)	Asvins
Bharani	"The Bearers"	δ Arietis	Mesa (Aries)	Yama

This chart contains all the information the worshiper might need to understand, if not their spiritual message, then the Nakshatras' inner essence. That essence is conveyed through their root names. As everything in the Vedic dharma, a "name" has its own specific, complicated, meaning. In the Vedas a name has meaning, it is something with power. This notion is contrary to the notion in other traditions, philosophical or otherwise, which hold that the assignment of a name is purely arbitrary. On the contrary, in the Vedas, a Name has an inherent power to effect transformation and change. The Name is foundational to the worshiper's understanding of the world and is related to the Word (Vak). Articulation, Name and the Word, are born from OM, the most auspicious of names. Articulation is Name and Word bound together, and they are inextricably related to the creation of the cyclic evolution and dissolution of the universe. Whenever the universe is dissolved and subsequently evolves, the Divine Sound, OM, resonates. (JUB 1.7.1, 1.9.1, 1.10.1.) But as R.L. Kashyap, the eminent Vedic scholar observes, a name in the Vedas is not simply an identifier, but a presence which may be revealed only as a result of yogic practice and meditation. Clearly, a name is at once the verbal articulation of a subject, but also the subtle basis of the subject. The name and the articulation of that name matters, because in its own way it affects and implicates the Divine Word, and by extension, the greater Vedic dharma. Thereupon:

- The asterism of Krittika took its name from the root krt, "to cut."
- The asterism of Rohini means "Red" or "Ruddy.
- The asterism of Mrgashirsha means "Deer's Head."
- The asterism of Ardra means "moist."
- The asterism of Punavasu means "who gives wealth again."
- The asterism of Pushya means "Flowered."
- The asterism of Ashlasha means the "embracer."
- The Asterism of Magha means the "bounties."
- The Asterism of Purva Phalguni means "Bright."
- The Asterism of Uttara Phalguni means "Bright."
- The Asterism of Hasta means "Hand."
- The Asterism of Citra means "Bright."
- The Asterism of Svasti (Srati) means "Self-Bound."
- The Asterism of Vasakra means "Without Branches."

- The Asterism of Anuradha means "Propitious."
- The Asterism of Jyestra means the "Eldest."
- The Asterism of Mula means the "Root."
- The Asterism of Purva Ashada means the "unconquered."
- The Asterism of Uttara Ashada means the "unconquered."
- The Asterism of Abhijit means "achieving victory."
- The Asterism of Sravana is the Ear.
- The Asterism of Dhanishta means "most wealthy."
- The Asterism of Shatabhisha means "having a hundred physicians."
- The Asterism of Purva Bhadrapada means "auspicious feet."
- The Asterism of Uttara Bhadrapada means "auspicious feet."
- The Asterism of Revati means "Wealthy."
- The Asterism of Ashvini means "the two horse-harnessers."
- The Asterism of Bharani means the "Bearers."

The Vedic astrologer will explain later the precise application of these names. Next there is the placement of the Nakshatras into their respective places in the Evening sky.

- The asterism of Krittika is fixed at the location of the constellation of the Pleiades, specifically at Star η Tauri in the constellation of Taurus.
- The asterism of Rohini is fixed at the location of the star α Tauri of the Pleiades in the constellation of Taurus.
- The asterism of Mrgashirsha is fixed at the location of the star β Tauri of the Pleiades in the constellation of Taurus.
- The asterism of Ardra is fixed at the location of the star γ Geminorum in the constellation of Gemini.
- The asterism of Punavasu is fixed at the location of the star Pollux, or β Geminorum in the constellation Gemini.
- The asterism of Pushya is fixed at the location of the star δ Cancri in the constellation of Cancer.
- The asterism of Ashlasha is fixed at the location of stars δ, ε, and ζ in the constellation Hydra.
- The Asterism of Magha is fixed at the location of the group of stars near Regulus, or stars α, η, γ, ζ, μ, and ν in the constellation Leo.

- The Asterism of Purva Phalguni is fixed at the location of the stars δ and θ Leonis in the constellation of Leo.
- The Asterism of Uttara Phalguni is fixed at the location of the stars β and 93 Leonis in the constellation of Leo.
- The Asterism of Hasta is fixed at the location of the star γ Virginis in the constellation of Virgo.
- The Asterism of Citra is fixed at the location of the star Spica or α Virginis in the constellation of Virgo.
- The Asterism of Svasti (Srati) is fixed at the location of the star π Hydrae in the constellation of Hydra.
- The Asterism of Vasakra is fixed at the location of the stars α2, β, and σ Librae in the constellation of Libra.
- The Asterism of Anuradha is fixed at the location of the stars β, δ, and π Scorpii in the constellation of Scorpius.
- The Asterism of Jyestra is fixed at the location of the α Scorpii in the constellation of Scorpius.
- The Asterism of Mula is fixed at the location of the stars ε through λ, and ν Scorpii in the constellation of Scorpius.
- The Asterism of Purva Ashada is fixed at the location of the stars δ and ε Sagittarii in the constellation of Sagittarius.
- The Asterism of Uttara Ashada is fixed at the location of the stars σ and ζ Sagittarii in the constellation of Sagittarius.
- The Asterism of Abhijit is fixed at the location of the Vega star, the most brilliant α Lyrae in the Lyra constellation.
- The Asterism of Sravana is fixed at the location of the β Capricornus star in the Capricorn constellation.
- The Asterism of Dhanishta is fixed at the location of the star δ Capricornus in the Capricorn constellation.
- The Asterism of Shatabhisha is fixed at the location of the star λ Aquarii in the Aquarius constellation.
- The Asterism of Purva Bhadrapada is fixed at the location of the star α Pegasi in the Pegasus constellation.
- The Asterism of Bhadrapada is fixed at the location of the star γ Pegasi in the Pegasus constellation.
- The Asterism of Revati is fixed at the location of the star η Piscium in the Pisces constellation.

- The Asterism of Ashvini is fixed at the location of the stars β and α Arietis in the Aries constellation.
- The Asterism of Bharani is fixed at the location of the star δ Arietis in the Aries constellation.

It is from this lofty perch that the Nakshatras spread their wisdom to the Vedic astrologer and the worshiper and to all persons living in the material world. The earth and its sentient beings is being bomb-barded by this stellar wisdom all the time. The worshiper and the Vedic astrologer is made up of the physical and subtle elements from these daily doses of external wisdom. It is only fair to assume that there is more than stellar dust and gas involved in the worshiper's spiritual journey, and the Vedic astrologer knows very well that the stellar population gives more to this material world than space debris. This is what this book will be about — the philosophical, religious and spiritual endowments given to the worshiper.

ooooooooooooo

What follows is a modest interpretation, an attempt to explain a riddle that has perplexed humans since they left their caves. This book is about the Vedic astrologer and the cosmos about which the Vedic astrologer attempts to understand. In this attempt the Vedic astrologer strives to present the lessons from the Stars, from the standpoint of Vedic literature and scripture in a coherent fashion. It provides one possible interpretation of the application of the Vedas to those things astrological. Whenever possible, assertions are supported by doctrinal references.

This volume is Part I of a companion set. The Vedic astrologer will release a second volume describing the effect the planets, the zodiac, the equinoxes, and constellations and other members of the Stellar Population has upon the spiritual journey.

It is the Vedic astrologer's sincere hope that you, dear Reader, will not be intimidated by the numerous citations in the text. The presence of the doctrinal citations in this text are as much for the benefit of the curious Reader for additional knowledge, for the Reader's future reference and study, as much as it is for the Vedic astrologer's own assurance that he is not falling into error. If the interpretation is incorrect, outlandish, audacious, foolish, unfounded, unorthodox, or simply mistaken, the fault lies not in the Stars or in the marvelous, moving, wisdom found in the Vedas, but belongs solely to this author.

THE VEDIC ASTROLOGER

COSMOLOGY
IN THE VEDIC DHARMA

In the Vedas, Dharma is the totality of the natural order. (VaS, 1.1.1.) What is the "Vedic dharma"? What does this actually mean? What does it consist of?

In the Introduction the Vedic astrologer described the origins of the Vedic dharma. Tilak, in his monumental commentary to the Bhavagad Gita, describes "dharma" as the "nature of things," and the "the order that holds society together," and that which "bind[s the] force of society." (Arun Tiwari, A Modern Interpretation of Lokmanya Tilak's Gita Rahasya (2017), pp. 113, 115.) At first there was a great mass of indiscriminate, undifferentiated, matter. Then, when Indra felled Vrtra with Vayra, he divided the world into two parts: one part, *adya/* ("What is") and the other *anyad* ("What is not"). (RV 6.24.5) and transformed "What is not" into "What is." The forces of Indra and Soma cast *asat* below the triple structure of the world. (RV 7.104.11.) From there, in the beginning stages of all creation, described in RV 10.190, *Satyam* and *Rta* are found at the highest level of Being. (RV 10.190.1.) Of the two, *Rta* prevailed over and pervades still over *Satyam*. As Hickman notes in his Toward a Comprehensive Understanding of *Rta* in the Rg Veda," *Satya* is "being" manifested by the establishment of the universe, but *Rta* is the mode of that being which promotes and supports the freedom and mobility of *Satyam*. The former, *Rta*, furnishes the framework for the latter, sat, and allows it, as well as all other subjects in the cosmic order, to function. *Rta* is the internal mechanism of the proverbial watch which regulates the ticking of the universe.

And so it is for the Vedic dharma. The Seven-Dimensional is a combination of the three upper and three lower levels of existence, conjoined together by the Svar. *Satyam* and *Rta* together create the second highest level of being, *Tapas*. (RV 10.190.1.) After *Tapas*, *Madhuunaam*, or Bliss, is on the bottom tier of the higher world. In the Arthavada, those highest stations are *Rta*, *Satyam* and *Brhat* (Infinity). (AV 12.1.1.) On the bottom level exists the three levels of sensible appearance: the earth, mid-world, and heaven. (RV 1.34.7; 1.154.4.) This schema is referred to differently. In some passages, these lower three regions have been referred to as "tridhaatu prthhvim," (RV 1.34.7; 1.154.4) which can be roughly rendered as the "three levels of the material plane." Sometimes these two general existential planes are referred in terms of the Ocean, one Higher and one lower. Other times, these two existential planes, one higher and one lower, are what are more commonly set forth as simply Heaven and Earth.

Whatever their denomination, each level contains three subdivisions. There are three levels of the Higher Ocean, Heaven, *dyaus*. (RV 1.35.6; AV 8.9.16.) The three divisions of this existential level are:

- *Uttama(m)* (RV 1.24.15; 1.25.21; 1.50.10; 1.91.8; 1.108.9; 1.156.4; 1.163.7; 2.1.2; 2.23.10; 3.5.6, 8; 4.315; 436.8; 4.54.2; 5.25.5; 5.28.3; 5.59.3; 9..22.6; 9.51.2; 9.63.29; 9.67.3, 28; 9.85.3; 9.107.1; 9.108.16; 10.75.1; 10.97.18; 10.159.3; 10.166.5; 10.78.3) or *uttame* (RV 1.31.7; 2.41.5; 5.60.4; 6.60.3, 8; 8.51.4; 9.61.29.)
- *Madhyama* (RV 1.24.15; 1.25.21; 1.108.9, 10; 2.29.4; 4.25.8; 6.21.5; 6.62.11; 7.32.16; 8.61.15;9.70.4; 9.108.9; 10.15.1; 10.81.5; 10.97.12) or *madhyame* (RV 1.27.5; 2.23.13; 5.60.6; 6.25.1); and
- *Avama* or *avame*. (RV 1.105.4; 1.108.9, 10; 1.163.5; 2.35.2; 3.54.5; 6.251; 6.62.11; 7.71.3; 1.185.11.)

Even here there are other expressions of Heaven. In the Atharva Veda there are also three levels of heaven. The highest level is that level where the ptrs (fathers) and angirasas reside. (AV 18.1.6; 8.2.48.) The second level is the "starry" heaven (AV 18.2.12, 48), and the third, lowest, level is the "watery" heaven. (AV 18.2.12, 48.)

In both the Rg Veda and Atharva Veda there are three levels to the atmosphere, the mid-world, firmament. (RV 1.34.8; AV 8.9.16.)

There is more uniformity when describing the Lower Ocean, or Earth. There is also in both the Rg Veda and Atharvaveda three levels to the lowest level of the material world. (RV 1.34.8; AV 8.9.16.) The Fire of Change, in its three aspects of Agne, Jatavedas, and Vasivanara, is the embodiment of the lower three regions. (BD, 1.6.6.) Agne is the embodiment of the earth; Jatadevas is the embodiment of the mid-earth (RV 1.77.5; 2.4.1; 3.1.20; 4.1.20; 4.58.8; 6.4.2; 6.10.1; 6.12.4; 6.15.13; 7.9.4; 7.12.2; 10.45.1; 10.61.14; 10.83.2; 10.88.4); Vasivanara is the embodiment of heaven. (RV 1.59.3, 4, 6, 7; 1.98.1, 2; 3.2.1, 11, 12; 3.3.1, 5, 11; 3.26.1, 2, 3; 4.5.1, 2; 5.15.13; 6.7.1, 2, 6, 7; 6.8.1, 2, 3, 4; 6.9.1, 7; 7.5.1, 2, 5; 7.6.6, 7; 7.13.1; 7.49.4; 8.30.4; 9.61.16; 10.45.12; 10.88.12, 13, 14.) Indra, in his representation of strength and vitality, embodies the mid-world. (BD 1.69.) The Purified Mind (Soma), the inherence of the Eternal Law of God-Realization and Purification, embodies heaven. (RV 9.22.51; 9.63.10; 9.48.1; 9.54.3; 9.63.9; 9.72.8; 9.86.29; 9.894.3; 9.113.2.)

There is an intermediary level binding the Upper Ocean and Lower Ocean. Materially, the binding level is represented by the Mid-World, the Firmament. In both the Rg Veda and Atharvaveda there are three levels to the atmosphere, the mid-world, firmament. (RV 1.34.8; AV 8.9.16.) The mid-world binds the two levels, the Upper Ocean and Lower Ocean. Subtly, these two levels of existence, the Upper Ocean and the Lower Ocean, are bound by the Svar.

The Svar is the transitory world of heaven and light. In the middle, the svar, is an intermediate world of heaven and light. (RV 1.35.6.) And here the Svar is bound by triads. There are three subdivisions to each region and has three subdivisions. (RV 3.56.8.) There are three regions of light in the svar. Those regions are *rocanna*, svar, and *raajati* (*raajati*). (RV 1.102.7; 2.27.9; 1.149.4; 4.33.5; 5.29.1; 5.69.1; 9.17.5.) These regions of light are sometimes indicated as general regions of light. (RV 1.102.7; 1.149.4; 3.56.8; 4.53.5; 5.69.1; 5.29.1; 9.17.5.) Those three regions of light are:

- *Rocanna.* (RV 1.49.1; 1.49.4; 1.50.4; 1.81.5; 1.93.5; 1.102.8; 1.146.1; 1.149.4; 2.27.9; 3.2.14; 3.5.10; 3.12.9; 3.44.4; 3.56.8; 3.61.5; 4.53.5; 3.61.5; 5.29.1; 5.56.1; 5.61.1; 5.69.4; 6.6.2; 6.7.7; 8.1.18; 8.5.8; 8.8.7; 8.14.7; 8.14.9; 8.93.26; 8.94.8; 8.98.3; 9.17.5; 9.37.3; 9.42.1; 9.85.9; 10.32.9; 10.46.3; 10.49.6; 10.65.4; 10.89.1; 10.170.4; 10.189.2.)

Rocanna is the highest sphere of light. (RV 1.6.1, 9; 1.19.6; 1.81.5; 1.86.1; 1.92.17; 1.113.7; 1.121.9; 1.124.3; 1.146.1; 3.2.14; 5.41.3; 6.7.7; 6.44.23; 8..1.8; 8.14.9; 8.25.19; 8.52.8; 9.42.1; 9.85.9; 9.61.10; 10.32.2; 10.70.5; 10.143.3.) The highest region of light is sometimes indicated as upa nam ketu. (RV 5.34.9.)

- The Svar.
- *Revati* (RV 1.164.12; 6.2.2; 6.66.7; 9.84.4; 9.108.2), also known as *rajas*. (RV 1.125.20; 1.36.12; 1.188.1; 5.8.5; 5.28.2; 5.81.5; 7.32.16; 8.13.4; 8.15.3; 8.15.5; 8.19.31; 8.37.3; 8.60.15; 9.66.2; 9.86.5, 28; 10.140.4; 10.167.1.)

It is a grand structure, and on top is *parame vyoman*, "the highest heaven." The parame vyoman is that highest level of heaven; it is where Divine Grace (Indra) and Transformation (Agni) were born RV 3.32.10); it is where the very source of Deification and Divination (Soma) dwells with the power of Divine Grace (Indra). (RV 9.86.15.) It is the place of origin where all the principles inherent in the divinities reside (RV 1.164.39.) It is a place beyond space and time. It is a region of Pure Being.

Parame Vyoma is also a psychological state. It is made of a psychological state through the agency of select divine attributes. The Fire of Transformation (Agni), as soon as it appeared in the realm of Pure Being (*parame vyoma*), placed the spark of consciousness in the firmament. (RV 4.50.4.) Brihaspati, as soon as it appeared in this region, created the seven layers of consciousness and the entire multitude of physical forms. (RV 5.15.2.) These divine qualities and others are crystallized in the place of the sacrificial alter (RV 5.15.2), where, once reborn, the worshiper is united with this highest place of Pure Being. (RV 1.143.2.) The Lunar house representing this highest state of Pure Being is Brihaspati. Brihaspati is the Supreme manifestation of consciousness. The appellation literally means "Lord of Infinity (the psychological state of Pure Being)."

Pure Being is infused in the Vedic dharma. The transition into the material world corrupts the pure state of Being and transforms it to a material state of Becoming. It is in this transition that this pristine state is transformed into the existential planes that we know today. Schematically, this edifice looks like this:

Parame Vyoma "the Highest Heaven"

UPPER HEAVEN (Upper Ocean):

ELEMENT	ATHARVA VEDA	RIG VEDA
Fire	Ptrs (Angirasas)	Uttama (Uttame)
Akasha Ether)	"Starry" Heaven	Madhyama (Madhyame)
Water	"Watery" Heaven	Avama (Avame)

THE SVAR

THE INTERMEDIARY REGION BETWEEN HEAVEN AND EARTH:

THE SVAR (REGION OF LIGHT)
Rocanna
Svar
Recast (Rajasic)

THE SENSIBLE WORLD (Lower Ocean):

Lower Heaven
Mid-World
Earth

It is in this cosmological framework that the stellar population is found. But as far as the sentient being is concerned, that population is composed of one thing — Light. The Vedic astrologer and the worshiper knows that it is not simply light. Light is composed of subtle elements, which is discussed next.

AND THERE WAS LIGHT

Light is a very important component in the Vedic dharma. The British astrophysicist, Sir John James, famously stated that the entire concepts, here of the Vedic dharma, reduce the whole world of the universe, potential or existent, to light. The Rg Veda is replete with light, in all its permutations. It is a religious and esoteric doctrine — nay, a religion — based on light. The Vedic astrologer counts upwards to five hundred different words expressing this very important concept. At a very basic level the Veda is a world divided between light and darkness, good and evil, us and them. At its most general overview, life is a battle between the agents of light and the forces of darkness. The final destination for the worshiper, what would be called millennia later "liberation," is the luminous region of light, to conquer darkness.

Light holds a very special significance to the Vedic astrologer, because it answers a crucial question. Granted, there is wisdom in the stellar population. But how is that wisdom communicated to the worshiper? An important component in this is the role of the Vedic forces and energies. It is through their offices that the stellar population's wisdom is communicated to the worshiper. Specifically, through the Vedic forces and energies at the sacrificial ritual. But it is through Light, the light of the stellar population through the Vedic forces and energies, that this wisdom is conveyed most of the time in conjunction with the Nakshatras and zodiacal houses over which the Vedic forces preside. Light is very much considered the wire, through which their wisdom is conducted to the Vedic forces and energies, who relay that wisdom to the worshiper.

All varieties of light are different in their own different way. Each variety of light has its own properties, intensities, origins, and benefits. All starlight appears alike to the observer on earth but they differ in purpose and intensity and have a different application for the worshiper during the spiritual journey. The common denominator is the manner in which that wisdom is conveyed to the worshiper. There is a wisdom contained in the light emitted from the Nakshatras. That wisdom is not held simply in the twinkling light of the evening sky. That wisdom is contained in the form of the types of light discussed in this chapter. This chapter discusses the subtle basis for that light. The worshiper then does not receive the spiritual endowments of Rohini, for example, or any other Nakshatra through "light." That wisdom is contained in that light's subtle basis. The worshiper does not learn the spiritual lessons of that light through simply observation. The spiritual endowments are obtained through sustained and concentrated *Tapas* and austerity on that light. This is true of the light of Rohini and true for all the other Nakshatras.

In the Vedas there are many forms of Light. What follows in this chapter are just very few of the most prominent examples of light.

Go, Gobhir

We have seen this type of light earlier. Kashyap renders *go* or *gobhir* as "rays of light." Indeed, in most situations they are. This is exactly the conventional interpretation of *go* or *gobhir*. Kashyap and other scholars follow this meaning first ascribed by Sri Aurobindo, and render *go* or *gobhir* "ray-cow," "rays of intuition," "rays of knowledge," or the like.

Monier Williams offers a more specific definition. If the contest is between the general and specific definition of the word, the specific meaning prevails. One specific definition Monier Williams gives for *go* or *gobhir* is "herds of the sky," or skylight or the light from the collective stellar population, from stars, planets, or other apparent astronomical phenomena or events. It really isn't difficult to understand why it would take this meaning, "herds of the sky." The "herd" implicates the group of physical cattle, but the collective grouping implicates the vastness of the esoteric knowledge to be found in the stellar population. It is difficult for the contemporary who lives in an industrial urban environment, where the firmament is covered in a perpetual hazy of smoke and particulates, to fully appreciate this herd of light. But go outside the city limits, to the mountains, and look at the sky without the cover of pollution. The evening sky is positively alive and lustrous with light, with tiny, discreet, drops of light punctuating the inky darkness of the background. These glittering flecks of light do not even flicker. A star which flickers indicates the presence of an environmental obstruction, blocking the image of the starlight above. In the evening sky unimpeded, the Milky Way is a clear, distinct band of milky blue traversing one end of the horizon to the other. In the same way witnessing the stellar population and this band of light creates a profound experience from which the worshiper gains a greater appreciate the Vedic dharma and its lessons. This more specific definition adds a greater understanding to both Agni and the Fire of Light. For example, it was earlier revealed that Agni the Mystic Fire is the Lord of Wealth and the Shining Herds. (RV 3.16.1.) Monier Williams would change this to say that Agni is the Lord of the light, the fire, the energy emitting from the stellar population. In a profound, esoteric sense this is exactly how *go* or *gobhir* should be applied to the Fire of Light. While cows represent this Bovine Knowledge, it is the knowledge obtained, derived, and learned from the stellar population. And what better way to communicate the fire of Agni than though *go or gobhir*, starlight? We see the stellar population in the cool of the evening as a flicker of light. In reality that faint light is millions of miles away. That tiny speck is as hot and massive as our own Sun, many times greater in bulk and heat. They are fire in the most pure, emblematic form.

So is it with the other passages in the Veda which reveal their mysteries of the fire of *go* and *gobhir*. It is upon the Rishiis to reveal these mysteries.

RV 1.23.15: Pusan, who endows the worshiper with the spiritual benefit of *Bhaga* (enjoyment) through the asterism of Revati and zodiacal house of Mina (Pisces), brings the worshiper the happiness and bliss of Soma at the spring season. The Rishii expresses the phrase "spring" in a highly stylized, cryptic manner. The rc (mantra) reveals that the pleasures of the Soma experience occurs when "the farmer tends his fields" and when he feeds his livestock. In other words, spring. The season has a special significance. Spring is the season when Sacrifices begin, it is the season of renewal of the earth and the worshiper. It is the time of year when the Vernal Equinox occurs, itself pregnant with meaning in the Vedic dharma. Pusan, as opposed to Surya, Sun gods both, confers the benefits to the worshiper. Both are associated with the Sun. This is indicated in these rcs (mantras):

RV 1.95.8: The fire of Agni assumes his effulgent, celestial form from the starlight emitted from the evening sky, from the zodiacal houses of Mesa (Aries) and Vrsabha (Taurus), and from the asterism of Krittika.

RV 3.1.12. The fire of Agni "gives birth" to the "herds of the sky," *go* or *gobhir*. This is the way of the Rishiis have in saying the fire of Agni supplies the material and subtle basis for the power that brightens the starlight appearing in the evening sky. This rc (mantra) highlights another reason Krittika holds so much significance to the Vedic astrologer. It is from this asterism that the subtle power of Agni is concentrated. That subtle power makes its physical appearance collectively in the "herds of the sky," *go* or *gobhir*. This subtle power is conveyed to the worshiper through the auspices of Indra, the incarnation of the fire of Agni. (RV 3.50.3.)

RV 6.65.5: The Words transmitting the mantras and revelations of the Angirasas smashed the mighty mountain releasing the *gobhir*, representative of the combined wisdom of the asterisms and Nakshatras in the Vedic dharma.

Indra, the incarnation of the fire of Agni, is instrumental is conveying knowledge obtained, derived, and learned from the stellar population:

RV 1.7.3: So, in a Sukta in which Indra, as the incarnation of the fire of Agni, presides, Indra destroys the mountain, releasing the cattle, *gobhir*, which, in the fire of the zodiacal houses of Dhanus (Saggitarius) and Vrscika (Scorpio), release not simply cattle, but happiness and bliss.

RV 1.16.9: For those same reasons, Indra, as the incarnation of the fire of Agni, provides happiness and bliss to the worshiper.

RV 1.53.4: Indra, as the incarnation of the fire of Agni, in conjunction with the fire of the zodiacal house of Vrscika (Scorpio), releases happiness and bliss held by Vrtra.

RV 1.62.5: Indra, as the incarnation of the fire of Agni, dispels the darkness with the light shining from the planet of Jupiter and the asterisms of Anuradha Jyestra.

This astronomical application is found in other rcs. In this context, Vrtra concealed, and Indra released, the "shining cows," the "herds of the sky," *go* or *gobhir*. (RV 3.31.10, 11; 4.3.11; 4.19.7; 6.17.7; 6.38.3, 5;

6.60.2; 9.87.3; 9.89.3.) Recall, in the struggle with Vrtra, Indra is acting as an incarnation of the fire of Agni and are thus functionally identical. In RV 1.36.8, as the creation of the energies inhered in starlight, the Bull as Agni reveal the "herds of starlight" after Vrtr is felled. Exactly what is the fuller implications of this rc (mantra) is clarified in RV 5.45.8. There, these "herds of starlight" lead the worshiper down the path of *Rta*, the inner essence of the Vedic dharma. We will be hearing more about Vrtr a little later.

Ghrta

Related to *go* or *gobhir* is ghrta. *Ghrta* is light, but specifically the Light of Knowledge derived from the Nakshatras. *Ghrta* is derived from the Sanskrit root, *gh*, meaning, to go, to hasten towards, + *Rta*. *Ghrta*, ghee, is "that which hastens towards or go to *Rta*," anything which supports the Vedic dharma.

According to RV 4.58.1 there are four aspects to *ghrta*:

- *Ghrta* is the highest form of offering to the divine.
- *Ghrta* is that which is recovered by Indra when battling Vala.
- *Ghrta* includes the cows recovered from the Panis, released by Indra typically with Vajra, and the waters released when Indra slew Vrtra.
- *Ghrta* is the inspired speech from the Rishis.

From these elements the Vedic astrologer summarizes *ghrta* to mean the primal light of knowledge. The Vedic astrologer maintains this is but another way of saying that *ghrta* is an aspect of Consciousness which is yet another way of saying "the Vedic dharma.

Ghrta also refers to the cows recovered from the Panis, released by Indra typically with Vajra. (RV 1.11.5; 2.24.6; 8.3.4; 1.93.4; 4.58.4.) The imagery is not difficult to imagine. The cow is a figurative symbol for light and for representative for knowledge and illumination. Cows came to be symbolic of these two word-concepts for a variety of reasons. One reason offered is their revered status in Indian society. A more likely reason is the simple fact that they are the animals who produce the milk which yields clarified butter, Ghee, *grhta*, which has its own special meaning. Cows produce the milk which yields clarified butter, *ghrta*, the clarity of illumination or knowledge. It is as if that because cows produce the milk (knowledge) that can also be made in butter and ghee (illumination), there must be something inherent in the animal-symbol itself which is capable of producing these attributes. For this reason, cows are said to be symbolic of the primal light. (RV 4.36.4.) As anyone who has cooked with ghee knows, it is practically impossible to clean ghee off a countertop, due to its oily, dense composition. There is an element of permanence to the substance, a permanence shared with knowledge once attained. But as anyone who has seen a clear bottle of ghee on the deli shelf can attest to, the oil portion of ghee, *ghrta*, has the ability to separate from the whey, such that the upper portion, the oil, is a crystal clear golden color, and the lower portion containing the congealed whey, is cloudy and bilious. This is also the nature of Consciousness: Clear at one moment, cloudy the next. The clear portion, however, is so brilliant, so crystalline, that this provides the metaphorical meaning for *ghrta*: Mental acuity, clarity and brilliance. In this state the mind is receptive; in its cloudy state, blocked in its own cloudy fog. The cloudy fog is created by Vrtra, the clear brilliant state of mental acuity and consciousness is removed by Indra, who with Tvastr, grants the Bliss which accompanies this state of consciousness through the power of the asterism of Chitra in conjunction with the zodiac house of Vrscika (Libra).

Ghrta is associated with several Vedic forces and energies.

- The lunar house of Agni, the Sun, who dispenses the secrets of yajna and Divine Response from the power of the Krittika asterism, in conjunction with the zodiacal houses of Mesa (Aries) and Vrsabha (Taurus).
- The lunar house of Soma, the Moon, who dispenses Bliss through the asterism of Mrgashirsha, in conjunction with the zodiacal houses of Mithuna (Gemini) and Vrsabha (Taurus).
- Vrtra, the concealer of the Vedic dharma.

There will be more about this synergy later in this book. For now, the next light from the Nakshatras is *Jyotis*.

Jyotis

Jyotis is an aspect of Agni and perhaps is the best known to the general public, if for the wrong reasons. There is and has always been an astrological component to the Vedic dharma. In the post-Vedic periods, after the influence of Hellenism to the Indian sub-continent, Jyotis became associated with predictive astrology. To the worshiper and to the Vedic astrologer, there is indeed a wisdom to the stellar population. That wisdom is not associated with the prediction of modern events or happenings. There is indeed a measure of prognostication from the stellar population. But just as the efforts at achieving siddhis, or supernatural powers, to the yoga practitioner is possible but to be avoided, so is milking the stars to tell the future in present time is a waste of other valuable lessons that may be learned. The yogi masters advise that the achievement of the siddhis are to avoided because they are an unnecessary distraction. In the same way the Vedic astrologer cautions that attempting to tell the future is vulnerable to all manner of quackery and ignores the real lessons that can be obtained from the stellar population.

Jyotis is not simply light. To the Vedic astrologer the wisdom of the stars is contained in the chart described above in AV 19.7.2 – 5. That wisdom is filtered through the light from the stellar population and heavenly bodies, and as that light is seen by the worshiper influences not only the worshiper but all sentient and non-sentient beings. Further, *Jyotis* carries specialized meanings. A subset of jyotis is *jyotir*. *Jyotir* carries specific meaning to the powers of Agni. Instead of the Fire of Agni subsuming the principles of the Light of Consciousness, Increase, the Waters, Purification — all those aspects discussed in the Introduction — *Jyotir* imbues the Fire of Agni with these specific meanings:

- Generally, as for the Fire of Agni, it is the light of the Sun.
- As to the Lunar house of Indra in his incarnation as Agni it is the light of the moon.

- As to the Lunar houses of the Asvins, applicable to Agni through the incarnation of Indra, it is the inner eyesight, the source of the "twinkle" in the eye.
- It is the light of heaven.
- It is that light which achieves for the worshiper freedom and liberation, the "guiding light."

These specific characteristics are united in the astrological position Agni occupies. The astrological/astronomical identification of Agni thus encompasses these capacities:

- Agni is the presiding deity ruling and presiding over the zodiacal houses of Mesa (Aries) and Vrsabha (Taurus).
- Agni is the presiding deity representing and presiding over the Sun.
- The lunar house of Agni represents the asterism of Krittika.
- In his capacity of ruling over the Krittika asterism, Agni dispenses the spiritual endowment of Divine Response.
- The lunar house of Agni, in conjunction with Indra, rules and represents the asterism of Vasakra.
- In his capacity of ruling and representing the asterism of Vasakra, the lunar houseof Agni, with Indra, dispenses the spiritual endowment of *radha* (Spiritual Increase, Great Achievements).
- The lunar house of Agni, in conjunction with Indra, rules and represents the zodiacal house of Mesa (Aries) and Vrsabha (Taurus).

The important portion of these capacities is the dispensation of spiritual endowments. The Fire of Agni dispenses the endowments of Divine Response and *radha* (Spiritual Increase, Great Achievements) both to the Vedic astrologer and to the worshiper. We already know that these capacities refer to two specific functions of the Fire of Agni. One, Divine Response refers to Agni's role as the Messenger and everything that role entails; two, *radha* refers to Agni's prime representation as the Principle of Increase and everything that means for the worshiper. What is different with the Fire of Jyotis is the agency through which these endowments are dispensed. Agni dispenses these endowments through the agencies of the Sun, the zodiacal houses of Mesa (Aries) and Vrsabha (Taurus), and through the asterisms of Krittika and Vasakra. Thus, through the study, learning, and consequent meditationaland religious austerities of the Sun, Krittika and Vasakra, the receipt, appreciation and integration of these spiritual endowments may be achieved.

This is generally how the Fire of *Jyotis* generally operates. For every Lunar house, the spiritual endowments associated with the Lunar house is conveyed to the worshiper through their astrological and astronomical portals. In other words, *Jyotis* is the course and movement of the heavenly bodies which exert influence on earth. It answers the question of just what is that influence on beings and events on this material world. It carrier of the light of sun and all the qualities therein. It is the light of the moon and all the inherent qualities of that light. It is the source of that mental capacity which supplies the spark of awareness to sentient beings. It is the edifying light of heaven. It guides the worshiper during the spiritual journey. By contrast it does not necessarily guide the worshiper to inform him what will happen next Tuesday, or any other related question posed in a natal chart.

For the specialized member of *jyotir*, Monier Williams assigns the following meanings:

- The light of the Moon.
- The light representing the divine principle of life or intelligence and/or the source of intelligence.

The creation of *jyotir* has an ancient history welled up in the beginnings of the Vedic dharma.

- The lunar house of Agni, as the presiding deity of the Krittika asterism and in conjunction with the zodiacal houses of Mesa (Aries) and Vrsabha (Taurus), set the Sun (Surya) in its place to bestow the light of *jyotir* to all sentient beings. (RV 10.156.4.)
- The light of *jyotir* was created by Surya for the spiritual benefit of all sentient beings. (RV 7.76.1.)
- Usas, the Dawn and the terrestrial manifestation of Agni, created *jyotir* to clear away the darkness. (RV 7.77.1.)

- At the same time, Indra acted in conjunction with Usas to install within the Sun the light of *jyotir* which would guide all sentient beings. (RV 6.44.23.)
- Later, the Ptrs decorated the heavens with the asterisms so that their light of *jyotir* can be showered on the worshiper. (RV 10.86.11.)

In many instances in this book a single English word will not convey the full meaning of a foreign word or phrase. In these instances, the better approach is to resort to the foreign word along with a full explanation. The non-English word will thus be a shorthand way of conveying a panoply of different meanings. This is the situation with *jyotir*. There are many elements to Jyotis, and *jyotir* is only one. While there are two distinct meanings for *jyotir*, they are not mutually exclusive. One is Intelligence, or Mind, which is frequently represented in terms of light or brightness. *Jyotir* is a special case because of its association with Moonlight, the second element. The Lunar house of Soma is also associated with the moon, and its primary function in the Vedic dharma — the source of religious ecstacy and liberation — is especially appropriate for the Vedic dharma. Not only is moonlight related to intelligence on the basis of the light reflected from the Sun, but Soma's religiosity forms the basis for the *divine* principle of life and Intelligence (Mind.) These two elements act together to produce a single meaning for *jyotir*, one that recognizes the Moon and the light transmitted therefrom as the source of the divine principle of life and intelligence (Mind). *Jyotir* then represents Moonlight (the light of Soma) which is the source of the divine principle of life and intelligence (Mind). This is the combined meaning of *jyotir*.

This is not to say that there are no other meanings for *jyotir*. *Jyotir* is closely associated with the *svadha*, the inherent and internal essence of the individual powers, of the Lunar houses. This *svadha* is communicated through light and results in a form of *jyotir*. Thus, *jyotir* becomes the version of light for many Lunar houses. *Jyotir* is thereby compared to the light of the following Lunar houses and Vedic forces:

- The light of Aditi. (RV 782.10; 7.83.10; 10.185.3.)
- The light of the fire of Indra. (RV 10.35.1.)
- The light of Soma. (RV 10.43.4.)

- The light of the Angirasas. (RV 1.57.3.)
- *Jyotir* is considered a distillation of these and other qualities of the Vedic forces. A well-known rc (mantra) relates how the worshiper drinks Soma to be like the gods. RV 8.48.3.) The complete recitation of this rc (mantra) reveals that the "immortality" of the Vedic forces and energies *is indeed* the light of *jyotir.*

Jyotir is also the light emitting from distinct parts of the heavenly bodies. Thus, *jyotir* becomes:

- The light of heaven. (RV 10.36.3.)
- Daylight. (RV 7.90.4)
- Sunlight. (RV 8.12.30.)
- The morning light at the beginning of the day. (RV 7.78.3.)
- Moonlight. (RV 1.123.1.)

Jyotir is also a combination of the two elements of Vedic force and heavenly body. The Vedic forces both presided over and personified the heavenly bodies. This should not be surprising since it is from the Vedic forces that the heavenly bodies obtain their spiritual strength. Nevertheless, *jyotir* derives in part from the synergy of the Vedic forces and the heavenly bodies with which they represent:

- The lunar house of Agni, as the presiding deity of the Krittika asterism and in conjunction with the zodiacal houses of Mesa (Aries) and Vrsabha (Taurus), is the light of the Sun (*jyotir*). (RV 6.3.1.)
- The Lunar house of Agni is contained in the light of *jyotir.* (RV 6.9.4.)
- *Jyotir* is the light of Surya. (RV 8.25.19.) Surya is primarily the astronomical body the Sun, but Surya's energy has the qualities of measuring the days, prolonging the days of life, driving away sickness, disease and other evils, and the Creator of all. Ancient commentators clarified the relationship of Surya and Savitr. Yaksa notes that Savitr appears when the darkness disappears. (Nir. 12.12.) Yet, commenting on RV 5.81.4, Sayana states before its

rising the Sun is called Savitr and from the rising of dawn to its setting the Sun is Surya. These two conflicting commentaries are reconciled by the Vedas in the dynamic force inherent in Savitr. Savitr "approaches" or "brings" Surya. (RV 1.35.8.) "Bringing" Surya" implies a similarity but also increase. In the hierarchy of Vedic dynamic forces, Surya is accorded a greater importance.

- The Vedic energy of Surya is the highest light (*jyotir uttaram*). (RV 1.50.10.)

- The lunar house of Savitr is bright with the light of *jyotir*. (RV 10.139.1.) Savitr is the Principle of Immortality. He bestows the benefit of immortality to other dynamic Vedic forces and to us, mere mortals. He also bestowed immortality to the Rhbus, who were previously mortal and acquired life immortal by virtue of their fine character. (RV 1.110.1, 2.) He bestows immortality to the gods and duration to humans. (RV 4.54.2.) After bestowing duration to the life of humans, Savitr conducts the remains of the worshiper's mortal coil, the smoke of the cremated body, upwards to the heavenly world (RV 10.17.4), under the guidance and protection of Pusan (AGS 4.4.7), another Sun deity and member of the Adityas (astrological houses). Savitr is also the Principle of Creation. This principle makes Savitr the ultimate giver of life. (RV 1.22.7.) This principle is responsible for all physical manifestation. (RV 6.71.2.)

- The lunar house of Savitr, the Sun, is lodged in the ray of intuition which creates *jyotir*, the divine light for us all. (RV 4.14.2.)

- The lunar house of the Asvins created the strength which is present in light of *jyotir*. (RV 1.92.17.)

The Vedic forces act together to endow the spiritual teachings of *jyotir* to the worshiper. In the Lunar house of Agni the fire of *Jyotir* is especially pronounced.

- Usas, a terrestrial manifestation of Agni, the presiding deity of the Krittika asterism and in conjunction with the zodiacal houses of Mesa (Aries) and Vrsabha (Taurus), created *jyotir* for the benefit of the worshiper. (RV 1.92.4.)

- Manu, the First Man (Adam), established the light of *jyotir* for the Lunar house of Agni, and this light is based on the inner essence of the Vedic dharma (*Rta/jaata*). (RV 1.36.19.)
- Agni, the presiding deity of the Krittika asterism and in conjunction with the zodiacal houses of Mesa (Aries) and Vrsabha (Taurus), is the very personification of *jyotir*, and in that capacity travels up and down the Vedic dharma as the Lord of Heaven, guiding the worshiper through the spiritual journey. (RV 1.59.2.)
- The lunar house of Agni, the presiding deity of the Krittika asterism and in conjunction with the zodiacal houses of Mesa (Aries) and Vrsabha (Taurus), is possessed of a triple ray (*tridaa/tuu*) of light (*jyotir*). The light of *jyotir* emits from his eye, and the light of immortality resounds from his mouth. (RV 3.26.7.)
- The lunar house of Agni, as the presiding deity of the Krittika asterism and in conjunction with the zodiacal houses of Mesa (Aries) and Vrsabha (Taurus), purifies the Sun (*jyotir*) with three filters. (RV 3.26.8.) The light of the Sun is available for all to see and enjoy. In this sunlight is *Jyotir*, the principal means for Agni to convey his powers of purification to the worshiper.

The worshiper's attainment of *jyotir* is a classic example of the give-and-take process of the *yajna*. There is first the desire to obtain the spiritual endowments of *jyotir*.

- The worshiper seeks the spiritual endowments of *jyotir* from Agni. (RV 7.35.4.)
- The worshiper seeks the spiritual endowments of *jyotir* from Indra. (RV 6.47.8; 7.32.26.)

Agni is the messenger. Agni is also the presiding deity of the Sun and derives his power of spiritual endowment through the Krittika asterism and in conjunction with the zodiacal houses of Mesa (Aries) and Vrsabha (Taurus) and has a singular purpose in conveying the spiritual endowments of *jyotir* to the worshiper. The Lunar house of Agni has primary task of presenting the light of *jyotir* to the worshiper:

- The lunar house of Agni, the Sun, through the Krittika asterism and in conjunction with the zodiacal houses of Mesa (Aries) and Vrsabha (Taurus) is himself the embodiment of the divine principle of life and intelligence found in *jyotir*. (RV 6.9.4.)
- The lunar house of Agni, the Sun, through the Krittika asterism and in conjunction with the zodiacal houses of Mesa (Aries) and Vrsabha (Taurus) presents this light of life and intelligence to the worshiper at the Sacrifice. (RV 6.9.5.)
- When incorporated in the worshiper's spiritual journey, the worshiper is enlightened in mind, body and spirit. (RV 6.9.6.)

The Lunar house of Agni, the Sun, in his capacity as the presiding deity of the Krittika asterism and in conjunction with the zodiacal houses of Mesa (Aries) and Vrsabha (Taurus), presents the light of *jyotir* in unison with the other Lunar houses to bring this light to the worshiper. Agni, in his capacity as the presiding deity of the Krittika asterism and in conjunction with the zodiacal houses of Mesa (Aries) and Vrsabha (Taurus), essentially coordinates the actions of the other Vedic forces and energies and places those forces in alignment. For example:

- Agni, the Sun, through the Krittika asterism and in conjunction with the zodiacal houses of Mesa (Aries) and Vrsabha (Taurus) brings the spiritual light of *jyotir* for the spiritual benefit of the worshiper. (RV 7.5.6.)
- Usas, the Dawn and a terrestrial manifestation of Agni, the Sun, through the Krittika asterism and in conjunction with the zodiacal houses of Mesa (Aries) and Vrsabha (Taurus), brings *jyotir*, the divine principle of life and intelligence to the worshiper. (RV 1.113.1, 16.)
- Usas brings *jyotir* as reflected Moonlight of the Sun to the worshiper. (RV 1.123.1; 1.124.3.)
- Usas brings the light of *jyotir* directly from the Sun. (RV 10.35.5.)
- Usas spreads the Daylight (*jyotir*) upon every new day. (RV 5.80.2.)
- The Asvins through the power of the asterism of Asvini and zodiacal house of Mesa (Aries) brings *jyotir* to the worshiper. (RV 1.117.7; 1.182.3.)

- The lunar house of Indra, the presiding deity over Jupiter, with the power vested through Jyestra, and in conjunction with the zodiacal house of Vrscika (Scorpio), takes *jyotir*, made it his own, and conveyed it to the worshiper. (RV 3.39.7.)

- The lunar house of Indra, the presiding deity over Jupiter, with the power vested through Jyestra, and in conjunction with the zodiacal house of Vrscika (Scorpio), brings *jyotir* to the Sacrifice to enable the worshiper to overcome evil. (RV 3.39.8.)

- The lunar house of Aditi, the head of the Adityas (zodiacal houses), through the power of Punavasu and the zodiacal houses of Mithuna (Gemini) and Karkata (Cancer), brings the light of *jyotir* to the worshiper. (RV 2.27.11.)

- The Adityas themselves, the zodiacal houses, bring the light of *jyotir* to the worshiper. (RV 2.17.14.)

Of course, Agni also acts on his own behalf to bring the spiritual endowments of *jyotir* to the worshiper. (RV 6.9.6.) The Lunar house of Agni also takes part in the grandest of all cosmic struggles.

Jyotir and the Clash of the Titans

RV 1.36.8 poses an interesting twist on the struggle with the serpent Vrtra. This rc (mantra) reveals how Agni as the Bull smote and killed Vrtra, making the Vedic dharma wide and broad. Aside from the fact that it clearly shows Indra to be the incarnation of Agni in matters dealing with Vrtr, it is interesting first because the force of Agni is the presiding deity on the Sukta in which the rc (mantra) is found. The force of Agni thereby applies to the revelations obtained therein. In this rc (mantra) the Rishiis reveal that when the force of Agni unveiled the shroud worshiper's worshiper's mortal coil of Vrtra the subtle foundation for the inner essence of the Vedic dharma was created. In its compact language pregnant with meaning, RV 1.36.8 reveals these basic elements:

- The lunar house of Agni, in his capacity as the presiding deity of the Krittika asterism and in conjunction with the zodiacal houses of Mesa (Aries) and Vrsabha (Taurus), creates the wide basis of

Heaven (*rodasi*) and Earth. These two worlds are stated in the collective and separately. In other words, the force of Agni not only created both Heaven and Earth, but he forged the union of these polar opposites. Indeed, in so uniting Heaven and Earth, Agni shows that these worlds are not so different after all. The very act of unification indicates how similar and unitary they really are.

- The lunar house of Agni, in his capacity as the presiding deity of the Krittika asterism and in conjunction with the zodiacal houses of Mesa (Aries) and Vrsabha (Taurus), releases the Water. Water is the ultimate basis of the Vedic dharma.

- The lunar house of Agni, in his capacity as the presiding deity of the Krittika asterism and in conjunction with the zodiacal houses of Mesa (Aries) and Vrsabha (Taurus), makes a sound (*ahuta*) uttering the Word.

- The lunar house of Agni, in his capacity as the presiding deity of the Krittika asterism and in conjunction with the zodiacal houses of Mesa (Aries) and Vrsabha (Taurus), releases the "herds of light," interpreted as the release of the light of knowledge.

RV 1.36.8 is an amazing rc (mantra) for another reason. It encapsulates the basic inner essence of the force of Agni described by Pandit David Frawley — speech (*vak*), prana and intelligence. It is the element of Speech which is the most remarkable. When Agni makes the sound uttering the Word, the Rishiis presage that which will be said millennia later. Later, it would be said that the sound of AUM is the primaeval sound which resonates after the emergence of a new cycle of creation which creates all sentient beings, things and objects in the Vedic dharma. (JUB 1.7.1, 1.9.1, 1.10.1.) The inner Vedic force of Agni is the energy which lies behind and is impels that resonance. This rc (mantra) further elaborates on the first steps in the evolution of the sentient beings, things and objects in the Vedic dharma. Those initial steps are very elemental and basic but provide the basis of the inner foundation of all sentient beings, things and objects in the Vedic dharma. Those elements are

- Agni wins the rays or "herds of starlight."

- Agni conquers and presides over the life energy (*ashvo*) of the Vedic dharma.

These two elements might as well be considered the constituent parts of *jyotir*. It is remarkable in that Agni, and not Indra, is the named Lunar house winning these benefits, but that the struggle with Vrtra has been posed in an astronomical context. Viewed in this light, Vrtra is seen to be more than simply a malevolent serpent. The basic nature of Vrtra, remember, is that of an enveloper, that which covers. Vrtra obscures and conceals. This is why, the Brahmanas remind us, he is called "Vrtra." (SPB 1.1.3.4.) Vrtra covers and obscures the inner truth and essence of the Vedic dharma, which is *Rta*, the second part of Vrtra's name. The act of concealment can be — and is — applied in many contexts, and these contexts have been used, certainly, in the Rg Veda. Aside from concealing the waters, Vrtra's the powers of concealment has been applied in other contexts:

- In a religious context, Vrtra has been associated with Evil. When Vrtra is felled by Indra's weapon, Vrtra's evil is driven away by the New Moon. (SPB 6.2.2.18.)

Astronomically considered, the subduing of Vrtra is seen as the emergence of the New Moon. "The full-moon oblation, assuredly, belongs to the Vrtra-slayer, for by means of it Indra slew Vrtra; and this new-moon oblation also represents the slaying of Vrtra, since they prepared that invigorating draught for him who had slain Vrtra. An offering in honor of the Vrtra-slayer, then, is the full-moon sacrifice. Vrtra, assuredly, is no other than the moon; and when during that night (of new moon) he is not seen either in the east or in the west, then he (Indra) finishes in destroying him by means of that (new-moon sacrifice), and leaves nothing remaining of him." (SPB 1.6.4.12-13.)

In the same way Vrtra endeavors the capture and restraint of the light of *jyotir*. It is not such a huge stretch to find that the clash with Vrtra brings consequences to the creation of the light of *jyotir*. The same Vedic titans, Agni and Indra, are involved, with Soma following close behind. Surya makes a surprise appearance. The import of Vrtra to *jyotir* is profound and far-reaching:

- The light of *jyotir* was released when Indra slew Vrtra. (RV 2.11.8.)
- With the dual Lunar houses of Agni-Soma, when Vrtra was slain, the divine light of *jyotir* was created for the benefit of all sentient beings. (RV 1.93.4.)
- The Lunar house of Indra is the winner of light (*jyotir*) as a result of being victorious over Vrtra. (RV 3.34.34.)
- The light of *jyotir* resulted from the death of Vrtra at the hands of Surya. (RV 10.170.2.) According to this rc (mantra) the struggle with Vrtra was very much seen as a struggle between two forces— *Rta*, the inner essence of the truth of the Vedic dharma and *Vrtra*, which, because he is in reality that which covers or obscures *Rta* is that which is not of the inner essence of the truth of the Vedic dharma.

All that is *jyotir* shines brilliantly. *Jyotir* explains from whence this brilliance originated. The next kind of light, *Bhanu*, describes and personifies this brilliance.

Bhanu

The Nagas are "a member of a class of mythical semidivine beings, half human and half cobra. They are a strong, handsome species who can assume either wholly human or wholly serpentine form and are potentially dangerous but often beneficial to humans. ... The creator deity Brahma relegated the Nagas to the nether regions when they became too populous on earth and commanded them to bite only the truly evil or those destined to die prematurely. They are also associated with waters — rivers, lakes, seas, and wells — and are guardians of treasure." (*https://www. britannica. com/topic/naga-Hindu-mythology*.) The operative words in the description of the Nagas are that they are "associated with waters — rivers, lakes, seas, and wells — and are guardians of treasure." The Vedic astrologer believes that both of these clauses — associated with the Waters and the guardians of the treasure — refer to the same object. The treasure in this instance are the Waters, the inner essence of the Vedic dharma, and this is the treasure bestowed upon the worshiper.

Specifically, in this instance the Naga is the guardian of *Bhanu*, a specific aspect of Light. The Vedas consist of a spiritual tradition based on Light. Monier Williams, the authoritative dictionary of Sanskrit, lists upwards to five hundred different words for "light," each containing its own specific meaning and context. *Bhanu* is only one such word. It is, of course, the light originating from the asterism Ashlasha. The Light of Ashlasha, however, carries with it so many other meanings. It can mean:

- Sunlight.
- Rays of light from the sky.
- The quality of this light, including the effulgence, resplendence, brilliance, brightness, or brightness of this light.
- The Beauty of this aspect of light.

Significantly, *Bhanu* continues the work of the previous asterism, Pushya. In Pushya, Beauty incarnate was the spiritual endowment given to the worshiper. Here, in Ashlasha, the spiritual endowment given is *Bhanu*, Beauty, with the properties of Light. Bhanu can be found in these manifestations:

- The lunar house of Agni as the presiding deity of and conveying the spiritual endowments from the asterism of Krittika, in conjunction with the zodiacal houses of Mesa (Aries) and Vrsabha (Taurus).
- The Maruts as a manifestation of the Fire of Agni in the Firmament. (BD, 1.103.)
- Usas as a terrestrial manifestation of the Fire of Agni. (BD, 1.108.)
- The lunar house of the Asvins as the presiding deity of and conveying the spiritual endowments of the asterism Ashvini, in conjunction with the zodiacal house of Vrishabha (Taurus).
- The lunar house of Naga itself acts in conveying the spiritual endowments of the asterism Ashlasha, in conjunction with the zodiacal house of Simha (Leo).

These are some formidable Lunar houses at work. These Lunar houses act in concert with Naga to convey the spiritual endowments of *Bhanu*. Agni as the presiding deity of and conveying the spiritual endowments from the asterism of Krittika, in conjunction with the zodiacal houses of Mesa (Aries) and Vrsabha (Taurus), represents the core spiritual qualities of the endowment itself:

- The Lunar house of Agni as the presiding deity of and conveying the spiritual endowments from the asterism of Krittika, in conjunction with the zodiacal houses of Mesa (Aries) and Vrsabha (Taurus) emits the shining brilliance of *Bhanu* with celestial splendor. (RV 10.6.2.)
- There are four elements to the shining beauty of Agni's *Bhanu* — *kavi*, the Fire of Revelation; *kratu*, the Fire of Divine Will; Food, the symbol of Consciousness; and *Bhanu*, the beauty of shining light. (RV 7.6.2.)
- *Bhanu* is the light of the Lunar house of Agni. (RV 1.92.5; 3.21.4.)
- The fuel powering the Lunar house of Agni is *Bhanu*. (RV 10.6.1.)
- Agni is the deification of the Beauty of *Bhanu* and shines like gold. (RV 7.3.6.)
- Agni's Beauty gleans with refulgence. (RV 7.9.4.)
- With this the Lunar house of Agni is armed with the *Bhanu* (sunlight) of the Great Impeller of the Vedic dharma. (RV 6.6.6.)

Bhanu has an ancient history:

- The lunar house of Agni as the presiding deity of and conveying the spiritual endowments from the asterism of Krittika, in conjunction with the zodiacal houses of Mesa (Aries) and Vrsabha (Taurus), was the first born of the Lunar houses, and was effulgent, the epitome of Beauty in its brilliance emanating from the light of *Bhanu*. (RV 8.7.36.)
- When the other Vedic forces created Agni, they made him resplendent in *Bhanu* (light). (RV 3.2.3.)

- Then, at this early stage of the Vedic dharma, the Lunar house of Agni gathered all traces of *Bhanu* and spread its effulgence to all corners of the dharma. (RV 6.16.2.)
- With his refulgent light of *Bhanu*, Agni, the presiding deity of and conveying the spiritual endowments from the asterism of Krittika, in conjunction with the zodiacal houses of Mesa (Aries) and Vrsabha (Taurus), overcame the Blackness which had permeated the indiscriminate, undifferentiated mass of inert matter which had enveloped the cosmos and with his Beauty and radiance bathed the Vedic dharma with light. (RV 10.3.2.)
- The radiance of Agni's *Bhanu* shines in waves, like sound waves, and in this manner reaches the highest reaches of heaven. (RV 10..3.5.) This is a clear reference to the waves of Saman discussed in the Introduction.
- Agni's light of *Bhanu* is also compared to the weaving which takes place in the subtle foundation of the Vedic dharma. As with the *disha* discussed in the introduction, Agni's shining light of *Bhanu* weaves like threads throughout the underbelly of the Vedic dharma. (RV 10.53.6.)

Bhanu is rightfully compared to sunlight. As sunlight, it is the only reason sentient sentient beings on earth. Without *Bhanu* (sunlight) the material world would be a very different place. Sunlight is the basis of all life on earth, it is the basis for the Vedic astrologer's existence and the reason for the worshiper's spiritual journey. *Bhanu*, sunlight, allows the stage for the worshiper's spiritual journey:

- The Lunar house of Agni shines in the light of *Bhanu* comparable to the sunlight of Savitr, and the power of this light lifts Agni high above to the heavens. (RV 4.13.2.)
- The Lunar house of Agni shines with the power of *Bhanu*, and, like the Sun, emits a fiery flame. RV 2.8.4.)
- And why is there a general equivalence between the simple sunlight of Savitr and the light of *Bhanu* from Agni? Savitr, like Agni, is the Child of the Waters. (RV 10.140.2.) The Vedas have been handed down in highly symbolic language. As discussed in

the Introduction, the "Child of the Waters" is coded language signifying from whence the Vedic forces of Agni and Savitr arose. The Waters is symbolic language signifying the essential nature of the Vedic dharma — the complete Vedic dharma. If Agni and Savitr are the "Child of the Waters," they arose from the same intrinsic forces which power the Vedic dharma. Thus, the Veda states that an aspect of Agni, Vaisvanara, was born at the "highest place," *parama vyoman*, an existential plane higher than the Seven-Dimensional Universe. (RV 7.5.7.) The "Child of the Waters" signifies "the germ (seed) of waters, germ (seed) of woods, germ (seed) of all things that move not and that move" (RV 1.70.3.) In that capacity Agni and Savitr become the Seed of everything in the Vedic dharma. The Lunar houses of Agni and Savitr thereby represent the latent potentiality of all things, alive or inert. That latent potentiality germinates and grows when nourished by the Waters.

Bhanu is a significant part of the worshiper's life and supports the world in which the worshiper lives and conducts the spiritual journey:

- The Vedic force of Agni, as the presiding deity of and conveying the spiritual endowments from the asterism of Krittika, and in conjunction with the zodiacal houses of Mesa (Aries) and Vrsabha (Taurus), fills the heart of the worshiper with the white light of *Bhanu*. (RV 10.1.1.)
- The Lunar house of Agni expiates the sins of the worshiper through the light of *Bhanu*. (RV 1.92.1, 2.)
- The Lunar house of Agni shines with the purifying light of *Bhanu*. (RV 6.15.5.)
- The Lunar house of Agni is the highest hotr (officiating priest) at the sacrifice and is resplendent in *Bhanu*.

The worshiper is not the only beneficiary of the light of *Bhanu*. The existential levels of earth, mid-earth and heaven in the Vedic dharma receives the blessings:

- The Lunar house of Agni spreads his light of his *Bhanu* over the three existential levels of earth, mid-earth and heaven. (RV 10.88.3.)
- *Bhanu* indeed is the force of light with which Agni binds Heaven and Earth (RV 3.22.2.)
- *Bhanu* is radiance itself and Agni invests this light on Heaven and Earth. (RV 4.17.)

In concert with Agni as the presiding deity of and conveying the spiritual endowments from the asterism of Krittika, in conjunction with the zodiacal houses of Mesa (Aries) and Vrsabha (Taurus), is the power of Usas, a terrestrial manifestation of Agni. These two Lunar houses act together in conveying the spiritual endowments of *Bhanu* to the worshiper. The daybreak dawn of Usas, a terrestrial manifestation of Agni, kindles Agni, and from there Agni emits its light of *Bhanu*. (RV 2.2.8.) The "kindling" of Agni is a term of art. Physical fire is "ignited," but Agni as the Sacrificial Fire is "kindled." Kindling imparts all those qualities and energies from the universe and channeled those qualities and energies into the Fire. The Sacrificial Fire plays a central role in the Sacrificial ritual, it is the center of attraction. Once kindled it is beheld by the worshiper, or, as in the Soma Sacrifice, the principal means of producing the Soma juice is to be consumed by the worshiper. In all sacrificial settings, the central fire is the means by which the worshiper is transformed spiritually. The Sun is the source of all life. It is the agent which destroys the old life of the worshiper, and like the phoenix rising from the ashes, a new worshiper emerges. Breath in this above passage is prana, the subtle essence of the life force permeating the universe and sustaining the life of the worshiper. In other words, in part, the fire of Agni is powered by and empowers the elements of the Vedic dharma, the natural order *(Rta)*

- Thus, the Vedic force of Usas shines the light of *Bhanu* to the worshiper at the Sacrifice. (RV 1.48.9.)
- The daybreak dawn of Usas conveys the light (*Bhanu*) of awareness to the worshiper. (RV 6.65.1; 7.7.5; 7.79.1.) "Dawn" should be read with both and literal and figurative meaning. It is both the beginning of each new day and the beginning stage of

self-realization, liberation, and salvation, which is the goal of the worshiper's spiritual journey.

- With the effulgence of *Bhanu*, the worshiper opens the doors of heaven. (RV 1.48.15.)

The Lunar house of Agni is asserted in other ways. The Maruts are a manifestation of the Fire of Agni in the Firmament. The Vedic forces of the Maruts are utilized to spread the light of *Bhanu* to the worshiper. The light of *Bhanu* is compared to the brilliance of the Maruts. (RV 5.52.6.) The Maruts are radiant and powerful. (RV 1.19.5.)

The Lunar house of the Asvins also play a part. The Asvins as the presiding deity of and conveying the spiritual endowments of the asterism Ashvini, in conjunction with the zodiacal house of Mesa (Aries), conveys the benefits of *Bhanu* to the worshiper.

- *Bhanu* is the light of Asvins. (RV 4.45.1.)
- The horses convey the Asvins like the light of *Bhanu*. (RV 7.72.4.)

With regards to *Bhanu*, and the other forms of light, the rcs (mantras) reveal what they reveal. The real spiritual endowment of Light is experienced and utilized by the worshiper during the spiritual journey. The light of *Bhanu* is important to open the eyes of the worshiper. Once opened the worshiper's eyes are trained to the spiritual journey. That journey is ruled by "rules of the road." These rules are the subject of the next spiritual teaching of the asterisms.

THE NAKSHATRAS

The Vedic astrologer knows that the center, the beginning, of the Vedic dharma in terms of the stellar population is located at the Nakshatras. Officially, Nakshatras are a stationary pattern or group of stars which, when viewed from Earth, are recognized in the night sky. To the Vedic astrologer, the Nakshatras are much, much more.

The Vedic astrologer knows that all of creation is a function of the interplay of the Nakshatras (asterisms), planets and zodiacal houses. The Nakshatras stand as the First among equals and prevail over the planets and zodiacal houses. In the Nakshatras rest the vast repository of wisdom, essence of the Vedic dharma. The Nakshatras exert an influence over human affairs by virtue of this wisdom of which the planets and zodiacal houses cannot compete. That power is unparalleled and stands head and shoulders above the planets and the zodiacal houses. In the passage of the millennia this wisdom has been forgotten and the Nakshatras' preeminence has been usurped by the zodiacal houses. Thus, contemporaneously, there is a modern preoccupation with reviewing a person's daily horoscope. This, however, is not the focus of the Vedic astrologer.

The most dramatic demonstration of the interrelationship between time and space are the Nakshatras. The Nakshatras are of divine origin. On a spiritual level the Vedic astral force of Usha represents Awareness; on a physical level Usha represents the Dawn. This is the Usha we witness on the material level. Usha's name is derived from "Ushi," also meaning "night," (Mikhailov, Rgvedic Studies (2001), p. 9) a direct consequence to the establishment of prana. Once established, Usha travels by day (and night), the ahoratra, from house to house (graha), changing names in each journey. (RV 1.123.4.) Thus there is a time element at work. The Nakshatras are based on "lunar mansions," which are in turn based on the orbit the Moon travels in relation to the Earth. That there are twenty-eight asterisms are due to the average days in the month. The difference, it seems, between a lunar house (i.e., asterism or Nakshatras) and a zodiacal house is the vantage point: With the Nakshatras that vantage point appears to be from the Moon. Be that as it may, the Vedic astrologer will use the terms "asterism," "Nakshatras," and "lunar house or mansion" more or less interchangeably.

The ancients had their own theories on the origin of the Nakshatras. According to one etymological meaning,

- "Nakshatra" means "to obtain." (Nir., 3.20.) By reason of the usurpation of their power by the houses of the zodiac (Adityas), the etymological basis for "Nakshatra" is the equivalent to "no power." (SBP 2.1.2.18, 19.) The influence of the Nakshatras were still to be enjoyed but expressed through the push and pull influences of the astrological houses (Adityas) and the presiding Vedic energies and principles in ascendant and descendant movements.
- Another tradition maintains that the word comes from "*na*," meaning "not" and "*ksarati*" meaning "ending." (Sw. Siva Priyananda, *Astrology in Art and Religion* (1990), p. 92.) Thus, the Nakshatras represent that which is never ending, the transcendental world which rules all that is located below.

The Vedic astrologer discussed in the Introduction the subtle basis for the creation of the Nakshatras. We still don't know how the Nakshatras we all see in the sky came to be. In this respect, the Vedic astrologer established a progression to the physical, gross Nakshatras in the sky. Their formation is intricately tied with the five gross elements:

- The element of Fire came into existence with the Earth element. (AV 19.19.1.)
- The element of Air (Vayu) came into existence with the arrival of the Mid-World. (AV 19.19.2.)
- The Sun (the Vedic force of Agni) came into existence with the Sky. (AV 19.19.3.)

- The Moon (the Vedic force of Soma) came into existence with the Nakshatras. (AV 19.19.4.) This in part explains why the Nakshatras are called "lunar mansions" or "lunar houses." They literally came into being at the same time.
- Soma, the juice extracted from the Soma plant, came into existence with the other plants. (AV 19.19.5.)
- The Sacrifice came into existence with the sacrificial act of Giving. (AV 19.19.6.)

Now that we know how the Nakshatras came to be, we need to know their spiritual significance. There is a spiritual aspect to the Nakshatras. The Vedas speak of them as "divine female beings." (VYS 11.61.) They are also described as the "lights of righteous men" who ascend to heaven. (SPB 6.5.4.8.) Through these correspondences above, this spirituality possessed by the Nakshatras are communicated to the worshiper.

The Vedic Astrologer knows the Nakshatras, the lunar mansions, represent a bundle of esoteric concepts, powers, and meanings that contain the secrets and benefits of the cosmos. The sky is where heaven resides. Each Vedic divinity — whether Agni, Indra, Soma, or whomever — represent their divine force and power. The asterisms (Nakshatras) is the place of the abode where the divine forces reside. (SPB 14.3.2.12.) The worshiper's goal in achieving salvation and liberation is to become integrated with that divinity inherent in those forces and return to whence it was born — the heavens. In addition, once the body expires, it must either proceed on one of two paths, the Path of the Gods or the Path of Prtrs.

The Vedas name twenty-seven asterisms. (SPB, 10.5.4.5.) Other texts contain some measure of variation of the specific names of the asterisms. Some scriptures ascribe different names, others give different numbers. There is also an issue of where and the asterisms begin. The newer system — that is for the period of time commencing from the date attributed to the war in the Mahabharata, c, 3500 B.C. — began with Ashwini. The older, original system began with Krttikas. This was because the Krttikas star is the first among the deva Nakshatras. (TB 1.5.2.9.) Be that as it may, the Tattiriya Samhita (TS 4.4.10.1-27; SPB 2.1.2.1-7, 11, 12), Tattiriya Brahmana (TB 1.1.2.1), Kathaka Samhita (KS 7.1), Maitrayani Samhita (MS 1.6.9), Arthavada (AV 19.7.1), and the Vedanga Jyotisa (R-VJ 15; Y-VJ17, collectively give a procession of the asterisms which look like this"

Asterism (TS)	Asterism (TB)	Asterism (KS)	Asterism (MS)	Asterism (Vedanga Jyotisa)	Asterism (AV)
Krttikas	Krttikas	Krttikas	Krttikas	Krttikah	Krttikas
Rohini	Rohini	Rohini	Rohini	Rohini	Rohini
Mrgashira	Mrgashira	Invaka	Invaga	Mrgashiram	Mrgashira
Ardra	Ardra	Bahu	Bahu	Ardra	Ardra
Punarvasu	Punarvasu	Punarvasu	Bahu	Punarvasu	Punaravasu
Tishya	Tisya (Pushya)	Tisya	Tisya	Pusyah	Pushya
Ashreda	Asresha	Aslesas	Aslesas	Aslesa	Ashlesha
Magha	Maghas	Maghas	Maghas	Maghah	Magha
P. Phalguni	P. Phalguni	Phalgunis	Phalgunis	P. Phalguni	P. Phalguni
U. Phalguni	U. Phalguni	U. Phalguni	Phalgunis	U. Phalguni	U. Phaguni
Hasta	Hasta	Hastau	Hasta	Hastah	Hasta
Chitra	Citra	Citra	Citra	Citra	Chitta
Svati	Svati	Nistya	Nistya	Svati	Srati
Vishakha	Vashaka	Visaka	Visaka	Visakhe	Vishakha
Anuradha	Anuradhas	Anuradha	Anuradha	Anuradhah	Anuradha
Rohini	Jyestha	Jyestha	Jyestha	Jyestha	Jyeshtha

Vichrtau	Mula	Mula	Mula	Mula	Mula	Moola
P. Ashadha	P. Asadhas	Asadhas	Asadhas	P. Ashadha	P. Ashada
U. Ashadha	U. Asadhas	U. Asadhas	Asadhas	U. Ashadha	U. Ashada
Shrona	Srona (Shravana)	Asvattha	Srona	Sravana	Abhijit
Shavishtha	Sravisthasta	Sravisthas	Sravistha	Dhanistha	Shravana
Shatabhisha	Satabhishak	Satabhisaj	Satabhisaj	Satabhisaj	Shravishtha
P. Proshthapada	Bhadrapada	Proasthapadas	Prosthapadas	Purvabharada	P. Proshthapada
U. Proshthapada	U. Proshthapadas	U. Proshthapadas	Prosthapadas	Uttarabharada	U. Proshthapada
Revati	Revati	Revati	Revati	Revati	Revati
Ashvayujau	Ashvayujau	Ashvayujau	Asvayujai	Asvini	Ashavayuja
Apabharani	Apabharanis	Apabharanis	Barahnis	Bharani	Bharani
	Abijit				

You, dear Reader, probably detected a slight variation in the classification of the asterisms among the various scriptures. Variations exist. Traditions vary as to the name of Nakshatras, Astrological houses, and their presiding deities. Whatever the tradition, recall that the Veda is the book of Knowledge. One of the goals of the Vedas is to impart knowledge; this knowledge is to be used for joy of learning that the worshiper may understand the world and the cosmos. With the astrological houses it is possible to understand the ascending and descending dynamic energies which preside over the astrological houses. Writing in the Fifth Century A.D. Varahamihira compiled the Brhat Samhita, a book of knowledge much like the Rg Veda, but incorporating elements of Hellenic and Roman knowledge. His denomination of the astrological houses were much different, but provided much insights to the influences of celestial bodies on human behavior:

Western Zodiac	Vedic Zodiac	Western Asterism	Vedic Asterism	Brhat Samhita
Gemini	Mithuna	Pleiades Aldebaran Orion	Krittika Rohini Mrgashirsha	Jutuma (BS, 1.8; 24.9); Manusa
Cancer	Karkata	Betelgeuse Castor, Pollux	Ardra Punavasu	Karkata (BS, 1.7.)
Leo	Simha	Cancri Hydrae	Pushya Ashlasha	Hari; Mrgaraja; Mrgendra; Mrgesvara
Virgo	Kanya	Regulus Leonis	Magha Purva Phalguni	Kanya; Manusa
Libra	Tula	Denebola Corvi	Uttara Phalguni Hasta	Manusa
Scorpius	Vrscika	Spica Arcturus Librae	Chitra Svasti Vasakra	Ali; Kaurpi; Vescika

Saggitarius	Dhanus	Scorpionis Scorpionis	Anuradha Jyestra	Karmukabrht; gurugrh; capa; tausika; Haya
Capricorn	Makara	Scorpionis Sagittarii	Mula Purva Ashada	Mrgamukha (BS, 2.0.)
Aquarius	Kumba	Sagittarii Lyrae-Vega Aquilae	Uttara Ashada Abhijit Sravana	Kumbha; ghata
Pisces	Mina	Delphini Aquarii Pegase	Dhanishta Shatabhisha Purva Bhadrapada	Jhasa; gurugrh
Aries	Mesa	Pegase-Andromedae Piscium	Uttara Bhadrapada Revati	Kriya (BS, 2.1.3.)
Taurus	Vrsabha	Arietis Arietis	Ashvini Bharani	Go (BS, 40.1); Vrsa; Vrsabha
Western Zodiac	Vedic Zodiac	Western Asterism	Vedic Asterism	Brhat Samhita
Gemini	Mithuna	Pleiades Aldebaran Orion	Krittika Rohini Mrgashirsha	Jutuma (BS, 1.8; 24.9); Manusa
Cancer	Karkata	Betelgeuse Castor, Pollux	Ardra Punavasu	Karkata
Leo	Simha	Cancri Hydrae	Pushya Ashlasha	Hari; Mrgaraja; Mrgendra; Mrgesvara
Virgo	Kanya	Regulus Leonis	Magha Purva Phalguni	Kanya; Manusa

Libra	Tula	Denebola Corvi	Uttara Phalguni Hasta	Manusa
Scorpius	Vrscika	Spica Arcturus Librae	Chitra Svasti Vasakra	Ali; Kaurpi (BS, 1.7); Vescika
Saggitarius	Dhanus	Scorpionis Scorpionis	Anuradha Jyestra	Karmukabrht; gurugrh; capa; tausika; Haya
Capricorn	Makara	Scorpionis Sagittarii	Mula Purva Ashada	Mrgamukha (BS, 2.0.)
Aquarius	Kumba	Sagittarii Lyrae-Vega Aquilae	Uttara Ashada Abhijit Sravana	Kumbha; ghata
Pisces	Mina	Delphini Aquarii Pegase	Dhanishta Shatabhisha Purva Bhadrapada	Jhasa; gurugrh
Aries	Mesa	Pegase-Andromedae Piscium	Uttara Bhadrapada Revati	Kriya (BS, 2.1.3.)
Taurus	Vrsabha	Arietis Arietis	Ashvini Bharani	Go (BS, 40.1); Vrsa; Vrsabha

So variations do, in fact, exist. They are not critical to the worshiper's spiritual journey. The Vedic astrologer would point out that demanding strict consistency in, for example, the classification of the asterisms distracts the worshiper from their primary purpose and leads to the kind of doctrinaire thinking which is so prevalent in predictive astrology. The asterisms and the rest of the stellar population are there for a higher purpose.

The asterisms are a function of the movements of the moon and the Sun. (AV 19.8.1.) The elliptical cycles of the equinoxes and solstices are a function of the Sun's apparent movement in relation with the moon. Bryant, in his *A History of Astronomy*, (1907), p. 3, states ancient priests "would notice that the moon followed roughly a certain path among the stars, and that the sun's path was nearly identical, and that at the same season of the year the sun's place in that celestial track was always the same. So that zone of the heavens came to be regarded as distinct, and the configuration of the stars in different parts of it were associated with different seasons and divided into groups called constellation and given names in order to define the sun's position, that is, the time of year. This zone has long been called the Zodiac."

Thus the stellar population acts as a whole organism, and the asterisms can be viewed as the most perfect conjunction of the Moon and the Sun. This conjunction is reflects the worshiper's life and conduct. More about conjunction later.

The precise nature of how the planets, stars, and the constellations, and the ecliptic relations thereof, effect salvation is a secret long obscured by the passage of time and the mysteries of the stars and will perhaps be forever beyond the grasp of the humans and worshipers alike who are influenced by their luster. Yet, somewhere deeply embedded in the rcs (mantras) of the Veda, those secrets are there waiting to be uncovered and with a proper interpretation are ready to be unlocked.

We saw in previous chapter that from the subtle and physical Life Force, prana, the Nakshatras were created. The Nakshatras attracted the planetary bodies on which they conjoin and over which they preside. The Nakshatras are ruled by the planetary bodies, which were themselves ruled by a specific Vedic astral power (*Http://www. denisharness.com/ vedicplanetarydieties.html*) in a specific zodiacal house (*http://www. academia. edu / 6437050/ Introduction_to_Vedic-_Astrology*). The Nakshatras occupy the primary position in the stellar landscape. The planets and the zodiacal houses derive their strength from the Nakshatras, as shown in this chart.

Vedic Asterism	Presiding Vedic Energy (Asterism)	Zodiacal House(s)	Planet Ruling Zodiacal House (Ruling Deity)
Krittika	Agni	Mesa (Aries) Vrsabha (Taurus)	Mercury (Saraswati)
Rohini	Prajapati	Vrsabha (Taurus)	Mercury (Saraswati)
Mrgashirsha	Soma	Vrsabha (Taurus) Mithuna (Gemini)	Mercury (Saraswati)
Ardra	Rudra	Mithuna (Gemini)	Moon (Soma)
Punavasu	Aditi	Mithuna (Gemini) Karkata (Cancer)	Moon (Soma)
Pushya	Brhaspati	Karkata (Cancer)	Sun (Agni)
Ashlasha	Nagas	Karkata (Cancer)	Sun (Agni)
Magha	Pitrs	Simha (Leo)	Rahu (Durga)
P. Phalguni	Bhaga	Simha (Leo)	Rahu (Durga)
U. Phalguni	Aryaman	Simha (Leo) Kanya (Virgo)	Venus (Indrani)
Hasta	Savitr	Kanya (Virgo)	Venus (Indrani)
Chitra	Indra (Tvastr)	Kanya (Virgo) Tula (Libra)	Mars (Rudra)
Svasti (Srati)	Vayu	Tula (Libra)	Mars (Rudra)

Vasakra	Indra/Agni	Tula (Libra)	Mars (Rudra)
Anuradha	Mitra	Vrscika (Scorpio)	Jupiter (Indra)
Jyestra	Indra	Vrscika (Scorpio)	Jupiter (Indra)
Mula	Nirrti	Dhanus (Saggitarius)	Saturn (Yama)
Purva Ashada	Apas	Dhanus (Saggitarius)	Saturn (Yama)
Uttara Ashada	Visvedevas	Dhanus (Saggitarius)	Saturn (Yama)
Abhijit	Brahma	Makara (Capricorn)	Saturn (Yama)
Sravana	Visnu	Makara (Capricorn)	Saturn (Yama)
Dhanishta	Vasus	Makara (Capricorn) *Kumba (Aquarius)*	Jupiter (Indra)
Shatabhisha	Varuna	Kumba (Aquarius)	Jupiter (Indra)
P. Bhadrapada	Ajikapada	*Kumba (Aquarius)* Mina (Pisces)	Jupiter (Indra)
U. Bhadrapada	Ahir Budhyana	Mina (Pisces)	Mars (Rudra)
Revati	Pusan	Mina (Pisces)	Mars (Rudra)
Ashvini	Asvins	Mesa (Aries)	Venus (Indrani)
Bharani	Yama	Mesa (Aries)	Venus (Indrani)

Given the largely unknown operation of the influence of the general stellar population upon the worshiper, the Rishiis of the Vedas decided that the effect of the heavens be reflected in the sacrifice itself. Therefore, as stated, the Tattiriya Samhita states that after the Nakshatras are completed so is the *yajna* (TS, 4.4.10.28), and by implication, so is the worshiper's grace and salvation derived therefrom. The asterisms provide a blue-print for the construction of the fire Altar. Nakshatras represent the bricks upon which the Fire Altar is constructed.

The Fire Altar is the centerpiece of Vedic sacrifice. The purpose of the Agnicayana ritual, the fire ritual is to actualize the rcs contained in the Rg Veda and to make flesh the deep principles contained therein. The Fire Altar is the focal means by which the worshiper realizes and understands the teachings of the rcs and implement them in the worshiper's life to assist the worshiper during the spiritual journey. The fire altar is so constructed in every way to facilitate this purpose — to facilitate and foster the sacrificial experience, to increase the worshiper's understanding, to implement those lessons in the Vedas and the secrets of the Vedic dharma into the worshiper's life and spiritual journey, and to enable the worshiper to surrender its Soul utterly to the fire which contain these spiritual endowments.

The Fire Altar is so constructed in order to enable the worshiper to instill that immortal body into the worshiper or sacrificer. The entire purpose of the Fire Altar is to provide a focal point to the worshiper's awareness and wherein the worshiper may discard the errors of previous ways of thinking, believing, and conducting, and become spiritually renewed, whether that is acquiring new insights, committing to new behaviors, or achieving liberation or salvation. The mystery of how this is accomplished is as ancient as fire itself:

> "The gods then established that (fire) in their innermost soul; and having established that immortal element in their innermost soul, and become immortal and unconquerable, they overcame their mortal, conquerable enemies. And so this one now establishes that immortal element in his innermost soul; and–though there is for

him no hope of immortality–he obtains the full measure of life; for, indeed, he becomes unconquerable, and his enemy, though striving to conquer, conquers him not. And, accordingly, when one who has established his fires and one who has not established his fires, vie with each other, he who has established his fires overcomes the other, for, verily, he thereby becomes unconquerable, he thereby becomes immortal." (SPB 2.2.2.14.)

Then:

"Now, when, on that occasion, they produce that (fire) by churning, then he (the sacrificer) breathes (blows) upon it, when produced; for fire indeed is breath: he thereby produces the one thus produced. He again draws in his breath: thereby he establishes that (fire) in his innermost soul; and that fire thus becomes established in his innermost soul." (SPB 2.2.15.)

The Fire Altar is also identified with the year, the 720 bricks represent the days and nights of the year. The Satapatha Brahmana (SPB 10.5.4.5.) states that

"Fire-altar also is the Nakshatras:–for there are twenty-seven of these Nakshatras, and twenty-seven secondary stars accompany each Nakshatra,–this makes seven hundred and twenty, and thirty-six in addition thereto. Now what seven hundred and twenty bricks there are of these, they are the three hundred and sixty enclosing-stones and the three hundred and sixty Yagushmatî bricks; and what thirty-six there are in addition, they are the thirteenth (intercalary) month, the body (of the altar); the trunk (consisting of) thirty, the feet of two, the (channels of the) vital airs of two, and the head itself being the (thirty-fifth and) thirty-sixth,– and as to there being two of these, it is because 'siras' (head) consists of two syllables;–and what (space) there is between (each) two Nakshatras that is the Sûdadohas; and what food there is in the Nakshatras that is the earth-fillings (between the layers of bricks), the oblations and the fire-logs; and what is called 'nakshatras' that is the space-filling (brick)."

The stage is then set to establish the spiritual influence of the Nakshatras.

WHEN YOU WISH UPON A STAR

If there is anything that the rcs (mantras of the Rg Veda), samans (mantras of the Sama Veda), and chhandas (mantras of the Yajur Veda) of the Vedas indicate after a careful and close reading, it is this: The Rishiis knew the Nakshatras contained a wisdom that could be conveyed to the worshiper. This was expressed in no uncertain terms in the Atharva Veda which outline the many ways the Lunar houses dispense spiritual endowments to the worshiper through their respective Nakshatras and zodiacal houses. The specific endowments will be discussed in a few moments.

The question is how does the worshiper receive this wisdom and endowments? The facile response is that the Lunar houses and energies in the Vedic dharma convey this wisdom. But just as sounds must travel through aether via the sound waves emitted therefrom to be received by the human ear, so there must be a medium through which the wisdom present in the Nakshatras arrive to the worshiper. In a similar fashion, the Lunar houses, Vedic forces, and energies transmit the wisdom of the Nakshatras through the powers of their respective Nakshatras. That power transmits the wisdom to the worshiper, in conjunction with the respective zodiacal houses belonging to the Lunar houses, Vedic forces, and energies, and, in those special cases, where the Lunar houses also act in the capacity as presiding deities to the several planets.

Once received by the worshiper the real work begins. The secret in fully implementing the wisdom contained in the Nakshatras is in their reception. The worshiper must fully experience the light emitted from the Nakshatras and implement that wisdom into the worshiper's life to derive their full benefit. It is not an issue of simple star-gazing. This requires a focused concentration and meditation of their light and the unimpeded entry into the worshiper's body, mind, and soul. The worshiper acquires the spiritual endowments inherent in the Nakshatras with the existing meditational techniques which are readily available through *Tapas* or religious austerity. It is important that the worshiper fully experience the wisdom which are the Nakshatras.

At the time of the Vedas, the Rishis believed the asterisms held sway over human affairs. The Rishiis believed the stellar population has their own wisdom. The lunar mansions (Nakshatras or asterisms) exert their many different powers over humans and over the sacrificial rituals. (SPB 2.1.2.17.) Over time and through divine intervention that power and influence was then usurped by Aditya, the astrological houses, who has since continues to possess that energy, power and influence (SBP 2.1.2.18, 19), and whose original influence continues. For the worshiper:

- Through participation in the construction or ceremony glorifying the fire altar the worshipers place that immortal element into their innermost souls. (SPB, 2.2.2.10.)
- By setting up the fire altar, the worshipers therefore dispels the evil from themselves;–the gods are immortal: he therefore, though there is for him no prospect of immortality, attains the (full measure of) life, whosoever sets up his fires during that time. (SPB, 2.1.3.4.)

At first, what the Rishiis had revealed were recorded in several passages from the Atharva Veda. The first revelations indicated that the Nakshatras primarily provide protection to the worshiper. That protection was dispensed through the dynamic between the asterisms, Nakshatras, the zodiacal houses and the Vedic forces which were presiding over selected members from the stellar population:

- From the Vedic force of Agni, the Sun, with the energy emitted from the forging of the forces of Heaven and Earth, protection to the worshiper from the enemies in the Western quarter is dispensed by the lunar house of Krittika, in conjunction with the zodiacal houses of Mesa (Aries) and Vrsabha (Taurus). (AV, 19.17.6; 19.18.5.)

- The Vedic force of Agni also works in alignment with the Vasus, protection to the worshiper from the enemies in the Southern and Mid-Eastern quarters are dispensed by the lunar house of Krittika, in conjunction with the zodiacal houses of Mesa (Aries) and Vrsabha (Taurus) and the zodiacal houses of Makara (Capricorn) and Kumba (Aquarius). (AV 19.17.2; 19.18.2.)

- From Prajapati, in conjunction with the Regenerative Principle, protection to the worshiper from the enemies present in the "fixed" quarter is dispensed from the lunar mansion of Rohini, in conjunction with the zodiacal house of Vrsabha (Taurus). (AV 19.17.9; 19.18.9.)

- From Soma in conjunction with the Rudras, protection to the worshiper is provided from the enemies present in the Southern quarter is dispensed by two lunar houses: Mrgashirsha (Soma) and Ardra (Rudra), in conjunction with their respective zodiacal houses of Vrsabha (Taurus) and Mithuna (Gemini). (AV 19.17.3; 19.18.3.)

- From Brhaspati and the visible material world protection to the worshiper from the enemies present in the "highest quarter" is dispensed by the lunar mansion of Pushya, in conjunction with the zodiacal house of Karkata (Cancer). (AV 19.17.9; 19.18.10.)

- From the Grand Architect, Tvastr, in conjunction with the Seven Rishiis (the Stars of the Big Dipper), protection to the worshiper from enemies in the Northern quarter is dispensed by the lunar mansion of Chitra, in conjunction with the zodiacal house of Kanya (Virgo) and Tula (Libra). (AV 19.17.7.; 19.18.7.)

- From Vayu and the Mid-World the worshiper is protected from the enemies in the Southern and Mid-Eastern quarters through the dispensing powers of the lunar mansion of Dhanistha. (AV 19.17.2; 19.18.2.)

- From the Waters (*Apas*), the subtle basis for the Vedic dharma, protection to the worshiper from the enemies in the Mid-Western and Northern quarters is dispensed through the lunar house of

Purva Ashada, in conjunction with the zodiacal house of Dhanus (Saggitarius). (AV 19.17.6; 19.18.6.)

- From Indra and the Maruts protection to the worshiper from the enemies present in the Mid-Northern and Easter quarters are dispensed by the lunar mansion of Jyestra in conjunction with the zodiacal house of Vrscika (Scorpio). (AV 19.17.8; 19.18.8.)\

- From Varuna, the Lord Protector of the Vedic dharma (Rta), in alignment with the "Suns from the twelve months," in other words, the Adityas, the zodiacal houses, protection is provided to the worshiper from the enemies in the Mid-Southern and Western quarters by the lunar house of Shatabhisha and presided over by the zodiacal house of Kumba (Aquarius). (AV 19.17.4; 19.18.4.)

At first this wisdom from the Nakshatras was not clearly revealed by the Rishiis, as that wisdom had largely been reduced to protection to and for the worshiper. Also, some, but not all, of the asterisms and their respective Vedic forces were revealed. Yet, there was a purpose to these directional protections. That the Nakshatras provide protection in all directions is simply another way of saying that the grace shining from the Nakshatras is omnipresent, protecting the worshiper everywhere and in all ways. The dynamic there most clearly demonstrated with the interactions of the dynamic Lunar houses and energies with Western and Vedic asterisms, the presiding astral energy (deity), and the spiritual benefits derived therefrom. It thereupon became necessary for the Rishiis to engage in more intensive meditation to discover further lessons to be obtained from the Nakshatras.

The Vedic astrologer knows, as in time the worshiper will know, there are other lessons to be learned from the stellar population. The Rishiis of the Vedas engaged in additional meditation and *Tapas* to reveal other secrets. The Rishiis revealed the wisdom found in Atharva Veda AV 19.7.2 – 5. The wisdom from other Vedic forces were revealed. This wisdom revealed other, more exacting, lessons derived from the asterisms existing in the evening sky. These lessons were based on their respective zodiacal house, presided over by their respective Vedi force or energy which rules the planets. Those lessons become the subject of the worshiper's meditations and study. The stellar population contain and dispense their own spiritual endowments. Those spiritual endowments are in the last column. The qualities in that column provide a near-complete definition of that most ambiguous terms in the Vedas usually translated as "riches," "treasures," or "wealth." These qualities consist of the spiritual treasures generally and the lessons the stellar population gives to the worshiper. When recording the revelations in the Atharva Veda, the Rishiis knew the significance of these spiritual gifts from the Stars. The asterisms, planets and zodiacal houses become objects of the worshiper's meditation. Whether upon gazing at the glittering ray of light in the sky, meditating on the asterism or star focused at the direction of its residence in the sky, or during auspicious times during the year, the worshiper meditates both on the presiding Lunar house and the esoteric meaning of the occasion to channel the message in the spiritual journey. Therefore much like the Fire or Sacrificial Fire becomes the focus of the worshiper's concentration, the *go* or *gobhir*, in their manifestation and particular meaning of the "herds of light" emitting from the star, or simply starlight, thereby become the focal point of the worshiper's meditation.

Vedic Asterism	Presiding Vedic Energy (Asterism)	Spiritual Endowment From Asterism	Zodiacal House	Planet Ruling Zodiacal House (Ruling Deity)
Krittika	Agni	*Yajna*, Divine Response	Mesa (Aries) Vrsabha (Taurus)	Mercury (Saraswati)
Rohini	Prajapati	*Yajna*, Divine Response	Vrsabha (Taurus)	Mercury (Saraswati)
Mrgashirsha	Soma	Bliss	Vrsabha (Taurus) Mithuna (Gemini)	Mercury (Saraswati)
Ardra	Rudra	*Sam*, union, conjunction,	Mithuna (Gemini)	Moon (Soma)

Punavasu	Aditi	*Sunrta*, Words of the "true speech," understanding of *Rta,* the Vedic dharma.	Mithuna (Gemini) Karkata (Cancer)	Moon (Soma)
Pushya	Brhaspati	Beauty	Karkata (Cancer)	Sun (Agni)
Ashlasha	Nagas	*Bhanu*, a shining rays of Light)	Karkata (Cancer)	Sun (Agni)
Magha	Pitrs	*Ayana*, guide to right conduct during the spiritual journey.	Simha (Leo)	Rahu (Durga)
P. Phalguni	Bhaga	Good Works	Simha (Leo)	Rahu (Durga)
U. Phalguni	Aryaman	Good Works	Simha (Leo) Kanya (Virgo)	Venus (Indrani)
Hasta	Savitr	Bliss	Kanya (Virgo)	Venus (Indrani)
Chitra	Indra (Tvastr)	Bliss	Kanya (Virgo) Tula (Libra)	Mars (Rudra)
Svasti (Srati)	Vayu	*Sukha*, deep Spiritual Fulfillment, Happiness	Tula (Libra)	Mars (Rudra)

Vasakra	Indra/Agni	*Radha,* Spiritual Increase, Great Achievements	Tula (Libra)	Mars (Rudra)
Anuradha	Mitra	Response	Vrscika (Scorpio)	Jupiter (Indra)
Jyestra	Indra	Happiness	Vrscika (Scorpio)	Jupiter (Indra)
Mula	Nirrti	*Amrtra,* the Eternal, Undying Principle	Dhanus (Saggitarius)	Saturn (Yama)
Purva Ashada	Apas	*Anna,* Food	Dhanus (Saggitarius)	Saturn (Yama)
Uttara Ashada	Visvedevas	Strength	Dhanus (Saggitarius)	Saturn (Yama)
Abhijit	Brahma	*Punya,* offering to Divine	Makara (Capricorn)	Saturn (Yama)
Sravana	Visnu	Nourishment	Makara (Capricorn)	Saturn (Yama)
Dhanishta	Vasus	Nourishment	Makara (Capricorn) Kumba (Aquarius)	Jupiter (Indra)
Shatabhisha	Varuna	Greatness	Kumba (Aquarius)	Jupiter (Indra)
P. Bhadrapada	Ajikapada	Protection	Kumba (Aquarius) Mina (Pisces)	Jupiter (Indra)
U. Bhadrapada	Ahir Budhyana	*Susarma,* Protection	Mina (Pisces)	Mars (Rudra)

Revati	Pusan	*Bhaga*, Enjoyment	Mina (Pisces)	Mars (Rudra)
Ashvini	Asvins	*Bhaga*, Enjoyment	Mesa (Aries)	Venus (Indrani)
Bharani	Yama	Spiritual Riches	Mesa (Aries)	Venus (Indrani)

What is the worshiper to make from the information in this chart? And how can this information assist the worshiper on the spiritual journey?

THE WORSHIPER'S GUIDE
TO THE GALAXY

These in brief are the true lessons of the Nakshatras. The remaining issue is how they are applied to the worshiper. The Nakshatras possess their own spiritual endowments which are made available to the worshiper, and a facile answer is that these endowments are obtained through meditation and stargazing. There are many types and levels and intensity to meditation, and stargazing is not a simple, passive act. Indeed, meditation is an active practice and stargazing, or at least that for the purpose of obtaining the endowments from the Nakshatras, is definitely a two-way street. It is one thing to identify the spiritual endowments of the Nakshatras in the last chapter, but the necessary next step is to provide guidance on how those spiritual lessons may be incorporated into the worshiper's life.

For the answer the Vedic astrologer obtains inspiration from the Yoga Sutras. The Yoga Sutras are noteworthy in providing a veritable roadmap to mental and spiritual liberation. The process in getting there requires the utilization of tools specifically designed to enable that liberation to occur. These are the same tools the worshiper will use to obtain the spiritual endowments possessed by the Nakshatras. The following is not meant to be an exhaustive list, but it will provide the raw materials for the worshiper to engage in something more than simple stargazing and release and incorporate the spiritual endowments held by Nakshatras. The meditative and contemplative devices which can be used by the worshiper to derive these spiritual endowments include the following steps, or limbs, of Patanjali Yoga. These three steps of Yoga—Dharana (concentration), Dhyana (meditation), and samadhi—are the final three rungs of Yoga.

Stages of attention. These three limbs constitute attention itself, which is progressively moving inward through these few stages. (Comm., YS, *http:// swamij.com/yoga-sutras-30103.htm.*):

- Dharana: Concentration is the process of holding or fixing the attention of mind onto one object or place. (YS, 3.1) (See also YS, 1.30-1.32) Attention leads to concentration (dharana). (YS, 3.1) In this step the worshiper fixes the gaze on the Nakshatra or heavenly body. It is more than simple stargazing; with stargazing one's attention is liable to be broken, or if not broken, moving the gaze to another planetary object or Nakshatra to another. With dharana, that concentration is steady and immovable for an uninterrupted, if limited, time. Sustained, uninterrupted concentration leads to meditation (Dhyana). (YS, 3.2) *With dharana, the worshiper will hold its attention on one Nakshatra, say, Krittika, and then after a short period of time move the attention to another, for example, Rohini. This is actually a good preliminary exercise for mediation on the Nakshatras. The worshiper should begin on one Nakshatras and move the attention to the next Nakshatra and then to the next, one after the other, in a deliberate exercise of practiced meditation of all the Nakshatras. All the while, the worshiper is mindful of the particular lessons offered by each Nakshatra.*

- Dhyana: Meditation is sustained concentration, whereby the attention continues to hold or repeat to the same object or place for a sustained period of time. (YS, 3.2) "This process of meditation is an ongoing series of individual concentrations, rather than one continuous concentration. If each of those concentrations is on the same object, that is called meditation. Whether you prefer to think of it as one continuous flow of concentration, or a series of individual concentrations on the same object, it is the unbroken or undistracted characteristic of attention that allows concentration to evolve into meditation. ... Crucially, with this meditation, there is still an observer observing an observed. When the observer becomes extremely absorbed in the process of observing the object, the three collapse such that all there is only awareness of the object. This is when meditation becomes samadhi." (Comm., YS, *http://swamij.com/yoga-sutras-30103.htm.) Therefore, while this level of concentration is higher than dharana, it does not rise to the level where the worshiper is able to derive the spiritual endowments inherent in the Nakshatras. Instead of moving the attention from one Nakshatra to another in tandem, the worshiper's attention stays fixed on one Nakshatra for a longer period of time, allowing the lesson that Nakshatra has to offer sink deep into the worshiper's psyche.*

- Samadhi: Samadhi is the deep absorption, wherein only the essence of that object, place, or point shines forth in the mind, as if the mind were devoid even of its own form. (YS, 3.3) Meditation leads to absorption (samadhi). (YS, 3.3) This process of meditation is an ongoing series of individual concentrations, rather than one continuous concentration. If each of those concentrations is on the same object, that is called meditation. Whether you prefer to think of it as one continuous flow of concentration, or a series of individual concentrations on the same object, it is the unbroken or undistracted characteristic of attention that allows concentration to evolve into meditation. Crucially, with this meditation, there is still an observer observing an observed. When the observer becomes extremely absorbed in the process of observing the object, the three collapse such that all there is only awareness of the object. This is when meditation becomes samadhi. (Comm., YS, *http:// swamij.com/yoga-sutras-30103.htm.) With samadhi the incorporation of the lessons from the Nakshatras become greater instilled and in a more permanent manner. While total absorption is not actualized as yet, the identification with the Nakshatra's lessons become ever more complete. The worshiper begins to experience the distinction between the worshiper, the perceiving agent, the Nakshatra, the object of perception, and the process of perception of the Nakshatra and the lessons it has to offer. The worshiper begins to move back and for the between these three states with ease and appreciates the differences between them, beginning to prefer the state of complete absorption.*

These steps are all fine and good, but the real benefits are found in samyama. Samyama is the collective practice of concentration (dharana), meditation (Dhyana), and samadhi, which are the sixth, seventh, and eighth of the eight limbs of Yoga. (Comm., *http://swamij.com/yoga-sutras-30406. htm.*) "Through samyama the true nature of the object is seen, and it is set aside with non-attachment, as it is seen to be another aspect of avidya or ignorance. In this process, the coloring of the kleshas is weakened through stages." (Comm., *http://swamij.com/yoga-sutras-30406.htm.*)

The defining characteristic of samyama is that through its correct practice, total absorption in the object of concentration is achieved. The other outstanding characteristic, one with the especial significance for the worshiper in this task, is acquisitions of siddhis, or super-human powers. A separate treatment can be devoted to these extra-ordinary powers. The siddhis have certainly gained a checkered reputation in the liberation game. Suffice it to say for our present purposes that siddhis are considered by many as "showing off," and not worthy of the merit for serious practitioners. The worshiper in this spiritual journey may well look into acquiring the siddhis which are specifically described in the Yoga Sutras:

- Yoga Sutra 3.28: Samyama on the Moon. When the worshiper exercises samyama on the Moon, knowledge of the inner stars can be known. *While the application of this missive may appear obvious, there is more than meets the eye. With the proper exercise of samyama, the worshiper acquires knowledge of the "inner stars." Thus, what is acquired is more than the knowledge of the movements of the stars, but knowledge of the inner qualities of the stars. Those inner qualities are none other than the spiritual endowments possessed by the Nakshatras themselves.*

- Yoga Sutra 3.29: Samyama on the Pole Star. When the worshiper exercises samyama on the Pole Star, the movements of those stars can be known. *The Vedic astrologer will reveal that the Pole Star is more than a simple star. The Pole Star is located at the very cusp of the Nakshatras, it is located in the zodiacal cluster which includes the Vedic forces of Agni, Prajapati, and Soma, and over the ages occupies an exalted position among the Nakshatras. Samyama over the Pole Star is thereby critical to mastery over the spiritual endowments offered by the Nakshatras.*

- Yoga Sutra 3.45: Samyama on the elements. When the worshiper exercises samyama on the elements, the worshiper achieves mastery over the elements. *Samyama over the elements is important but not critical. It has value in enabling the worshiper to traverse over the elements of the Vedic dharma, with the ultimate goal of transcending those elements, the very purpose of samyama of the Nakshatras.*

These were the only instances of siddhis the worshiper acquires on the practice of samyama. *With a sustained practice dharana, Dhyana, and samadhi, the worshiper is encouraged to use the tools of samyama to each of the Nakshatras which follow. The purpose is initially to derive the spiritual endowments found therein.* In a nutshell according to the Vedic astrologer this is how the worshiper obtains the wisdom and guidance from the Nakshatras. Once the proper exercise of samyama is practiced the worshiper will obtain total absorption of the particular spiritual endowment and finally achieve all the Nakshatras have to offer. However, according to the Vedic astrologer whatever works for the worshiper is sufficient. The important element is that the worshiper knows that there is wisdom in the Nakshatras which is there to be obtained.

In his Capacity of Ruling the Krittika Asterism, the Lunar house of Agni Dispenses, and the Worshiper Learns, the Spiritual Endowments of *Yajna*, Divine Response, and Increase.

Agni is simply an awesome Vedic force in its own right. The astral power powers of Agni are equally so. Agni represents the Vedic element of Fire. The Vedic astrologer knows that the Vedic force of Agni receives its power and in turn presides over several members of the stellar population. Its astral powers are many:

- The Vedic force of Agni resides in the zodiacal houses of Mesa (Aries) and Vrsabha (Taurus).
- The Vedic force of Agni is the presiding deity representing the Sun.
- The Vedic force of Agni represents the asterism of Krittika.
- In his capacity of ruling the Krittika asterism, the Vedic force of Agni dispenses the spiritual endowment of Divine Response.
- In his capacity of ruling and representing the asterism of Vasakra, the Vedic force of Agni, with the Vedic force of Indra, dispenses the spiritual endowment of *radha* (Spiritual Increase, Great Achievements).
- The Vedic force of Agni, in alignment with the Vedic force of Indra, resides in, rules and represents the zodiacal house of Mesa (Aries) and Vrsabha (Taurus), and dispenses the spiritual endowments of these astral bodies therein to the worshiper.

These cosmic forces act together to create the lunar mansion of Agni, Krittika. In conjunction with these stellar players Agni dispenses three important, interrelated, spiritual endowments.

- From the asterism of Krittika, through his powers as its presiding deity, Agni dispenses the inner, esoteric secrets of *yajna* (Sacrifice).
- From the asterism of Krittika, through his powers as its presiding deity, Agni dispenses the endowment of Divine Response.
- From the asterism of Vasakra, through his shared powers as its presiding deity in alignment with the Lunar house of Indra,

the lunar house of Agni dispenses, with Indra, *radha* (Spiritual Increase, Great Achievements).

Krittikas is first among the Nakshatras, and it, with Vasakra, is the deva Nakshatras. (T.B. 1.5.2.7.) It is for this reason perhaps that Krittikas is so named. Its name is derived from the Sanskrit root meaning "to cut." This is why it is distinguishable from other lunar mansions; it is literally a "cut" above. This is so because Krittikas and Vasakra are located north of the celestial equator. (Subhash Kak, *The Astrological Code of the Rig Veda*, (2011), p. 177.)

Krittikas gives the Vedic force of Agni great astral credentials:

- Agni, in his manifestation as the Principle of Change, is identified with the Sun, Surgher, Savitr. (RV 1.57.1; 4.11.1; 3.11.1; 4.13.1.)
- On an astronomical level, Agni, in his manifestation as the Principle of Change, moves the celestial sphere where the sky is fixed, and with the help of the Rishis (stars) leads this sphere like a horse. (RV 3.2.7.)
- In addition, Agni, in his manifestation as the Principle of Change, holds the rim of the celestial sphere that holds the sun. (RV 2.5.1.)

Krittikas and the Pole Star

The primacy of Krittikas should be recognized for another, more important, reason. In Vedic times, the Pleiades, the constellation where reside the stars of the Big Dipper, served as a marker in the sky, guiding travelers, stargazers, and mariners. It also guided priests and mendicants, who sought exact times of the year to begin their *yajna*. It held a revered place among the ancients. This reverence is demonstrated modernly in the HBO series, The Young Pope. During one scene, the young pope is having a conversation at night on the rooftop of the Vatican Palace. with one of his aides. The Young Pope, played by Jude Law, at one point asks his aide. "Do you know where God lives?" "No, Holy Father," answers his aide. "There," the Jude Law Character replies, pointing to the Big Dipper, "in a house and a small pool." The Pleiades, where the Big Dipper is located, are located in the zodiacal house of Vrsabha (Taurus), where the lunar houses of Krittikas belong to Agni, the Rohini asterism belonging to Prajapati, and the asterism of Mrgashirsha belonging to Soma are located. (Om Shanti, Vastu Shastra (2011), p. 42.) Since during Vedic times, the Pleiades were located at Krittika. (*https://en.wikipedia.org/wiki/Pleiades.*) The Vedic priests, demanding exactitude to determine the beginning of the year-long *yajna*, and determined Krittika to be the reference point of those sacrifices. Thus, the rcs (mantras) of the Rg Veda confirm this conclusion:

- Agni, the Sun, whose lunar house of Krittika, enjoys food in the form of light and the trees. (RV 10.27.18.) *Drvanna*, the "trees," which according to Monier Williams, is a derivative of *dhruva*, "pole," which is representative of the steadiness of the Pole Star, the Pleiades. That Agni is the "Eater" of the light emitted from the "trees," the Pole Star, emphasizes in coded language that Krittikas, the lunar mansion of Agni, should be considered the beginning point for the yajna sacrifices.
- The "Eater" itself is coded, hidden, language. The "eater is used to signify the processor of, here, the light emitted from the Pole Star, and the main source of power of that light.
- Agni, the Sun, as the "Eater," is also symbolic for Atman, the Absolute Self, the Universal Subject. This meaning is consistent with how the Pleiades have been interpreted. The seven daughters or sisters (RV 1.164.3; 1.191.14 6.61.10; 6.61.12; 8.41.2, 9; 9.61.8; 9.86.36; 10.5.5) refer to the Pleiades.

This interpretation is confirmed in other rcs (mantras) of the Veda:

- Agni, through the Nakshatra of Krittikas, is the "Eater" of the tree (i.e., the Pole Star). (RV 2.7.6.)
- Agni feeds on the tree. (RV 6.12.4.)

Agni, the Sun, through the lunar mansion of Krittikas, is the astral representative of the Seven-Dimension Universe through the symbolic language of the Rg Veda:

- The seven-priests (RV 3.4.5; 3.10.4; 3.29.14; 3.31.5; 3.4.5; 8.49.16; 9.7.4; ; 9.8.4; 9.10.7; 9.114.3; 10.3, 7; 10.35.10; 10.61.1; 10.63.7;

10.64.5), which on one level represents the ministrants at the ritual, but on a deeper level the worshiper's seven spiritual levels. Alternatively, the seven priests are symbolic of the Pleiades.

- The seven rishis (RV 3.7.7; 3.31.5; 4.2.15; 6.22.2; 9.92.2; 10.82.2; 10.109.24; 10.114.7; 10.130.7), which refer to the Vedic Seers who authored the Rg Veda, and/or the asterisms in the Vedic sky, or the Big Dipper constellation. The seven priests are symbolic of the Pleiades.
- The seven rivers, many of which are implicated with The Purified Mind (Soma)(RV 3.1.4; 3.1.6; 1.32.12; 1.34.8 ("the mother streams"); 1.35.8; 1.71.7; 1.72.8 ("floods from heaven"); 1.100.2; 2.12.3; 2.12.12; 4.19.3; 4.38.1; 6.7.6; 7.18.24; 7.36.6; 7.67.8; 8.24.8; 8.58.12; 9.54.2; 9.61.6; 9.66.6; 9.92.4; 10.43.3; 10.49.9; 10.64.8; 10.67.12; 10.75,1; 10.104.8), also signifying the Milky Way, or the Pleiades.

In these rcs (mantras), Agni, the Sun, whose lunar mansion is Krittikas, is repeatedly associated with the Pleiades, the Pole Star, and the Big Dipper. All of these stellar members holds a special place for the Vedic astrologer, but especially to the Pole Star. The references to the Pole Star are of course clouded and hidden, but there are clear references to the Pole Star in the following rcs (mantras). In these references the Vedic force of Agni is mentioned more or less in the same breath with the Pole Star.

- In RV 2.3.1, the Pole Star is described as "the purifying flame." The Pole Star takes on religious connotations in this rc (mantra), intimating that the worshiper discovers the path to inner purification when relying on the guidance of the Pole Star.
- In RV 3.1.20 calls the Pole Star the "ancient flame." The antiquity refers to the ancient practice of using the Pole Star as a calibration of when the year-long yagna should commence as well as the long use of the Pole Star to provide direction on travels.
- In RV 3.1.21, the Pole Star is called the "eternal" flame.
- Significantly, in RV 3.56.2 the Pole Star is called "immovable." This moniker refers to all the interpretations mentioned thus far.
- In RV 6.9.5, the Pole Star is called "immortal."

The Nakshatra of Krittika represent the sacrificial powers to the Vedic force of Agni that are concentrated in the North Star.

- The principle of Change and Transformation (Agni) is communicated in "the form of light." (RV 6.9.5.)
- This light is diffused as the central point in the Natural Order which empowers all that which moves, and which are stationary. (RV 5.62.1; 10.5.3.)
- This light is centered in the North Star, Polaris, in the Orion constellation. (RV 1.146.1; 8.41.9.)
- Polaris, in turn, becomes the focal point of all events in the sacrifice. (RV 1.36.5; 1.73.3; 1.146.1; 3.54.8; 4.5.4; 8.41.9.)
- The principle of sacrifice thereby becomes another constant in the Natural Order. (RV 1.36.5; 1.73.3; 1.146.1; 6.9.4; 6.15.7.)

These epithets emphasize the importance of the Pole Star. It also points to the centrality of the Vedic force of Agni in this religious system. Agni occupies a critical position. According to RV 1.79.3, the Lunar house of Agni, the Sun, through the power obtained from the asterism of Krittika and in conjunction with the zodiacal houses of Mesa (Aries) and Vrsabha (Taurus), aligns with several other Lunar houses and asterism powers to act in furtherance of the path of *Rta*, the Vedic dharma:

- The Lunar house of Aryaman, whose power is derived from the Nakshatra Uttara Phalguni, in conjunction with the zodiacal houses of Simha (Leo) and Kanya (Virgo), and whose spiritual endowment is Good Works.
- The Lunar house of Mitra, whose power is derived from the Nakshatra Anuradha, in conjunction with the zodiacal house of Vrscika (Scorpio), and whose spiritual endowment is Response.
- The Lunar house of Varuna, the Lord Protector of the Vedic dharma, whose power is derived from the asterism of Shatabhisha, in conjunction with the zodiacal house of Kumba (Aquarius), whose spiritual endowment is Greatness.

Krittikas and the Sacrifice

In keeping with his capacity as the Messenger, Agni works to steer these Vedic astral powers to act in alignment to further both the goals of *Rta* and the conveyance of the spiritual lessons of these Nakshatras. This is a power the Lunar house of Agni, with that which is given to Agni through the asterism of Krittika, in conjunction with the zodiacal houses of Mesa (Aries) and Vrsabha (Taurus), itself directs. (RV 1.128.3.) Each of these stellar members carry their own spiritual power. These powers coalesce in the Lunar house of Agni, who dispenses the spiritual endowments therefrom to the worshiper.

The first spiritual endowment is *yajna*. Agni represents *yajna*, the Sacrifice. Agni is the presiding Lunar house and guiding principle of *yajna*, Sacrifice. The principle behind the Vedic sacrifice ritual is to demonstrate a fundamental truth of the universe: that there is a give-and-take in the universe, between the Microcosm (humankind) and the Macrocosm (the universe), of every object therein, encompassing the process from creation to dissolution. The Fire of Agni is the "give" in this equation of the Vedic sacrifice. (RV 8.102.1.) This give-and-take is the essence of how the Vedic dharma (*Rta*) operates. This give-and-take is an outgrowth of the binary, dualistic Two-Dimensional universe. On the one hand, the worshiper seeks and offers obligations to the chosen Lunar house, Vedic force, or energy. On the other hand, the force and energy of the chosen Vedic force is channeled to the worshiper. On a rudimentary level, this give-and-take is the bargained for exchange for the condition of life in the universe: One being dies so another may live. The dynamics of the exchange takes many forms and is premised on a fundamental assumption that if it is accurately performed sacrifice has a secret power to produce the desired effect. The dynamics in this new level demonstrates the give-and-take process which has been operating every moment in the material universe for eons.

Agni's Fire of giving and taking is grounded in the Two-Dimensional Universe which serves as the basis for the material world. The rising of the Sun gives rise to the appearance of the Moon, Day rises to bring in the night, Hot is the flip side of Cold. This dynamic was not unknown in Vedic literature. The Chandogya Upanishad recognizes the dichotomy of pleasant and unpleasant smells, Truth and Falsity, pleasant and unpleasant sounds, and even pleasant and unpleasant thoughts. This dichotomy is grounded on the existence of Good and Evil. But even with these polar opposites there comes a point where there is unification. This is the purpose of Increase and implies the importance of Soma in the resolution of this push and pull.

The chaotic Two-Dimensional universe is resolved with the worshiper's spiritual awakening. In the process of spiritual awakening, the world and its perception are different because the worshiper is different. The old worshiper is discharged in exchange of the new. The sacrifice of the higher element produces an increase of the lower is called an out-and-out increase: it indicates the spirit that alone has power to help the world. Sacrifice thus becomes a prominent feature of increase, because it is a product of a give and take process.

The second endowment related to *yajna* is Increase. Basically, the Lunar house of Agni represents in the broadest possible terms the principle of Change and Transformation; Agni is the Fire of Change and Transformation. Related to the Vedic concept of Change and Transformation is Increase. Increase is an esoteric, yet important, element in the Vedic dharma. Increase is what it is all about. There can be no development—upward movement, downward movement, spiritual or otherwise—without Increase. Increase is the practical means of the worshiper to gain the spiritual endowments provided in the Vedas. More generally the only means by which the fire of Change and Transformation may occur. Agni is the guiding force for the power of Increase.

The idea of Increase is expressed in the fact that the spiritual development of the worshiper admits to the addition of qualities not present before of characteristics not previously exhibited. In many cases, previous views are modified, some are outright discarded. It is the very essence of sacrifice. Sacrifice is basically a giving and taking. In a similar way, Richard Wilhelm, commenting on the I-Ching, once observed, "Sacrifice on the part of those above for the increase of those below fills the people with a sense of joy and gratitude that is extremely valuable for the flowering of the commonwealth. When people are thus devoted to their leaders, undertakings are possible, and even difficult and dangerous enterprises will succeed. Therefore in such times of progress and successful development it is necessary to work and make the best use of time. This time resembles that of the marriage of heaven and earth, when the earth partakes of the creative power of heaven, forming and bringing forth living beings. The time of increase does not endure; therefore it must be utilized while it lasts."

Here however is where the I-Ching and Vedas depart. The I-Ching credits the worshiper for this increase, while in the Vedic dharma, in the Vedas Agni is the agent for increase. (RV 5.16.7, 5.17.5.)

Krittikas and the Power of Increase

Agni obtains his powers of Increase from the Waters, from the foundation of the Vedic dharma itself. (RV 1.95.5.)

- The Lunar house and energy of Agni is the means of increase in every aspect of the worshiper's life. (RV 5.10.3.)
- We will soon meet Parjanya, the Fire of Regeneration. This fire Increases the spiritual fire of Agni. (RV 7.101.3.)
- The Vedic force and energy of Agni in its manifestation as the Bull increases the life of the worshiper. As the Bull, the change and transformation effected by Agni is accomplished through regeneration, which the Bull symbolizes. (RV 1.31.5.)
- Agni's means for Increase in the worshiper is also sourced from his light. (RV 1.71.8.) It seems rather self-evident that there should be some correspondence between fire, flames and light. But this is another exercise in symbolic speech. Light is associated with Illumination and Consciousness, and as we will see in the next discussion in this Introduction, Agni is the Light of Consciousness.
- The divine force and energy of Agni, in its manifestation as Jatavedas, is the source of Increase to the Vedic dharma as a whole. (RV 1.87.5.)

Agni's capacity of Increase is a demonstration of the give-and-take displayed at the sacrifice. Agni as the Sacrificial Fire is itself increased when the fire is kindled by the worshiper. (RV 2.35.11.) The "kindled" fire carries with it an entire bundle of mystic properties. The Veda states that the kindled, transcendent Agni does not simply have the characteristics of the Maruts, but those characteristics multiplied twice or three times. (RV 6.66.2.) The Maruts, even though they are more commonly associated as the "cleaners" of the Lunar house of Indra, were first empowered with their divine Vedic energies from Agni, in his manifestation as Vanaspati, the Terrestrial Agni. (BD, 1.103.) We will later see those seven characteristics of the Maruts. Briefly, those qualities are:

- The Maruts encapsulate the knowledge of how to cause the waters to descend. (RV 1.19.3.)
- Ferocity (*ugra*). (RV 1.19.4.)
- The Maruts are radiant and powerful. (RV 1.19.5.)
- They live in the heaven above the Sun. (RV 1.19.6.)
- The Maruts have the psychic and physical strength to move mountains. (RV 1.19.7.)
- The Maruts spread and expand with the rays of an ocean (i.e.,
- Consciousness.) (RV 1.19.8.)
- The Maruts drink Soma. (RV 1.19.9.)

These are a powerful set of qualities, you can imagine the awesome strength of these characteristics when Agni is fully empowered. After the worshiper kindles the Sacrificial Fire, these augmented powers are concentrated into the light produced therefrom and becomes food. This food is thereupon consumed by the worshiper and is incorporated into spiritual lessons the worshiper gains and incorporates for travel in the spiritual journey. In turn, Agni as the Fire Altar thereafter gives Increase in the form of strength to the worshiper. (RV 8.75.13.) It is an intricate symbiosis which ultimately accounts for the spiritual inspiration of the worshiper during the spiritual search. As a result of this give-and-take process Agni bestows much more to the worshiper:

- The worshiper's increase results from being "bathed in the flames" of Agni. (RV 1.71.6.) This is symbolic speech referring to the fire of purification. In addition to being the agent for Increase, Agni is the purifying agent. This aspect of the Vedic force of Agni will be explored later in this Introduction.

- Agni provides Increase to the worshiper to battle the enemies encountered in the spiritual journey. (RV 1.79.11.)
- Agni provides this Increase by awakening the worshiper's consciousness, driving and guiding the worshiper's thoughts and providing expression to the worshiper's words. (RV 3.3.8.)
- Agni provides increase by bestowing spiritual endowments and benefits to the worshiper. (RV 5.10.7.)
- The worshiper indeed depends on the spiritual strength and illumination of Agni for the Increase. (RV 8.60.10.)

Krittikas and the "Herds of the Sky"

The Lunar house and energy of Agni also "increases the Kine." (RV 1.93.2) This is another exercise of symbolic speech but illustrates the power of Increase in the worshiper. The cow, however, represents more than an animal. The Cow is normally a very placid mammal, interested more in chewing cud than in anything else. Monier Williams translates *go* or *gobhir* as "cow." It also offers a more specific definition. If the contest is between the general and specific definition of the word, the specific meaning prevails. One specific definition Monier Williams gives for *go* or *gobhir* is "herds of the sky," or skylight or the light from the collective stellar population, from stars, planets, or other apparent astronomical phenomena or events. It really isn't difficult to understand why it would take this meaning, "herds of the sky." The "herd" implicates the group of physical cattle, but the collective grouping implicates the vastness of the esoteric knowledge to be found in the stellar population. It is difficult for the contemporary who lives in an industrial urban environment, where the firmament is covered in a perpetual hazy of smoke and particulates. But go outside the city limits, to the mountains, and look at the sky without the cover of pollution. The evening sky is positively alive and lustrous with light, with tiny, discreet, drops of light punctuating the inky darkness of the background. These glittering flecks of light do not even flicker. A star which flickers indicates the presence of an environmental obstruction, blocking the image of the starlight above. In the evening sky unimpeded, the Milky Way is a clear, distinct band of milky blue traversing one end of the horizon to the other. The worshiper will gain a greater appreciation of the ancient Greek explanation of how the Milky Way was created. It was created when Hercules was violently pushed away while he was suckling Hera's breast, spilling her milk across the sky, giving rise to its name. In the same way witnessing the stellar population and this band of light creates a profound experience from which the worshiper gains a greater appreciate the Vedic dharma and its lessons. This more specific definition adds a greater understanding to both Agni and the Fire of Light. For example, it was earlier revealed that Agni the Mystic Fire is the Lord of Wealth and the Shining Herds. (RV 3.16.1.) Monier Williams would change this to say that Agni is the Lord of the light, the fire, the energy emitting from the stellar population. In a deep, esoteric sense this is exactly how *go* or *gobhir* should be applied to the Fire of Light. While cows represent this Bovine Knowledge, it is the knowledge obtained, derived, and learned from the stellar population. It takes a lot to infuriate a cow, and once riled, quickly calms down. The ancients no doubt superimposed their own aspiration on the cow's demeanor. Its stoic calm indisputably indicated a deeper understanding which stood as a stark contrast to the great penchant for mischief in humans. In keeping with these aspirations, cows, the *go* or *gobhir,* as the "herds of the sky, were subsequently interpreted as these:

- The *go* or *gobhir* represent the inner illumination of the rays of knowledge. (RV 2.24.6, 4.1.16 (glory of the cow of light discovered after meditation of the supreme name of the milch cow.)
- The *go* or *gobhir* represent consciousness as knowledge. (RV 3.30.20, 3.39.6.)
- Indra finding meath (empirical knowledge) in the cows. (RV 10.92.10 (inspired knowledge), 3.31.10, 3.31.11.)
- According to Sri Aurobindo, the *go* or *gobhir* represent the power of consciousness, discrimination, and discernment. (See also, RV 2.11.2, 2.15.10, 2.16.9, 2.34.15 (right-thinking), 3.31.11, 10.92.10.) In recognition of this meaning, some English translations render *gobhir,* as "Ray-Cows," signifying the rays of knowledge.
- *Go* or *gobhir* figure prominently in the Ninth Mandala, is the presiding divinity of Soma Pavamana. (RV 9.2.4, 9.6.6, 9.8.5, 9.10.3, 9.14.3, 9.32.3, 9.43.1, 9.50.5, 9.61.13, 9.66.13, 9.68.9,

9.74.8, 9.85.4, 9.85.5, 9.86.27, 9.91.2, 9.97.15, 9.103.1, 9.107.2, 2, 9, 18, 22.)

- Kine, generally referred to in the Vedas as the milking cow, is the source of truth, essence, and knowledge. The imagery is inescapable. Just as just as there is the milk of knowledge so is the Kine, the milking cow, its symbol.
- Kines are also representative of the union of heaven and earth.

The Jaiminiya Brahmana (JB 1.19.) makes the following correspondences of the *go* or *gobhir* to knowledge:

- The agnihotra cow is speech.
- The calf of agnihotra cow is mind.
- The milk of the mother cow flows to her calf.
- The milk of agnihotra cow produces the speech that causes the mind to flow.
- This mind of the calf is followed by speech.
- For this reason, the mother cow runs after the calf who walks in front.

Agni is the embodiment of Divine Response. In this capacity, he is called in the Rg Veda the "Messenger." The Vedas frequently call Agni the "Messenger of the gods." Taken on a surface level, this means that Agni summons the gods to participate in the sacrifice. On a deeper level, it signifies that in his capacity as the Messenger, the cosmic force of Agni seeks and consolidates other Lunar houses to provide the pervasion of consciousness. Agni as the Messenger has its own give-and-take aspect resulting in the spiritual increase of the worshiper, and in its aspect as the Fire Altar is the starting point in this process.

- The Lunar house of Agni brings all of the other Vedic forces and Lunar houses to the sacrifice and gives these forces life. (RV 5.26.8.)
- The worshiper begins by approaching the Fire Altar with thoughts of Self-Surrender. (RV 1.1.7.)

- The worshiper surrenders before the Fire Altar. In this context the Fire Altar represents the fire of the Vedic dharma, its natural laws and processes. (RV 10.92.4.) The Fire Altar also represents the fire of the Word. (RV 10.115.4.) The Fire Altar also presents the fire of Impulsions and Knowledge. (RV 10.165.5.)

- The worshiper then send the "streams" — thoughts, prayers, meditative austerities — to the Fire Altar, seeking its protection. (RV 7.94.4.) The worshiper's self-surrender may be for different purposes. The worshiper may self-surrender, conscious of the worshiper's sins, but seeking expiation from here, the Visvedevas and the One, seeking their expiation.

- Agni in its aspect as the Fire Altar accepts the worshiper's self-surrender. (RV 1.65.1.)

- Agni in its aspect as the Fire Altar thereupon surrenders to the worshiper. (RV 1.71.6.)

- From that point forward, the worshiper follows and surrenders to the Lunar house or energy, the force and energy of Agni, or of any other Lunar house or energy before which the worshiper prostrates. These include any one from the vast array of Vedic forces, such as Rudra, the fire of the firmament (RV 3.54.3; 7.36.5); Heaven and Earth (RV 3.54.3); the Angirasa Seers (RV 1.62.2); Indra, the supporter of the Vedic dharma (RV 4.21.5; 4.23.4); the ancestors, ptrs (RV 10.15.2); and Rudra, the fire of the firmament, and the Maruts, Mitra, Varuna, Aditi, Sindhu, Earth and Heaven. (RV 3.51.4.)

With these stellar powers Agni dispenses the spiritual endowments on the worshiper. The fire of Agni contains the essence of these endowments which are reined upon the worshiper. As its presiding force, Agni supplies these endowments through the flames of the Sun, Agni's domain. The Lunar house of Agni, the "God of Fire," moves the flame. Flame moves to Light, in the form of *bhanu* and others; from Light, the imbued meaning contained therein moves to the worshiper. The source of this power is the Krittika asterism; Vrscika (Scorpio) provides a secondary source; that power is communicated to the worshiper through the rays of the Sun; these endowments are housed in zodiacal mansion of Mithuna (Gemini). Agni in this capacity teaches Response. Agni as the Messenger in a procedure similar to what we had just witnessed teaches Response in its aspect as the Fire Altar. It is a two-way street.

- The Lunar house of Agni brings all of the other Lunar houses or Vedic forces to the sacrifice and gives these forces life. (RV 5.26.8.)
- The worshiper begins by approaching the Fire Altar with thoughts of Self-Surrender. (RV 1.1.7.) The worshiper surrenders before the Fire Altar. In this context the Fire Altar represents the fire of the Vedic dharma, its natural laws and processes. (RV 10.92.4.) The Fire Altar also represents the fire of the Word. (RV 10.115.4.) The Fire Altar also presents the fire of Impulsions and Knowledge. (RV 10.165.5.)
- The worshiper then send the "streams"—thoughts, prayers, meditative austerities—to the Fire Altar, seeking its protection. (RV 7.94.4.) The worshiper's self-surrender may be for different purposes. The worshiper may seek self-surrender, conscious of the worshiper's sins, but in seeking expiation from here, the Visvedevas and the One, give their expiation.
- Agni in its aspect as the Fire Altar accepts the worshiper's self-surrender. (RV 1.65.1.) Agni in its aspect as the Fire Altar thereupon surrenders to the worshiper. (RV 1.71.6.)

From that point forward, the worshiper follows and surrenders to the Lunar house or energy, the force and energy of Agni, or of any other Vedic force or energy before which the worshiper prostrates. The same dynamics are present in the next category, the Lunar house of Prajapati. It is the same lesson taught by Prajapati in the next Nakshatra.

In his Capacity of Ruling the Rohini Asterism, the Lunar house of Prajapati Dispenses, And the Worshiper Learns, the Spiritual Endowment of *Yajna*, Divine Response.

The Vedic astrologer knows that Prajapati receives its power and in turn presides over the asterism of Rohini. The spiritual endowment dispensed by Prajapati is a complex one. The Vedic Astrologer believes there are two greater concepts that identifies the spiritual endowment dispensed by Prajapati. One is the name of this asterism itself. Rohini is known as "Reddish One" or "Growing One." (*https://www. astroved.com/freetools/rohini-nakshatra.*) Two, is the role of color. The different schools of Classical Alchemy differed widely. There was general agreement, however, on the meaning ascribed to the change in color of base metals to the higher metals during the transmutation process. The base metals began the journey upwards on the color chart, beginning with the colors

- Black, called Melansis or Nigreda, representing Death. A case can be made that this was the vast, indiscriminate, undefined mass of matter described in RV 10.129, wherein began the process of evolution of the Vedic dharma.
- White, called Leukosis or Albedo, representing Resurrection.
- Yellow, Gold, called Xanthosis, representing Immortality.
- Red, or Ruddy Brown, called Iosis, representing Rebirth. Other traditions include a further step. The color in this additional step is Green, or Green-tinted, called Verditas.

Prajapati dispenses the spiritual rebirth of the worshiper from energy originating from the source, Rohini. In the Vedas, the worshiper is born three times: One is in the physical birth of the worshiper; one is when the worshiper dies and is physically reborn; the third is where the worshiper is spiritually reborn at the sacrifice. (SPB, 11.2.1.1.) The worshiper once initiated into the mysteries of the Vedas becomes "born again," a new and different person, or *dvija*. Soma and the cosmic order play their intimate role in effectuating the second birth of the worshiper. Being "born again" is a quality of internal divinization.

There are two processes at work which generate the principle of change in the worshiper's spiritual growth to being born again.

- One is the inherent ability of the Agni as the Sun dispensing spiritual increase from the power of Krittika to take multifarious forms. (RV 1.1.2; 2.16;3.47.5.) This ability to change forms enables the worshiper to be spiritually transformed through the agencies of Agni's various powers, e.g., the force of the light of consciousness. (RV 3.3.2.)
- The second process is through the agency of the Light of Consciousness to pervade all manifestation, including the worshiper who is transformed to a new person. (RV 1.95.10; 3.1.20.)

This process of rebirth coincides with the symbol associated with rebirth and regeneration which exists in the Vedic dharma — The Bull. The Rohini Nakshatra is the Bull, not simply because it spreads from 10°-0' to 23°-20' in the zodiacal house of Vrsabha (Taurus).

The Bull is the Rainmaker, not just because the Bull's seed is the rain and as rain brings water to renew the earth, but because the Rainmaker replenishes the worshiper's soul, replenishing the soul with strength, vigor, and other benefits, while traveling on the Vedic path to salvation and liberation. There are three aspects to the Bull:

- *Vrasanaa*, the Showerer of benefits.
- *Vrsaa*, the Bull in its active principle of regeneration.
- *Vrsabha*, the Bull, in its aspect of the Purusa, in its personification of strength and might. It is this last aspect of the Showerer the serves as the inspiration for the zodiacal house of Vrsabha (Taurus).

The Lunar houses or Vedic forces or energies displaying *vrsanaa*, the Showerer of benefits, are:

- The lunar house of Indra. (RV 1.7.6,7; 1.52.23; 1.108.3, 7, 8, 9, 11, 12; 2.17.8; 4.50.10; 5.33.2; 6.22.8; 6.33.1; 6.44.20; 7.31.4; 8.85.7; 10.153..2.)

- The lunar house of Agni. (RV 1.112.8; 3.27.25; 6.1.1; 8.73.10; 10.191.1.)
- The lunar houses of Agni-Soma. (RV 1.93.6.)
- The Vedic force of Indragni. (RV 1.108.3, 7, 8, 9, 11, 12.)
- The Vedic forces and lunar houses of Indra-Soma. (RV 7.104.1.)
- The Vedic forces and lunar houses Indra-Varuna. (RV 6.68.11; 7.60.9; 7.82.2; 7.83.9.)
- The lunar house of the Asvins. (RV 1.112.8; 1.116.22; 1.117.3, 4, 8, 12, 15, 18, 19, 25; 1.118.1, 6; 1.119.4; 1.157.5;1.158.1; 1.180.7; 1.181.8; 1.183.1; 1.184.2; 2.41.8; 5.74.1; 5.75.4, 9; 6.62.7; 7.70.7; 7.71.6; 7.73.3; 7.74.3; 8.5.24, 27, 36; 8.22.8, 9, 12, 16; 8.26.1, 2, 5, 12, 15; 8.35.15; 10.39.9.)
- The Vedic forces and lunar houses of Mitra-Varuna. (RV 1.151.2, 3; 1.151.2; 7.60.9, 10; 7.61.5.)
- The Vedic energies of the Maruts (RV 2.33.13; 7.56.18, 20; 7.58.6; 8.20.16; 10.93.5) and
- The lunar house of Soma. (RV 2.40.3; 8.93.19; 9.5.6; 9.19.5; 9.64.2.)

Precisely the Vedic forces and energies which we will see are the epithets to Prajapati. What are the benefits conferred? The benefits conveyed to the worshiper are those obtained at the sacrifice. (RV 1.93.6; 1.151.2, 3; 1.151.2.) What are the benefits conferred?

- Granting all desires. (RV 1.7.6.)
- Opening the world to the Angirasas, which is symbolic of the light of consciousness emanating from the principle of Change (Agni). (RV1.51.3.)
- Provides the germ or seed of life to the world and "all moving creatures." (RV 1.157.5; 6.22.18; 6.33.1.)
- The benefits conferred from Soma, which is divine ecstasy and union. (RV 1.13.1; 5.75.4, 9; 8.22.7; 8.93.19; 9.5.6; 9.19.5; 9.64.2.)
- Vigor and strength, represented in various rcs as vitality, youth, and life-force. (RV 1.151.2, 3; 1.153.2; 1.158.1; 1.180.7; 1.181.8; 1.183.1; 1.184.2; 2.17.8; 2.33.13; 2.40.3; 2.41.8; 3.27.15.4.14.4.35.6; 6.1.1; 6.44.20.)

- An appreciation and understanding of the laws of *Rta*. (RV 8.22.7.)
- The benefits conferred are those of regeneration itself. (RV 8.22.9; 8.26.1, 2, 5, 12, 15.)
- Perhaps the most significant, one of the benefits is the power of pranayama which raises the waters (*apana*) upwards. (RV 1.116.22.)

In the Rigveda, Prajapati appears as an epithet for Savitr, Soma, Agni, and Indra, who are all praised as equal, same and lord of creatures. (Sukumari Bhattacharji, *The Indian Theogony* (2007) pp. 322 – 323.) Other Vedic forces and lunar houses inhere in, spring from, and act in conjunction and in alignment with Agni. (RV 10.61.9.) Agni as the Sun dispensing spiritual increase from the power of Krittika guides the worshiper to spiritual renewal. Agni, the Sun, is predominant. Agni as the Sun dispensing spiritual increase from the power of Krittika, is *dvijanam*, that which is "twice born." (RV 1.60.1; 1.140.2; 1.149.4, 5.)

- Just as Indra is reborn when as the sacrificer he kills Vrtra, so is the worshiper reborn when an offering is made at the sacrifice. (KB 15.3.)
- Just as the Soma plant is "killed" when they are pulverized to make the Soma juice, so does the divine essence of that admixture produce the Vedic principle of Soma, divine union, during the Soma sacrifice. (KB 3.32; SPB 3.2.6.6; 3.9.4.3; 3.9.4.8; 3.9.4.23; 4.3.4.1.)
- Prajapati in offering and reproducing himself at the sacrifice, saves himself from Death, is re-born, and achieves life eternal. (SPB 2.2.4.7; 2.3.3.2; 3.9.4.17; 11.1.2.1.)
- Indra asked Agni, the Principle of Change, and Brhaspati, to sacrifice him, and they did so.
- As a result, each was reborn: Indra, as *indriyam*, articulation; Agni, as *tejas*, the source of divine energy; and Brhaspati, as brahman, the divine speech. (MS 2.4.6; 43.12.)
- As a result of the animal sacrifice, modernly that most odious form of sacrifice, the sacrificer renews his fires, and thus himself, when he cooks the victim. (SPB 11.7.1.1.)

The lesson from Prajapati's self-sacrifice is to show the worshiper the path to being born again. When Prajapati sacrificed himself at the sacrifice, so too will the worshiper, who lives on with the remaining progeny. (SPB 2.2.4.8.) These examples also underscore the importance of sacrifice in spiritual renewal and rebirth:

- The worshiper is born again through the sacrifice. (RV 10.61.19; 10.101.11.)
- To arrive at this place of personal transformation, the worshiper must have a belly full of Soma. (RV 10.101.11.)
- The worshiper is thereby reborn through *yajna* to observe and follow the dictates of the Vedic dharma, *Rta*, through the tongue of change (Agni). (RV 6.50.2.)
- As a result of being "twice born" the worshiper attains Divine Union (Soma) and becomes one with the God(s) and drinks the milk from the cup of the cosmic order, *Rta*. (RV 10.61.19.)

The process of being reborn is accomplished through the agency of the Vedic divine dynamic forces at work during the sacrificial rite. (RV 1.148.1.) This aspect is termed as the "Showerer" for a reason, for just as the blood flows from the sacrificial victim during the animal (or human) sacrifice, so do the benefits to the worshiper. Like rain, this rainmaking capability creates new life materially and spiritual rebirth in the worshiper. Where does this rebirth occur? The Svar, the subtle region wherein the essence of the cosmic order (*Rta*), is the culmination of the give-and-take process of the sacrifice.

Dvija is the capacity or quality of being born again. It is present in the dynamic forces just mentioned, and it is a quality present primarily in Agni, the Fire of Change. This aspect of spiritual rebirth inherent in the principle of change is conveyed to the worshiper as well, and the worshiper's soul is transformed, born again, such that he or she has been made a wholly new and different — a purified — person, one conjoined with the cosmos and the divinities. This transformation clearly allows the possibility of the worshiper being spiritually reborn. In its most complete manner this transformation is what is meant by Divine Union; the worshiper shares the qualities of divinities, i.e., immortality.

The sacrifice was established when the subtle region wherein the essence of the dynamic cosmic order was placed in the Vedic cosmos.(RV 5.66.2.)

- The sacrifice subsumes the qualities of the subtle region wherein the essence of the Vedic dharma. (RV 1.148.1.)
- These dynamic Vedic forces and forefathers guide the worshiper in the ascent to the region where the essence of dynamic force of cosmic order resides and during the Vedic path to salvation and liberation. (RV 1.71.2.)
- The worshiper seeks access to the region where the essence of dynamic force of cosmic order, the taking aspect of the sacrificial rite. (RV 4.40.2; 5.60.1; 7.90.6.)
- Through the sacrifice and during the journey on the Vedic path to liberation, the worshiper seeks to know the inner truth of the Vedic dharma (*Rta*) and its essence (Svar). (RV 10.66.4.)
- The worshiper seeks the assistance of the Duad (Asvins) in the Vedic Path to liberation and to the region where the essence of dynamic force of cosmic order. RV 8.76.4.)
- The worshiper requests access to the region where the essence of dynamic force of cosmic order with a purified mind (Soma)(RV 9.4.2; 9.59.4; 9.61.18; 9.73.1; 9.90.4; 9.98.8), with the help of the powers and grace of Bala (Indra)(RV 6.72.3; 8.3.13), which confer the essence of the dynamic cosmic order (*Rta*) to the worshiper
- The Principle of Change (Agni) confers the inner essence of the Vedic dharma (*Rta*) to the worshiper (RV 2.2.7, 10; 8.48.8), in conjunction with Bala (Indra). (RV 8.48.8.)
- The worshiper ascends to the region where the essence of dynamic force of cosmic order resides through the sama chant. (RV 1.52.9.)
- Once reborn, the worshiper acquires all the attributes of the inner essence of the Vedic dharma: food (immortality), horses (discrimination), and the rays of the essence of the Vedic dharma (*Rta*) (knowledge). (RV 4.45.6.)
- Once reborn, awareness (Usas) in the worshiper grows, whether that self-awareness is derivative of the rebirth, or awareness of the worshiper's place in the cosmic order and shines throughout the world. (RV 3.61.4; 7.81.4.)

The Svar is the new abode for the worshiper after rebirth. The Svar is both a subtle and material region.

- As a result of this spiritual rebirth, the worshiper resides in the sphere of the Svar. (S.P.B., 9.3.4.13; 13.2.8.5; VS 23.20.)
- The Svar is the Region of the Eternal Light. (RV 9.113.7.)
- This is the region where the eternal Vedic forces reside (RV 4.16.4) and where the spiritually reborn worshiper resides.

Rohini provides the ultimate spiritual destination for the worshiper and designates the Svar as its destination. The next asterism, Mrgashirsha, provides the means by which that destination is made.

In his Capacity of Ruling the Mrgashirsha Asterism, the Lunar house Of Soma Dispenses, and the Worshiper Learns, the Spiritual Endowment of Bliss

Soma receives its power and in turn presides over these members of the stellar population:

- Soma is the presiding deity and personification of the Moon.
- Soma is the presiding deity, in alignment with the Lunar houses of Agni and Prajapati, of the zodiacal houses of Vrsabha (Taurus) and Mithuna (Gemini).
- Soma rules over and dispenses the spiritual endowments from the asterism of Mrgashirsha.

The Vedic astrologer knows that Soma occupies a position much exalted in the astrological Vedic dharma. With the lunar house of Indra, Soma represents the Vedic element of Akasha. Soma is situated in the Lunar mansion of Mrghashira, which is itself in an exalted position. The eminent Vedic scholar, Bal Ganghadar Tilak, postulated in The Orion, of the Antiquities of the Vedas, that Mrghashira was identified by the ancients as the Orion Star, signified the beginning of the Vernal Equinox, and subtly was associated with the devayana, the Northern Path trod by the worshiper's soul after death. (Tilak, *Orion, or the Antiquities of the Vedas* (1898), p. 107.) In an interpretative note, in much the same way that the Big and Little Dippers are represented as bears, Tilak deduces that the references in the Vedas of deers and antelopes are references to Orion or the Mrghashira asterism. (RV 2.34.3, 4; 2.36.2; 4.21.8; 5.53.1; 5.55.6; 6.75.11; 7.40.3; 7.87.6; 8.2.6; 8.7.36.) Tilak's deductions further a deeper understanding to the message of the Vedas. The reason the Vedas reveal that the Maruts in their dazzling, blazing, glory traveled the skies on the deer was because Orion itself is the brightest Star in the evening sky. (RV 1.37.2; 5.58.6; 5.60.2.) The deer is identified with Soma. (RV 10.94.5.) The deer is *mrgam* (RV 8.5.36), so it is not a huge stretch to call Soma's Lunar house "Mrghashira." *Mrgam*—which references either collectively or individually the Vernal Equinox, Orion, the devayana, the Northern Path, the Lunar house of Soma, Mrghashira, or Soma itself—is found in many other passages in the Rg Veda. (RV 1.80.7; 1.105.7; 2.33.11; 5.29.4; 8.1.20; 8.2.6; 8.5.36; 8.69.15.)

But we are getting ahead of ourselves. The impact of the Nakshatras to the Northern Path will be explained far later in this piece. The significance of the equinoxes and the like will be set forth in the Vedic astrologer's next book on the subject. For now, suffice it to say the Vedic astrologer knows Soma as the Lunar house dispensing Bliss as the personification of the Moon, dispensing these the spiritual endowments through the power from the asterism of Mrgashirsha and in conjunction with the zodiacal houses of Mithuna (Gemini) and Vrsabha (Taurus).

Other Lunar houses dispense Bliss to the worshiper.

- The Vedic force of Savitr is the dispenser of the spiritual endowment of Bliss through the asterism of Hasta and the zodiacal house of Kanya (Virgo).
- The lunar houses of Indra and energy of Tvastr are the dispensers of Bliss, through the asterism of Chitra and the zodiacal houses of Kanya (Virgo) and Tula (Libra).

What accounts for these shared responsibilities?

- The lunar house of Savitr is known in the Vedic dharma as the presiding deity of Creation. As part of his work, Bliss is created and is manifested for the worshiper to experience.
- The Vedic force of Indra and energy of Tvastr are supplicants for the Lunar house of Agni. Indra, the Lord of the Mid-World, is the incarnation of Agni both specifically (RV 2.1.3) when battling Vrtra. (RV 3.14.7; 10.80.2; Mikhailov, (2001) RgVedic Studies, p. 14.), and generally when this Vedic force is the incarnation of Agni Vasivanara when battling the "enemies," whomever they are.
- Tvastr is the Architect, "Fashioner of Forms," (BD 1.84) of the Universe. Tvastr is a manifestation of the terrestrial fire of Agni. (BD, 1.108.) Together these supplicants of Agni dispense Bliss to the worshiper through the asterism of Chitra and in conjunction with the zodiacal houses of Kanya (Virgo) and Tula (Libra).

Through the lunar house of Soma's spiritual endowment of Bliss, this Lunar house provides the raw energy to propel the worshiper towards the path of liberation and salvation. While other Vedic forces and lunar houses also provide this spiritual endowment, the spiritual strength of Soma is the primary source. This is accomplished in the asterism of Mrghashira. Mrghashira triggers the commencement of the year-long sacrificial rites. Initially, Vrtra represented the Nakshatra Mrghashira (Orion), which in turn triggers other aspects of the sacrifice such as the commencement of the year-long sacrifice and construction of the sacrificial altar. In RV 4.18.9, 8.6.7, 5.34.2, and 8.93.14, Indra, the dispenser of Happiness through the asterism of Jyestra and in conjunction with the zodiacal house of Vrscika (Scorpio), cuts off Vrtra's head, as symbolic of cutting off of the head of Prajapati, the symbol reflected in this Nakshatra, Mrgashira, closing the first phase of the Vernal Equinox, the "Antelope's Head", the English correlate of the constellation Orion. (SPB 2.1.2.8.)

- Salvation and liberation in the Vedic dharma is accomplished in two stages containing seven stages. The first stage of salvation and liberation consists in acquiring the mental state of mind to withstand the intense feeling of salvation and liberation.
- The Awakening is the first step in the journey towards salvation and liberation.
- From the Awakening, or Enlightenment, the worshiper acquires Knowledge; from Knowledge, the worshiper gains Consciousness;
- From Consciousness, the worshiper has the capacity to be engaged in Contemplation or Deliberation.
- From the act of Contemplation or Deliberation the worshiper gains Insightful Knowledge.
- From this Insightful Knowledge, the worshiper obtains Discernment.
- From Discernment, the worshiper obtains Divine Vision.

From there, Soma provides the raw material for the second stage of salvation and liberation. That second stage is Bliss. In this second stage, the worshiper experiences rapture and bliss.

- From Divine Vision, the worshiper experiences Joy.
- From Joy, the worshiper is completely overcome by Rapture.
- From there, Rapture, the worshiper gets a taste of Liberation.

Liberation is the goal. Now the worshiper's spiritual journey begins.

Awakening

Each separate level of this spiritual awakening has its own separate category. Soma informs each category. Soma is also the vehicle which takes the worshiper through all these different points of entry. So, much like the ladder of spiritual of ascent to heaven, Mrgashirsha guides the worshiper on the path to salvation and liberation. In the Awakening Mrgashirsha gives the worshiper the first taste of Liberation in Rapture.

The Awakening is sometimes described in terms of simile. The Ninth Mandala likens the Awakening as the Dawn (RV 9.86.19), personified by the divine force of Usas. It is also described as Illumination. (RV 9.84.5.) Since the Awakening is symbolized in terms of light and illumination, in cosmological terms it is found in the Svar, (RV 9.61.18), the intermediary region of light, between Heaven and Earth. All these aids the worshiper in the journey to salvation and liberation.

Knowledge

Knowledge occurs early in the worshiper's spiritual journey. It is often said that knowledge is power. The same can be said about Soma. Soma is the Knower of all things (RV 9.8.9), All-Knowing (RV 9.87.3), and is guided by knowledge. (RV 9.69.3.) In a simile used throughout the Vedas, Soma is the milk of knowledge. (RV 9.96.24.) This is one of the reasons why the Cows are said to be symbols for knowledge. (See, RV 2.40.2.) It was explained earlier that the inner essence of Soma is the Knower of the two levels of existence of Heaven and Earth. "Knower" in this context was taken to mean that Soma is both the Subject, the Universal Atman, superimposing its nature on the perceiving Object of mortal consciousness and the Object of that knowledge. As the "Knower of All Things," Soma is acting as the Universal Atman.

Power obtained is ineffectual if not acted upon. This is completely consistent with the Universal Atman, which essentially does not act, but simply "is." Thus, knowledge without the appropriate discernment or appreciation is sterile. Think of a computer supplied with all the knowledge in the world operating without an algorithm. With the proper algorithms, the capabilities are very powerful indeed. Just ask the folks at Cambridge Analytica. Similarly, when knowledge and proper discernment are coupled, when applied to worshiper's spiritual journey, the quest is complete. It is under these conditions that Soma is capable of expiating sins. (RV 8.79.4.) Having said this, it should be noted that Soma also nourishes. Soma accordingly imparts its knowledge to the worshiper in the spiritual journey. Thus, Soma discovers the brilliance of Knowledge for the worshiper. (RV 9.86.39.) Soma acts through the agency of Mrgashirsha to aid and foster the worshiper's spiritual development. Knowledge is an essential part of that journey.

Consciousness

From the Awakening, or Enlightenment, the worshiper acquires Knowledge and from Knowledge, he worshiper gains Consciousness. Soma plays a huge role in the elevation of consciousness. (RV 9.86.42.) Soma plays a great role in the field of consciousness. The worshiper becomes conscious by consuming Soma. (RV 9.108.2.) Thought and thinking are by nature subtle. (RV 9.15.1.) Thought and thinking may be viewed as electrical impulses traveling through the synapses in the brain. Soma can be viewed as the Bull which fertilizes the seed which invigorate those electrical charges. (Nir., 3.3.) Soma is consciousness itself. (RV 9.106.4.) In Soma through the agency of Mrgashirsha the worshiper acquires the Universal Consciousness of Atman. (RV 9.20.3.)

Contemplation, Deliberation

Contemplation and Deliberation are an important part of the worshiper's journey to liberation and salvation.

Contemplation is defined as that activity of *Tapas* or askeseis, which are defined as intense thought or meditation. (RV 6.47.3.) In this way, contemplation has an obvious mental aspect. Soma through the agency of Mrgashirsha is responsible for providing for the capability of humans to think, deliberate and become aware. (RV 9.8.9.) In addition, Soma gives birth to human thoughts and is that human thought. Soma is the Contemplator of Men. (RV 9.8.9.) This is a very telling saman (mantra). The Veda recognizes that the worshiper is a thinking subject. However, the worshiper is a thinking subject because Soma superimposes the worshiper's thoughts for the worshiper. If this sounds like Classical Vedanta, you're correct. Soma thereby becomes the subject and the object of human thought. This reconciles the notions in which Soma impels—is the Efficient Cause—humans' thoughts, the Contemplator of humans and is inside human thought. (RV 9.21.7.) It also leads us to the next step.

Insightful Knowledge (Cows)

From the Awakening, or Enlightenment, the worshiper acquires Knowledge; from Knowledge, the worshiper gains Consciousness; from Consciousness, the worshiper has the capacity to be engaged in Contemplation or Deliberation; from the act of Contemplation or Deliberation the worshiper gains Knowledge; from Knowledge the worshiper is elevated to Inspired Knowledge. Cows are intimately related to Knowledge in general and the knowledge necessary for liberation and salvation.

The cows are an important part of the Vedic dharma. They represent knowledge, wisdom and illumination, most likely because these qualities are representative of their products: milk, butter and ghee. Cows are symbolic of the principle or precept of existence. Cows are also symbolic of some aspect of universality, usually in association with other Vedic divine dynamic forces. It is their aspect to this stage of liberation that interests us at this point. Because the cows produce several by-products, different cows in the Vedas represent different aspects of knowledge, mind, and/or consciousness. This was covered at length in the introduction but justifies repetition. That essence is the following:

- A barren or immature cow is taken to mean the lack of consciousness, incomplete or faulty knowledge, because of its unripe milk. (RV 3.30.14 (unripe milk); 2.7.5; 1.112.3; 1.116.22; 1.117.20; 1.61.9 (raw cows); 6.72.4; 4.19.7; 7.68.8.)

- Red or ruddy cows are said to represent the onset or beginnings of illumination. (RV 1.92.2; 10.68.6; 6.64.3; 1.49.1; 8.7.7).

- The ray-cows represent Aditi, the infinite consciousness. (RV 4.58.4; 4.1.6.)

- The Ray-Cows also represent hidden or occult knowledge. (RV 4.53; 4.58; 4.5.10).

- A cow's calf represents jiva, or the individual soul. (RV 4.33.4; 4.34.5; 1.110.8; 1.111.1; 1.164.5; 1.164.9, 17, 18, 27; 2.7.5; 2.16.8; 2.28.6; 2.24.8; 3.33.3; 3.41.5; 1.55.'4; 6.45.25; 5.30.10; 7.87.5; 8.43.17; 8.59.14, 15; 8.61.5; 9.41.14; 9.86.2; 9.100.1,7; 9.104.2; 9.105.2; 9.111.14; 10.8.2, 9; 10.53.11; 10.119.4; 10.145.6; RV 10.10.75.4; 10.123.1).

The result of this insightful knowledge is the worshiper's ultimate liberation. This is again symbolically reflected in what the Vedas have to say about the Cows in the number Seven as contained in the Seven-Dimensional Universe. The Seven Dimensional Universe is the transcendent world of Liberation and Salvation. The Vedas associate the Cows with this Seven-Dimensional Universe. Thus, to this level of existence the Cows symbolize the dawn of consciousness or truth. (RV 1.71.1). They represent the seven principles of existence. (RV 1.164.3), the seven rivers. (RV 1.32.12; 2.34.15), the "seven sisters." (RV 2.7.1), the very expanse of Heaven and earth itself. (RV 3.6.4; 9.86.2).

The Cows — and insightful knowledge — are ubiquitous. The insightful knowledge of the Cows, with Soma through the agency of Mrgashirsha greatly aides the spiritual journey of the worshiper. For this there is little wonder. In gaining insightful knowledge the worshiper acquires the divine knowledge and wisdom of God which has obtained that insightful knowledge from the cows. Thousands, says the Satapatha Brahmana, are the number of cows taken from the gods. (SPB 3.3.1.13.)

Discernment

Discernment is another stage of consciousness which leads the worshiper to liberation in the spiritual journey. This is an important stage. From Discernment, the worshiper obtains Divine Vision, the precursor stage to rapture and ultimate liberation. (RV 10.25.1.) Soma has penetrating Wisdom. (RV 9.1.9.) The worshiper receives discernment from Soma. (RV 10.25.1.) Soma through the agency of Mrgashirsha has this discernment. (RV 8.48.8.) That discernment is eternal. (RV 9.4.3.)

Divine Vision

Divine Vision is an important building block in the spiritual aspect of the Vedic dharma. Divine Vision is a beginning stage towards liberation. Not only is it an important stage of liberation but is also a symbol of the pervasion which is the natural order, the Vedic dharma.

Soma not only permeates all creation, it permeates *Rta* itself. *Rta* is the underlying principle which empowers the entire Vedic dharma. Soma is *Rta*/van, born or possessed of *Rta*. This is no mean characteristic, as the only other Lunar house so completely possessed of *Rta* is Agni, the personification of the element of the fire of Change. (RV 1.72.1, 2, 5; 2.35.8; 3.13.2; 3.20. 4; 4.2.1; 4.6.5; 4.2.1; 4.7.7; 5.1.6; 5.25.1; 6.12.1; 6.15.1; 6.15.13; 7.3.1; 7.7.4; 5.28.2; 10.2.2;10.6.2; 10.7.4.) Agni is also Rta/jata: 1.36.19; 1.144.7; 1.189.6; 3.6.10; 6.13.3.)

One of the most common characteristics assigned to Soma is vi/shvaa, or "pervasion," its ability to pervade and permeate the cosmos, the sacrificial hall and the world. (RV 9.1.10; 9.3,4; 9.4.2; 9.8.7; 9.14.8; 9.16.6; 9.18.6; 9.20.1, 3; 9.21.4; 9.23.1; 9.25.4; 9.28.2, 5; 9.29.4;9.36.5; 9.40.1, 4; 9.42.5; 9.43.2; 9.9.54.3; 9.55.1; 9.57.2, 4; 9.59.3, 4; 9.61.19, 24, 25, 28, 30; 9.64.6, 8, 18; 9.65.2, 9, 10; 9.66.1; 9.73.8; 9.80.3, 4; 9.84.2; 9.85.11; 9.86.6, 15, 24, 26, 30, 41, 48; 9.87.6; 9.88.2; 9.89.6; 9.90.1, 6; 9.94.3, 5; 9.97.51; 9.98.7; 9.100.2; 9.102.1; 9.107.23; 9.108.11; 9.109.4, 8, 9, 14; 9.9.110.9; and 9.111.5.) Not only does it permeate or pervade the universe, it is "all pervading," *vishvacakSa*. In this regard a common adjective used in connection with Soma is sahasra. Subject to several meanings, Wilson translates sahasra as "thousand" but it can also mean "innumerable." Keshav Dev Verma has given this word in the Vedas a gloss in terms of modern particle physics and interprets sahasra simply as "the universe." (Verma, *Vedic Physics* (2008) Motilal Banarsidass). A rendering with this gloss gives much more meaning to ordinary translations, for example in RV 1.10.11, Soma through the agency of Mrgashirsha is said to give the worshiper a "thousand gifts." Those "thousand gifts" point to the enormity of the specific spiritual benefits originating from the Vedic dharma. Having drunk the Soma Juice, the worshiper is given the essence of the world, the universe, the Vedic dharma.

Joy, Bliss

Joy, or Bliss, is the category most associated with Soma. Joy is the very essence of the aspect of Soma expounded in the Rg Veda. Soma is joyful (RV 9.98.7) and joyous (RV 9.65.25.) It is the very incarnation of Joy and Bliss. (RV 9.108.8.) Soma is rapture, a related building block. (RV 9.69.3.) Soma releases its rapture like waves (RV 9.12.3), and those waves makes the worshiper happy. (RV 9.63.5.) Mere happiness should be distinguished with spiritual bliss. Soma is not only possessed of Joy and Bliss, but it is also imbued with a higher expression of Spiritual Bliss. (RV 9.63.13.)

A significant part of the blissful aspect of Soma is the Word, articulation. In the bliss generated by Soma, the "rhythmic word" is spoken. (RV 9.113.6.) The meaning of this saman is that joy and bliss is generated simply by the chanting at the Soma Sacrifice. Like all things Vedic, displaying its love of classification, there are different levels to Joy:

- There is *Mada*, the generic, ground level, category to Joy. It is the simple joy experienced by the worshiper, either as a result of a spiritual awakening or otherwise and associated with the Three-Dimension Universe of the material world. In the Rg Veda there are well over one hundred references to this type of Joy.
- There is *madhya*, the joy experienced as a result of a spiritual awakening. In the Rg Veda it is the joy experienced by the vast array of Vedic divine forces after consumption of the Soma juice. Again, there are upwards to one hundred and more references in the Rg Veda to madhya and its derivatives. Because it is associated

with the Vedic divine forces, this is the form of Joy associated with the Five-Dimension Universe.

- There is *madhummatanam*, the highest form of Joy. *madhummatanam* is that Joy experienced at the acme of spiritual development. Accordingly associated with the Seven-Dimension Universe, it is ananda which is the third member of the three-part experience, along with cit and sat, of the ultimate unchanging reality in Hinduism called Brahman. References to *madhummatanam* can be found in the following passages of the Rg Veda: 1.47.3; 5.11.5; 6.68.11; 7.42.2, 7; 7.102.3; 8.3.15; 8.9.7; 9.12.7; 9.30.5, 6; 9.51.2; 9.62.21; 9.63.16, 19; 9.64.22; 9.67.16; 9.80.4; 9.100.6; 9.101.4; 9.105.3; 9.106.6; 9.108.1, 15; 10.14.15; 10.122.7.)

The experience of Joy is specifically defined and its scope is vast. Joy contains elements of Bliss (RV 9.5.10, RV 9.63.13.), Rapture (RV 9.12.3), Happiness (RV 9.63.5.), Delight (RV 9.5.9.), and Rapture (RV 9.12.3.) Least we delude ourselves we must be clear on the basis for Joy. It is not a hedonistic experience but one grounded from and the result of virtuous means. (RV 9.76.1.) The Source of Joy is Soma. Soma is Joy incarnate. (RV 9.108.8.) Soma is joyous (RV 9.65.25) and joyful (RV 9.98.7) by nature. The worshiper experiences Joy with two means. One, on a sacrificial level, the worshiper consumes the Soma Juice to experience the divine. This is the import of the saman which says that Soma makes the worshiper happy with "waves of Juice." (RV 9.63.5.) Two, the worshiper may experience Joy, Bliss, by hearing the "rhythmic word," the ritualistic chanting, at the sacrifice. (RV 9.113.6.)

Rapture

If one knows anything about Soma, it is this, Rapture. Rapture and Bliss, Joy. Madhu, the exhilarating experience of the bliss of divine union, is a central element to Vedic salvation and a necessary companion in the Vedic path to salvation. In the classical English translations it has been rendered variously as "bliss," "ecstasy," "rapture," "fervor," or even "madness." All these words indeed are synonymous with madhu, rapture.

These synonyms can be reduced to "Theosis" or "divine union." Soma is the symbol of divine rapture, that level of existence, the Satya/m pavamana, is that level of existence and reality wherein divine rapture is found. Indeed, the highest of the seven planes of existence in Vedic cosmology.

Rapture is sweet. (RV 6.47.1.) The prepared Soma is sweet. (RV 6.47.2.) But we should understand the real meaning of sweetness. The Vedic dharma has been compared to honey. The Brhanaranyaka Upanishad in 2.5 gives the deeper meaning of honey and sweetness. Sweetness and honey form the very basis of the Vedic dharma:

- Water—the fundamental essence of the Vedic dharma—is the honey of all sentient and non-sentient beings. Thus, Soma emanates rapture in water-like waves.
- Honey thereupon forms the basis of the divine existential levels in the Seven-Dimension Universe and physical and sentient-based existential level in the Two-, Three-, and Five-Dimensional Universes.

The sweetness accordingly consists of both the divine and the physical. It consists of

- This earth.
- All sentient and non-sentient beings.
- The First Cause of all sentient and non-sentient beings. Soma upholds Everything with its Ecstasy. (RV 9.18.1.)
- That Self, the Immortal, that Brahman, that All. Thus, Soma is the Great Rapture of the universe. (RV 9.108.1.)

F. Max Muller, the German scholar who was one of the first translators of Hindu and Vedic scriptures in the West, recognized that honey is not simply sweetness. In these passages honey and sweetness is a metaphor for the dependent processes of cause and effect. Just as the bees both make and are supported by honey, both earth and all living beings therein are mutually dependent, and the material and the intangible, the divine, where the latter is the cause of the former.

As this Upanishad recognizes, the processes of cause and effect are in reality one process carried out in two steps. This is indicated by the consumption of Soma. Through the rapture of purified Soma, the worshiper does directly to the divine. (RV 9.98.7.) The worshiper consumes Soma, and the worshiper experiences the divine. This is the Divine Ecstacy spoken of in the Vedas. (RV 9. 80.2.)

The great misconception is that the sweetness is associated with the state of being happy. The samans (mantras) in the Ninth Mandala give some credence to this belief by saying that Some gives a happy mind. (RV 10.25.1.) Happiness, however, is not the same as Joy or Bliss, a related topic, nor is the equivalent to Rapture. Again, this happiness should be put in its proper context. Soma is modernly associated with pleasure and recreational altering of mental states. But Soma is not simply the joy experienced by ingestion of mind altering substances as is understood today. It is the joy encountered by the worshiper while experiencing the divine mental awareness found in the Seven-Dimensional Universe. In the language of the Ninth Mandala, the greatness of Soma opens up in the worshiper with its rapture. (RV 10.25.5.) The totality of the Vedic dharma is what is opened up to the worshiper.

Liberation

Yes, this is the purpose of the worshiper's spiritual journey. Just as the main purpose of a parent is to allow the child to leave when the time comes, so is the purpose of living in the material world to be liberated from it.

In the final third stage, the worshiper is saved through Soma's ability to expiate sins. These stages taken together are roughly equivalent to the path of liberation formulated millennia later with Vedanta. This formulation itself consists of three elements: Reality, "Sat" + Understanding, Consciousness, "Cit" + Ananda, or "Bliss." The last two elements are the first two methods to liberation as far as Soma is concerned. This is a recognition that the final liberation of the worshiper's soul is ultimately an act of Grace.

The Influence of Soma by and through Mrgashirsha

Soma exerts a tremendous influence on the worshiper, because it gives birth to the Illuminated State. It describes the process required to obtain the illuminated state. The notion of release, whether it is of the waters, cattle, or the clouds, is closely related to illumination; it is only when the shackles of ignorance have been loosened or released that the mind and heart are illuminated. This illuminated state is described in the language of the Rg Veda: The cattle are released when the rocks are shattered. (RV 4.1.13, 14.) Cattle, remember, is symbolic for the conscious state and the powers of consciousness. While Indra is the primary liberator, (RV 5.30.4 (Indra tore apart the rocks and rescued the cattle), Soma also is the Lunar house responsible for this mental and spiritual release. For instance:

- Soma's dispensation of Bliss through the Moon, Mrgashirsha, and Mithuna (Gemini) releases the cattle (read, knowledge) concealed in the rocks. (RV 5.30.4 (Indra rent the rocks and rescued the cattle).)
- In this respect, Soma's dispensation of Bliss through the Moon, Mrgashirsha, and Mithuna (Gemini) is seen as the giver of the cattle. (RV 9.72.9; 9.86.39; 1.91.20.)
- Soma's dispensation of Bliss through the Moon, Mrgashirsha, and Mithuna (Gemini) is also responsible for the releasing of the waters. (RV 9.76.1 (Soma, golden hued, like a cursor winning the waters); 9.78.4 (winning the waters and the light); 9.86,27 (the waters flow to the golden-hued Soma); 1.93.5 (with Agni); 9.42.1 (Soma, robed in waters).)

The influence of Soma, through the power vested in it through Mrghashira, extend far beyond merely sharing responsibilities with other astral Vedic forces or energies. Every Vedic force or energy dispenses a spiritual endowment to the worshiper. Soma, through the power vested in it through Mrghashira, teaches, instructs and informs other astral Vedic forces and energies the act of Dispensation.

Dispensation is the category dealing with one of the two elements in the greater category of Sacrifice. The Vedic sacrifice ritual is intended to demonstrate a fundamental truth of the universe: that there is a give-and-take between the Microcosm (humankind) and the Macrocosm (the universe), of every object therein, encompassing the process from creation to dissolution. (Sannyasi Gyanshruti, Sunnyasi Srividyananda, *Yajna, A Comprehensive Survey* (2006), pp. 84 – 85.) This give-and-take process is the essence of the natural order (*Rta*) and how it operates.

This give-and-take is an outgrowth of the binary, dualistic Two-Dimensional universe. On the one hand, the worshiper seeks and offers obligations to the chosen Vedic force or energy. On the other hand, the force and energy of the chosen Vedic force is channeled to the worshiper. On a rudimentary level, this give-and-take is the bargained for exchange for the condition of life in the universe: One being dies so another may live. The dynamics of the exchange takes many forms and is premised on a fundamental assumption that if it is accurately performed sacrifice has a secret power to produce the desired effect. The dynamics in this new level demonstrates the give-and-take process which has been operating every moment in the material universe for eons. This give-and-take is reflected in several ways. In the sacrificial level, an offering is made to receive blessings. The left-handed movement of the giving is based on a simple premise. Divine powers are associated with and inherent to the action of giving. The right-handed movement of discernment is reflected in and a product of the sacrifice itself, which establishes consciousness, mind and thought.

This give-and-take is carried out in the simple act of giving of an offering and the invoking of a divinity so that the sacrificer may also take his or her reward, which is redemption, being born again, purification, or obtain the divinity's grace. In the Soma sacrifice this give-and-take is played out by the "killing" of the Soma plant, the giving its own life literally squeezing its life out through the pressing process, so that the sacrificer receives spiritual redemption and divine bliss.

On an individual level, the essence of yajna, the sacrifice, is the interchange between the embodied soul and conscious human nature and the eternal spirit. It is stated plainly in the Vajaseneyi Yajurveda Samhita that by worshiping Bala (Indra) the worshiper acquires and Increases their own individual Indra-powers (*Indriyam*), specifically by giving powers of knowledge for the worshipers willing to put forth the effort.

Dispensation is instrumental in this grand, cosmic interplay. Soma is the grand puppet-master. Just as in traditional Christian liturgies, bread is given to the congregation to symbolize the sharing of the body of Christ, the distilled Soma juice is consumed by the worshiper to experience the ecstasy of liberation with the Universal Atman. Consumption, though, is one building block, dispensation is another. Dispensation is the subtle element of the act of giving. The act of Dispensation is calculated to elevate the consciousness of the worshiper. (RV 6.41.3.) It enables the worshiper to enter the realm of heaven. (Epithet No. 89.) It is through this act of Dispensation that the worshiper unites with the Universal Consciousness. (RV 9.20.3.) On a broader note, the act of Giving dispenses energies to the worshiper. (RV 9.63.18.) Specifically, through the act of this Dispensation, Soma

- Conveys vigor. (RV 7.91.4.)
- Gives Health. (RV 9.80.2.)
- Fosters physical strength. (RV 9.64.14.)
- Gives long life. (RV 9.80.2.)

Soma exerts its influence on other members of the Stellar Population. The consumption of Soma is seen as another means to achieve the great fusion of galactic forces. The mere consumption of Soma is another one element to the metaphor of the battle between Indra and Vrtra. Indra released the waters after destroying Vrtra with a stone and under the exhilaration of Soma. (RV 1.56.6; 1.93.5 (Agni-Soma).) In essence, the consumption of Soma is but the external vehicle by which the worshipers obtain that union with the divine and by which the divinities battle against evil. Consumption of Soma confers divine consciousness, or, the process of illumination. Divine consciousness can take many forms. In the general Vedic sense, it is represented by the drinking of Soma by the various Vedic divinities. Each divinity represents their own separate inner principle. The act of drinking Soma confers divine properties to whatever principle that particular divinity represents, which ultimately corresponds to the worshiper in the microcosm. So Soma, through the Moon, Mrgashirsha, and Mithuna (Gemini) is consumed by

- The lunar house of Vayu, who dispenses *sukha* (Profound Spiritual Fulfillment, Happiness), through Svasti (Srati) in conjunction with Vrscika (Scorpio). (See, RV 1.2.1, 2; 1.14.10; 1.23.1, 2; 1.134.1, 6; 1.135.1; 2.41.1, 3, 14, 21; 4.61.1; 4.47.1-4; 5.51.6; 7.90.1; 7.91.4, 6; 7.102.1; 9.25.1.)

- The lunar house of the Asvins, who dispense *Bhaga* (Enjoyment) through Asvini and in conjunction with Mesa (Aries). (See, RV 1.15.11; 1.22.1; 1.34.10, 11; 1.44.14; 1.46.5, 15; 1.47.1, 3, 5, 9; 1.112.15; 1.116.21; 1.180.1, 2; 1.18.2; 3.58.7, 9; 4.44.3, 4; 45.3; 5.77.1; 6.63.2; 7.59.3-5; 7.67.4; 7.69.3; 7.70.2; 7.74.2, 3; 8.8.1, 3, 5; 8.10.4; 8.22.8, 17; 8.26.20; 8.35.1-3, 10, 16-21 (with Surya and Usas), 23, 24; 8.74.1-9; 8.75.2, 4, 5; 9.67.3; 10.24.1; 10.40.13; 10.41.3.)

- The lunar house of the Visvedevas ("All Gods"), who dispense Strength through the asterism of Uttara Ashada. (See, RV 1.3.7; 1.14.7; 1.14.8; 1.156.40; 3.57.6; 5.43.3, 6; 5.44.11; 5.51.1 (with Agni), 2; 7.44.4; 9.97.21; 9.109.27.)

- The lunar house of Agni, the Sun, who dispenses the inner secret of *Yajna* and Divine Response through the asterism of Krittika in conjunction with the zodiacal houses of Mesa (Aries) and Vrsabha (Taurus). (See RV 1.14.7; 1.14.10; 1.19.1; 1.21.1, 2; 1.44.9; 1.45.9, 10; 1.141.3, 6; 5.1.3; 5.60.8 (with the Maruts); 6.16.44; 10.16.8; 10.53.9; 10.88.1; 10.91.14; 10.102.2; 10.115.1; 10.122.4.)

- The Maruts. (See, RV 1.15.2, 3; 1.19.1; 1.86.1; 1.88.4; 1.166.7; 4.34.7; 5.60.8 (with Agni); 5.61.11; 6.83.4, 5, 9, 10, 11, 12; 9.54.24; 10.773.)

- The lunar houses of Mitra-Varuna. Mitra, who dispenses Response through the asterism of Anuradha and Vrscika (Scorpio), and Varuna, who dispenses Greatness through the asterism of Shatabhisha and the zodiacal house of Kumba (Aquarius).(See, RV 1.23.4; 1.136.4; 1.137.2, 3; 1.143.4; 5.71.2, 3; 5.72.1-3; 6.67.7; 7.67.18; 9.54.24; 9.100.5.)

- The lunar house of Varuna himself. (See, RV 1.44.14; 4.34.7.)

- Usas ("dawn"). (See, RV 1.44.14; 1.92.18.)

- The Ray-Cows. (See, RV 1.84.10; 6.27.7 (drinking sweet water); 9.101.8; 10.119.1 (drinking sweet water).)

- The lunar house of Indra-Agni, who dispenses *radha*, spiritual increase and great achievement, through the asterism of Vasakra in conjunction with the zodiacal house of Tula (Libra). (See, RV 1.108.1, 2, 5, 8-12; 3.12.2; 3.25.4; 6.59.10; 6.20.7, 9, 15.)
- Ribhus. (See, RV 1.110.3; 1.51.1, 5, 8; 3.60.5; 4.33.11; 4.34.1, 10; 4.35.2, 4, 5, 7, 9; 4.36.2.)
- Indra-Vayu. (See, RV 1.135.1, 4, 5; 4.46.1-3, 6; 4.47.1-3.)
- Indra-Brihaspati. (See, RV 4.44.2, 3, 5, 6; 4.50.9.)
- Indra-Varuna. (See, RV 6.68.10, 11.)
- Indra-Vishnu. (See, RV 1.155.2; 6.69.7.)
- The Adityas. (See, RV 7.51.2.)
- Brihaspati. (See, RV 7.102.1.)
- Surya. (See, RV 10.37.11; 10.85.5 (Surya's bride); 10.170.1.)
- The lunar house of Yama, who dispenses spiritual riches through the asterism of Bharani and in conjunction with the zodiac house of Mesa (Aries). (See, 10.135.1.)
- Most prominently, Soma was consumed by Indra, who was its main purveyor. (See, RV 1.4.2; 1.5.5, 6; 1.87.10; 1.9.3; 1.10.3, 5, 11; 1.14.10; 1.15.1; 1.16.1, 3, 6, 7, 8; 1.21.1, 3; 1.23.7; 1.28.1, 2; 1-4, 6, 8; 1.29.1; 1.30.11, 12; 1.51.7, 9; 1.55.2, 7; 1.56.1; 1.84.4; 1.104.7, 9; 1.130.2. 1.139.6; 1.155.2; 1.175.1, 2; 1.77.4; 2.11.11, 14, 15, 17; 2.12.13; 2, 5, 2.14.1; 2.16.2, 5, 6; 2.18.4, 5; 2.22.1; 2.35.5; 2.36.1, 2, 4, 5, 6; 3.22.1, 15; 3.1, 3, 6, 8, 9, 10; 3.36.2, 3; 3.37.8; 3.40.1; 1, 2, 6, 7; 3.41.1, 5; 3.42.2, 4, 7, 9; 3.43.7; 3.47.1-4; 3.49.1; 3.50.1, 2; 3.51.7, 8, 9; 3.52.7; 3.53.8, 10;4.20.4, 5; 4.23.1; 4.25.3, 7; 4.27.5; 4.32.14; 4.31.1, 6, 7; 4.35.1; 5.29.3; 5.32.8; 5.36.1; 5.37.4; 5.40.1; 5.51.6; 6.17.1, 2, 3; 6.23.2, 3, 4, 7; 6.24.9; 6.37.2; 6.40.1; 6.41.1, 2, 4; 6.41.2; 6.52.1, 2; 6.43.1-4; 6.44.14, 15, 16, 21; 6.47.6; 6.57.2; 7.22.1; 2.24.3; 7.32.4; 7.107.1, 2, 3; 8.1.21, 24, 26; 8.2.1, 4, 23, 26; 8.3.1, 7, 17; 8.4.3, 4, 8, 10, 11, 12, 14; 8.15.11, 14, 19, 26, 40, 45; 8.12.12, 16, 20; 8.13.21; 8.14.12; 8.17.1, 4, 5, 11, 15; 8.21.4; 8.24.13; 8.32.20, 21, 24; 8.33.4, 7, 13; 8.36.1-5 (father of cattle and steeds), 6; 8.37.1;8.45.22, 24; 8.46.26; 8.50.1; 8.54.3, 5, 8; 8.55.7, 12; 8.57.7; 8.59.10; 8.65.4, 6, 7, 9; 8.66.11; 8.81.1, 5; 8.82.20, 33; 8.84.3; 8.86.8, 11; 8.89.10 (with Vak); 9.1.1, 9; 9.4.4; 9.6.9; 9.8.9;9.15.8; 9.12.2; 9.16.3; 9.9.17.3; 9.18.3; 9.24.3;

9.30.5; 9.32.3; 9.37.2; 9.43.2; 9.45.1; 9.50.5; 9.51.1, 9; 9.52.8, 14; 9.53.16; 9.9.54.2, 12; 9.55.8,14; 9.74.9; 9.80.2; 9.85.2; 9.87.1; 9.94.3; 9.96.3,13; 9.97.32; 9.99.3; 9.100.5; 9.104.5; 9.108.2, 14, 15; 9.109.2; 9.113.1;10.22.15; 10.24.1; 10.25.10; 10.28.1, 3; 10.29.6; 10.30.9 (drinking the waters); 10.43.2; 10.76.8; 10.84.2, 19; 10.96.1, 6, 9, 12; 10.100.1; 10.101.7, 8; 10.104.1, 2, 6; 10.112.1, 2, 6; 10.116.1, 2, 7; 10.144.2; 10.160.)

We have not started discussing the zodiacal houses yet, but every member of the Lunar houses presiding over those houses consume Soma.

Through the consumption of Soma the powers of Divine Union are invested in the principles which inhere in the various Vedic divinities. That Soma was to be consumed only by the Vedic divinities and not mortals is not exactly for accurate. Allowances were made that Soma could be consumed by the worshipers. Soma was consumed by

- Manu, the First Man. (RV 10.82.7.)
- The ptrs (RV 10.15.10), the decedents or forebearers of the worshiper.
- Soma was described as a never ending well for men to drink. (RV 9.110.5.)
- Worshipers beseeched Soma that it would confer benefits, both inner and material.

In its own way, the consumption of Soma produces its own alchemy based on synthesis and transformation—both to the Vedic dharma and to the worshiper.

In his Capacity of Ruling the Ardra Asterism, the Lunar house of Rudra Dispenses, and the Worshiper Learns, the Spiritual Endowment of *Sam* (Conjunction, Union)

Rudra is more commonly known today as the harbinger of death, closely aligned with Siva. Indeed, Rudra is more commonly recognized as a pivotal deity in Shaivite traditions or as belonging to its own Tantric cult, not as a Vedic force or energy. While the lunar house of Rudra's power is filled with awe, it does not have the diabolical connotations of later traditions.

The lunar house of Rudra is not the only asterism which dispenses conjunction or union. One prominent lunar house, for example, is that of Agni, which dispenses the inner secrets of yajna, the Sacrifice. The powers of dispensation originate through the Nakshatra of Krittika, but these powers are conjoined and unified with the kindle spark. (RV 1.36.4, 7.) When kindled, the Vedic force of Agni, through the power conferred in his lunar house, conjoins divine and human consciousness. (RV 1.44.7.) This aspect of conjunction illustrates the effect on the worshiper. The act of conjunction and union melds two distinct properties to form a unitary whole. The Vedic force of Agni, through his lunar house Krittika, dispenses in the worshiper spiritual riches, divine mind and intelligence to the worshiper. (RV 1.31.18.) These three disparate qualities thereby coalesce into one in the worshiper. A prominent feature in Agni is the powers of conjunction of Heaven and Earth. By virtue of these powers of unification, a supreme force is created. (RV 1.103.1.)

Another prominent example is the lunar house of Indra. The Vedic force of Indra owes his very being in uniting with the strengths acquired through the lunar house of Soma, by drinking the Soma juice. (RV 1.30.3, 4; 1.38.6; 1.53.4; 1.82.6; 2.14.12; 2.15.4, 6; 2.16.4, 5; 2.18.4, 5; 2.22.1; 2.36.1, 4, 6; 2.37.1 – 6; 2.41.3, 4, 21; 3.32.1, 2, 3, 5, 15; 3.35.1, 6, 8, 9, 10; 3.36.2, 3; 3.37.8; 3.39.7; 3.40.1, 2, 6; 3.41.1, 5; 3.42.3, 4, 7, 8, 9; 3.43.1, 3, 7; 3.46.5; 3.47.1 – 4; 3.48.1, 2; 3.49.1; 3.50.1 – 3; 3.51.7 – 10; 3.52.7, 8; 3.53.6, 8, 10; 3.57.5; 4.20.4; 4.23.1; 4.27.5; 4.32.14; 4.33.11; 4.34.7; 4.35.7; 5.29.3, 5; 5.32.8; 5.36.1; 5.37.4; 5.40.1, 4; 5.43.3;5.44.11; 6.17.14; 6.23.3, 6, 7; 6.24.1, 9; 6.37.1; 6.28.7; 6.37.2; 6.38.1; 6.40.1, 2, 4; 6.41.2, 3; 6.42.1, 2; 6.43.1 – 4; 6.44.7, 8, 14 – 16; 21; 6.45.10; 6.47.6; 7.22.1; 7.24.3; 7.29.1;

7.31.1; 7.32.4, 8; 7.33.2; 7.97.1; 7.98.2; 8.1.21; 8.2.1, 4, 7, 23, 26, 37; 8.3.1, 7, 11; 8.4.3, 8, 10 – 12; 8.6.36, 40, 44; 8.12.12, 20; 8.13.1, 21, 27; 8.14.12, 15; 8.17.1, 3, 4, 11, 15; 8.21.1, 3, 4, 14; 8.22.6; 8.26.15; 8.32.7, 16, 20, 21, 24; 8.33.7, 13, 15; 8.34.5 10; 8.36.2 – 6; 8.37.1, 6.)

Thus, it appears paradoxical that the lunar house of Rudra should dispense *sam*, conjunction or union. Dichotomy is the nature of the lunar house of Rudra. On the one hand, it dwells within the sphere of Agni. (BD, 1.67; 7.142). The lunar house of Rudra is a manifestation in the Mid-World, the Firmament, of the Fire of Agni. (BD, 1.103.) On the other hand, it belongs to the divine sphere controlled by the lunar house of Indra. (BD, 1.122.) On the one hand, the lunar house of Rudra is the Healer and forgives the worshiper's sins; on the other hand, it is a fierce wild animal. This dichotomy would serve as the inspiration to the essential natures of not only to Shiva, but to Kali, Shiva's consort, as well. Yet, Rudra is an integral part of the original Vedic dharma and is more closely associated with the Lunar house of Agni (SSS, 4.29.1.)

Agni himself is a drinker of Soma. (RV 3.12.2; 4.14.4; 5.51. 1, 5; 6.16.44.) For that matter, so is Rudra. (RV 2.36.2.) This therefore is the key to resolving the paradox of Rudra's powers. Conjunction and unification owes not so much with the lunar house of Rudra, but Rudra owes its powers of dispensation when working in unison with the lunar house of Soma. This is perhaps the most extreme example of mutual dependence among Vedic powers, yet the powers of the lunar house of Mrgashirsha which empowers Soma empowers Rudra as well.

The spiritual endowment dispensed by Rudra is a particularized aspect of Bliss, *sam*. In this context *sam* is the unifying aspect in Bliss. While the spiritual power of Mrgashirsha rested in the physical embodiment of Soma as the Moon, the unifying power of Ardra comes from the spiritual efficacy of the Soma plant. These are not separate powers but act in unison.

The spiritual power of Ardra is demonstrated most prominently in the epic battle with Vrtra. Vrtra is more known as the enveloper, that which conceals the truth and the inner essence of the Vedic dharma. In this respect, Vrtra has been compared to the indeterminate mass at the very beginning of the material world, prior to the evolution of the cycles of existence, which did not consist in sat (existence) and did not consist of asat (non-existence). According to the eminent Vedic scholar, R.L. Kashyap,

RV 6.24.5 relates that the world was thereupon divided into two parts: one part, *adya/* ("What is") and the other *anya/d* ("What is not"), and when Indra felled Vrtra with Vayra, he transformed "What is not" to "What is," thereby beginning the evolution of cycles of universes in the Vedic dharma. Lifting the veil of concealment can be applied in many contexts, and these contexts have been used, certainly, in the Rg Veda.

One of the most enduring icons of the Vedic dharma is Indra's battle with Vrtra. Astronomically, the Vedic astrologer considers the subduing of Vrtra as the emergence of the New Moon explained earlier in the Satapatha Brahmana, 1.6.4.12 to 13. This astronomical application is found in other rcs and in other contexts. For example, Vrtra concealed, and Indra released, the "shining cows," the "herds of the sky," *go* or *gobhir.* (RV 3.31.10, 11; 4.3.11; 4.19.7; 6.17.7; 6.38.3, 5; 6.60.2; 9.87.3; 9.89.3.) Recall, in the struggle with Vrtra, Indra is acting as an incarnation of the fire of Agni and are thus functionally identical. In RV 1.36.8, the creation of the energies inhered in starlight, the "herds of starlight." In a religious context, Vrtra has been associated with Evil. When Vrtra is felled by Indra's weapon, Vrtra's evil is driven away by the New Moon. (SPB 6.2.2.18.)

To set the record straight, Agni is the initial killer of Vrtra. (RV 3.14.7; 10.80.2.) As Rudra is a manifestation of Agni, Indra is the incarnation of Agni Vasivanara when battling the "enemies." (RV 1.59.6.) Indra acts as the incarnation of Agni as he commits those actions. (Mikhailov, (2001) *RgVedic Studies*, p. 14.) Specifically, Indra acts in that aspect of Agni in the form of the Sacrificial Fire when Vrtra is slain (RV 2.12.4) in every instance in which Indra comes in contact with Vrtra and its aftermath.

We will be learning about Conjunction in a later installment in this series. For now, the Vedic astrologer views union and conjunction as the outcome of the battle between Indra and Vrtra. This battle is seen very generally as a conflict between good and evil. But instead of this battle being simply one in which one side or another wins, it is viewed by the Vedic astrologer as a dialectical process. Therefore, instead of either good or evil prevailing in the battle, the end result is a third element which is a synthesis of the two battle sides. This third element, this result of the battle between good and evil, is neither wholly good and neither wholly evil but a combination of the two. Therefore, the killing of Vrtra the beginning of the cycles of evolution and devolution of the universes resulted from synthesis of two different, disparate elements of *adya* ("What is") and *anya/d* ("What is not"), so Vrtra's the powers of concealment has been applied in other contexts. The slaying of Vrtra and the subduing of the other demons does not merely release the waters or begin the process of evolution. It also produces the Sun above and places it in the sky.

What is going on here is an elaborate dialectic. The elements of Thesis and Antithesis are present with the disparate elements of *adya* ("What is") and *anya/d* ("What is not"). The Synthesis, the union, from these elements are produced on the death of Vrtra. Essentially, the death of Vrtra results in the birth of the universe and the entire cosmos. Vrtra's death also produced the dawn (awareness), the awakening of consciousness and awareness, together with the birth of the sun. There are other consequences from the killing of Vrtra:

- Vrtra's death fixes the dawn and the rays of the sun under heaven dispelling the darkness. (RV 1.62.5.) "Dawn" is understood in both the macrocosmic and microcosmic meaning. In the macrocosm, Dawn is the beginning of a new day; in the microcosm it is the beginning of mental awareness. The su rays refer to the powers of Krittika.
- Vrtra's death gives birth to the dawn and the sun. (RV 2.12.7; 4.17.5; 1.32.4.)
- Vrtra's death generates the sun, the sky and the dawn. (RV 1.30.5.)

The Vedas describe the death of Vrtra is other ways:

- Having slain Vrtra, Indra places the Sun on high and for all to see. (RV 1.7.3; 1.51.4.)
- The death of Vrtra gives birth to the sun and facilitates the discovery of the ray-cows. (RV 2.19.3; 6.17.3.)
- With the birth of the Sun, the ray-cows, the *go* or *gobhir*—the "herds of the sky" are released, gaining the sun and the dawn. (RV 1.62.5.)

By placing the Sun on high, Indra also releases the waters. (RV 1.52.8.) (having slain Vrtra Indra placed the sun on high for all to see and released the waters for all).) "The Waters" are understood as the truth and inner essence of the Vedic dharma.

- By slaying Vrtra, Indra won the light and released the celestial waters. (RV 3.34.8.)
- Indra slew Vrtra who lay against the celestial waters. (RV 4.17.7.)
- Indra killed Susna and released the celestial waters. (RV 8.40.10, 11.)

The real beneficiary from this process is the physical universe. Because from this union the stellar system is created. The Nakshatras and the lunar houses benefit. The Lunar houses dispense their spiritual endowments in part from the action of conjunction with the powers of the zodiacal houses. That power of conjunction is supplied by Rudra through the asterism of Ardra. The worshiper benefits, however, from the wisdom imparted from this stellar system. From this particular area the worshiper learns union, so important for the spiritual journey. It is a power conferred not only through the plant and astrological object of Soma, but through Rudra, who is a supplicant of Agni and who conveys this power from Ardra. We will later return with more about this cosmic struggle with Vrtra and how it is resolved.

In his Capacity of Ruling the Punavasu Asterism, the Lunar house Of Aditi Dispenses, and the Worshiper Learns, the Spiritual Endowment Of *Sunrta* ("True Speech," Understanding of the Inner Essence of the Vedic Dharma (*Rta*).)

We will learn more about Aditi in a later installment concerning the zodiac. In the Nakshatra Punavasu Aditi occupies an important function. Aditi dispenses the spiritual endowment of *sunrta*, which is the understanding and speaking of the truth underlying the inner essence of the Vedic dharma. Aditi dispenses this truth through the power of the Punavasu Asterism. What that inner essence and truth actual consists of would fill volumes and much of it alludes the modern worshiper, the kernel of that truth lost to the eons. Accordingly that truth and inner essence must be personal applied to the worshiper, according to the worshiper's personal situation and requirements, but subject to a conceptional framework which is familiar to students of the Veda.

Aditi herself is the representation of the highest infinitude. According to the Veda, Aditi consists of the following (RV 1.89.10.):

- Heaven and Earth;
- Father and Son;
- The collective energies of the dynamic Vedic energies;
- All that was, all that is, and all that will be; and
- The expanse of the Five-Dimensioned Universe.

The light of the "herds of the sky, the *go* and *gobhir*, represent Aditi, the infinite consciousness of the Vedic dharma. (RV 4.58.4; 4.1.6.) As such, Aditi represents the collective wisdom of the lunar houses, the Nakshatras. From the standpoint of the worshiper or any other sentient being, that wisdom must be articulated in Speech.

Without Speech no form could exist. (SB, 2.5.) Without speech, material forms could not be known and the worshiper would be bereft of intelligence (SA, 5.7.) Speech and the Word distinguishes all human sentient beings from the animal world and indeed sets these human sentient beings from other forms of creatures. The worshiper by necessity travels in the spiritual journey with the use of speech. This spiritual journey through the existential levels of the Vedic dharma as reflected in the worshiper's level of speech are summarized in the following chart:

Level of Speech	Dimensional Existential Level	Type of Speech
Vaikhari	Two-Dimensional Universe	Spoken, Articulated Speech (Gross Speech)
Madhyama	Three-Dimensional Universe	A Combination of Subtle and Gross Speech
Pasyanti	Five-Dimensional Universe	The all-perceiving State of Brahman
Para	Seven-Dimensional Universe	The purely subtle region of the logos, The Word, total, subtle Speech

The mechanics of this four-step process, while rarified to its most elemental components, have a practical application to the worshiper and all other sentient beings in the acquisition of speech and language:

- The stage of *Vaikhari* in the material world in the Two-Dimensional Universe is the world of verbal speech between sentient beings. The acquisition of speech in the beginning is purely in the gross level. This gross materiality may appear in a couple of ways. More commonly, this is reflected in conversation, or you learn a new word, either through print media or by verbal instruction. Thus, on this level the worshiper hears or reads or speaks the words, "cat" or "dog." Transposed to a level of personal austerity and discipline, this is where the worshiper learns of a mantra.

- *Madhyama* is where all the action is located. It is described as a combination of gross and subtle elements. The gross element comes in with the verbal communication or visual reflection of the word. In the subtle element the sentient being attaches the mental idea of the word seen or conversation heard. On this level the worshiper establishes the mental activity involved in conceiving of "cat" and "dog." In personal austerities this is where the worshiper mentally and silently utters the mantra used in their disciplines.

• In *Pasyanti* there is also a combination of material and subtle elements, but that combination is placed in a different framework. In Madhyama, the subtle element is in the sentient being. In Pasyanti, the subtle element is in Brahman or the Absolute Self, the Atman. In this level, the subtle meaning of speech and language is reposed in the Atman and that meaning is superimposed to the sentient beings in the material world. It is here that the Atman superimposes the idea of "cat" and "dog." Significantly, on the level of personal discipline, it is here that the mantra has been repeated to the extent that mental activity is not necessary to give the mantra its full edifying effect. The meaning and power of the mantra has been so infused in the being of the worshiper that no mental effort is needed to give it effect on the life and practice of the worshiper.

• *Para* is a higher level of Pasyanti. Here, the meanings of the words in speech and language are reposed in a completely subtle region. It is not conveyed to sentient beings, but the meanings are there for sentient beings to discover in meditation or reflection, but not totally. These words are all words, actual and possible, and encompass all sentient beings, things, and objects, and the interrelations thereof. Heraclitus and the Stoics called this region logos, Λογος, but the worshiper calls this region *Rta*, and this is the meaning of the phrase used so many times in this and other books in this series — the inner essence or truth of the Vedic dharma.

These levels of speech correspond to existential levels in the greater Vedic dharma, *Rta*, the natural order. Those four existential levels are Earth, the Mid-World, the Svar, and Heaven. Just as the quality of Speech becomes more rarefied the higher the worshiper travels the different Dimensions in the Vedic dharma, so higher the worshiper travels up the existential levels in the Vedic dharma, the more subtle the worshiper's speech becomes. At the terminus point, Heaven or the Seven-Dimensional World, Speech here is at a very fine, subtle level. At that level, the worshiper arrives at a place where what the Vedic astrologer calls "the Word" resides. According to Heraclitus, the Word the Logos, is the link between rational discourse (the Word, Speech) and the world's rational structure. (*Wikipedia, https:// en.wikipedia. org/wiki /Logos#Heraclitus.*) This same usage is applied famously in the Gospel of John, where it was revealed that "In the beginning was the Word, and the Word was with God, and the Word was God." While traditionally the phrase "the Word," a translation of "Logos," is widely interpreted as referring to Jesus, in a wider sense it is closer to the meaning of Heraclitus, the Word as it relates to the world's rational structure. *Rta* is the concept subsuming the Word (the logos) and the other subtle categories, which works as the subtle foundation operating the Vedic dharma, the Word.

As the spiritual endowment implies, however, the Word is no ordinary word. Aditi dispenses the Words contributing to and containing the understanding of the Vedic dharma, *sunrta*. The Veda speaks of *sunrta*. As with all subtle energies found in Vedic dharma, all Lunar houses participate in its creation, formation and articulation. For example:

- The lunar house of Vayu, with the power of the asterism Svasti (Srati) and the zodiacal house of Tula (Libra), inspires the articulation of *sunrta*. (RV 1.113.18.)

The Vedic energy of Dawn, the beginning of mental and spiritual Awareness, figures prominently in the articulation of *sunrta*.

- Dawn (*Usas*), the beginning of mental and spiritual Awareness, informs *sunrta* with *go* and *gobhir*, the light of "herds in the sky," the wisdom of the Stars, and strength (horses.)(RV 1.92.7.)
- Dawn (*Usas*), the beginning of mental and spiritual Awareness, inspires the development of sunrta in the worshiper and all sentient beings. (RV 1.113.4.)
- Dawn (*Usas*), the beginning of mental and spiritual Awareness, is also marks the beginning of *sunrta*. (RV 7.76.7.)

While Dawn (*Usas*) may mark the beginning of the articulation of *sunrta*, another Lunar house, Indra, with the power of the asterism of

Jyestra and the additional power of the zodiacal house of Vrscika (Scorpio), allowed for the emergence of *sunrta*:

- We will later see that the elements of *sunrta*, the specific elements of the articulation of the Vedic dharma and hence the means to speak of and understand the Vedic dharma, were created when Indra overcame and killed Vrtra. (RV 3.31.8.)
- For this reason it is said that Indra is possessed of *sunrta* as a component of his *svadha*, his internal, essential nature. (RV 8.32.15.)

The Vedic force conveying the Word to the worshiper through the asterism Punavasu is Aditi. Once articulated, in addition to contributing to the worshiper's spiritual journey, that speech expresses the beauty of the Vedic dharma, as explained in the next lunar house.

In his Capacity of Ruling the Pushya Asterism, the Lunar house of Brhaspati Dispenses, and the Worshiper Learns, the Spiritual Endowment of Beauty

We saw earlier that the Lunar house of Brhaspati assisted the Lunar house of Indra to sacrifice Prajapati, and as a result Brhaspati was reborn as the Word. (MS 2.4.6; 43.12.) We also saw that through the power of the asterism of Punavasu the Word is dispensed to the worshiper by the Lunar house of Aditi. We also learned that the Vedic astrologer attaches great symbolic significance to the "herds of the sky," the *go* and *gobhir*, the Cows, if you will.

The synergy of these great cosmic forces produce Beauty. Cows are symbolic of the Word, prayer characterized by beauty, truth and devotion. (RV 8.14.3.) Elsewhere in the Vedas Vanaspati is defined as the "Lord of Beauty." (RV 10.172.1.) Vanaspati is not simply "plants" or "wood" as found in some translations, but a much more deeper and complex Vedic force. Vanaspati is a bundle of concepts and Vedic forces which concern the very essence of the material world and its link with the divine, psychic, and subtle, and affirms that there is a link and essential sameness between these two worlds. That psychic link delves deep into the essential truth and inner essence of the Vedic dharma, *Rta*, the Word.

The roots of Beauty run deep.

- All living beings and creatures were created by Prajapati as a result of his intense meditation and religious austerity. (SPB 11.4.3.1.)
- From that initial creation, Sri, Fortune and Beauty arose, and stood resplendent, shining and undulating before the Vedic forces in the dharma. (SPB 11.4.3.1.)
- Saman, the pulse of the Vedic dharma, was established as sri, fortune and beauty. (Kaus. Up., 2.6.)
- Far earlier, in the very beginnings of the Vedic dharma, when the cosmos was enveloped with indiscriminate and undeterminable matter, Viraj, the recurring cycles of indiscriminate darkness, was *sri*, fortune and Beauty. (SPB 11.4.3.18.)

What Brhaspati offers the worshiper, through the asterism of Pushya, runs to the very pith and marrow of the Vedic dharma: Knowledge (Cows) of the internal mechanism and workings of the Vedic dharma, resplendent, shining and undulating Beauty.

In his Capacity Of Ruling the Ashlasha Asterism, the Lunar house of Naga Dispenses, and the Worshiper Learns, the Spiritual Endowment of *Bhanu* (Shining Beauty Of Light).

The Nagas are "a member of a class of mythical semidivine beings, half human and half cobra. They are a strong, handsome species who can assume either wholly human or wholly serpentine form and are potentially dangerous but often beneficial to humans. ... The creator deity Brahma relegated the Nagas to the nether regions when they became too populous on earth and commanded them to bite only the truly evil or those destined to die prematurely. They are also associated with waters — rivers, lakes, seas, and wells — and are guardians of treasure." *(https://www.Britannica.com/topic/naga-Hindu-mythology.)*

The operative words in the description of the Nagas are that they are "associated with waters — rivers, lakes, seas, and wells — and are guardians of treasure." The Vedic astrologer believes that both of these clauses — associated with the Waters and the guardians of the treasure — refer to the same object. The treasure in this instance are the Waters, the inner essence of the Vedic dharma, and this is the treasure bestowed upon the worshiper.

Specifically, in this instance the Naga is the guardian of *Bhanu*, a specific aspect of Light. The Vedas consist of a spiritual tradition based on Light. Monier Williams, the authoritative dictionary of Sanskrit, lists upwards to five hundred different words for "light," each containing its own specific meaning and context. *Bhanu* is only one such word. It is, of course, the light originating from the asterism Ashlasha. The Light of Ashlasha, however, carries with it so many other meanings. It can mean:

- Sunlight.
- Rays of light from the sky.
- The quality of this light, including the effulgence, resplendence, brilliance, brightness, or brightness of this light.
- The Beauty of this aspect of light.

Significantly, *Bhanu* continues the work of the previous asterism, Pushya. In Pushya, Beauty incarnate was the spiritual endowment given to the worshiper. Here, in Ashlasha, the spiritual endowment given is *Bhanu*, Beauty, with the properties of Light, whose Beauty is an essential property of its light. Beauty and *bhanu* are intricately and intimately connected.

Naga, perhaps because it is semi-human, must rely on the assistance of other Vedic forces and lunar houses to dispense the spiritual wealth to the worshiper. For whatever reason, other Vedic forces predominate the conveying of spiritual benefits to the worshiper. Those forces are:

- The lunar house of Agni as the presiding deity of and conveying the spiritual endowments from the asterism of Krittika, in conjunction with the zodiacal houses of Mesa (Aries) and Vrsabha (Taurus).
- The Vedic energies of the Maruts as a manifestation of the Fire of Agni in the Firmament. (BD, 1.103.)
- The Vedic force of Usas as a terrestrial manifestation of the Fire of Agni. (BD, 1.108.)
- The lunar house of the Asvins as the presiding deity of and conveying the spiritual endowments of the asterism Ashvini, in conjunction with the zodiacal house of Mesa (Aries).
- Naga itself acts in conveying the spiritual endowments of the asterism Ashlasha, in conjunction with the zodiacal house of Karkata (Cancer).

These are some formidable Vedic forces at work. These Vedic forces act in concert with Naga to convey the spiritual endowments of *Bhanu*. Agni as the presiding deity of and conveying the spiritual endowments from the asterism of Krittika, in conjunction with the zodiacal houses of Mesa (Aries) and Vrsabha (Taurus) represents the core spiritual qualities of the endowment itself:

- The Lunar house of Agni, the Sun, emits the shining brilliance of *Bhanu* with celestial splendor when dispensing his spiritual endowment of the inner secret of *yajna* and divine response through the asterism of Krittika and the zodiacal houses of Mesa (Aries) and Vrsabha (Taurus). (RV 10.6.2.)
- There are four elements to the shining beauty of Agni's *Bhanu*—kavi, the Fire of Revelation; kratu, the Fire of Divine Will; Food,

the symbol of Consciousness; and *Bhanu*, the beauty of shining light. (RV 7.6.2.)

- *Bhanu* is the light of the Lunar house of Agni, the Sun, when dispensing his spiritual endowment of the inner secret of *yajna* and divine response through the asterism of Krittika and the zodiacal houses of Mesa (Aries) and Vrsabha (Taurus). (RV 1.92.5; 3.21.4.)
- The fuel powering the Lunar house of Agni, the Sun, is *Bhanu*. (RV 10.6.1.)
- The lunar house of Agni, the Sun, dispenses his spiritual endowment of the inner secret of *yajna* and divine response through the asterism of Krittika and the zodiacal houses of Mesa (Aries) and Vrsabha (Taurus), is the deification of the Beauty of *Bhanu* and shines like gold. (RV 7.3.6.)
- The lunar house of Agni's Beauty gleans with refulgence when he is dispensing his spiritual endowment of the inner secret of *yajna* and divine response through the asterism of Krittika and the zodiacal houses of Mesa (Aries) and Vrsabha (Taurus). (RV 7.9.4.)
- With this the Lunar house of Agni, the Sun, is armed with the *Bhanu* (sunlight) of the Great Impeller of the Vedic dharma when he is dispensing his spiritual endowment of the inner secret of *yajna* and divine response through the asterism of Krittika and the zodiacal houses of Mesa (Aries) and Vrsabha (Taurus). (RV 6.6.6.)

Bhanu has an ancient history:

- The Lunar house of Agni, the Sun, the dispenser of the inner secret of *yajna* and divine response through the asterism of Krittika and the zodiacal houses of Mesa (Aries) and Vrsabha (Taurus), was the first born of the Vedic forces, and was effulgent, the epitome of Beauty in its brilliance emanating from the beauty of *Bhanu*. (RV 8.7.36.)
- When the other Lunar houses created Agni, the Sun, the dispenser of the inner secret of *yajna* and divine response through the asterism of Krittika and the zodiacal houses of Mesa (Aries) and Vrsabha (Taurus), they made him resplendent in *Bhanu* (light). (RV 3.2.3.)

- Then, at this early stage of the Vedic dharma, the Lunar house of Agni, the Sun, the dispenser of the inner secret of *yajna* and divine response through the asterism of Krittika and the zodiacal houses of Mesa (Aries) and Vrsabha (Taurus), gathered all traces of *Bhanu* and spread its effulgence to all corners of the dharma. (RV 6.16.2.)
- With this refulgent beauty of *Bhanu*, Agni, the Sun, the dispenser of the inner secret of *yajna* and divine response through the asterism of Krittika and the zodiacal houses of Mesa (Aries) and Vrsabha (Taurus), overcame the Blackness which had permeated the indiscriminate, undifferentiated mass of inert matter which had enveloped the cosmos and with his Beauty and radiance bathed the Vedic dharma with light. (RV 10.3.2.)
- The radiance of Agni's *Bhanu* radiated in undulations, like sound waves, and in this manner stretched to the highest reaches of heaven while dispensing his spiritual endowment of the inner secret of *yajna* and divine response through the asterism of Krittika and the zodiacal houses of Mesa (Aries) and Vrsabha (Taurus). (RV 10.3.5.) This is a clear reference to the waves of Saman discussed in the Introduction. Agni's beauty of *Bhanu* was also comparable to the weaving which takes place in the subtle foundation of the Vedic dharma when he is dispensing his spiritual endowment of the inner secret of *yajna* and divine response through the asterism of Krittika and the zodiacal houses of Mesa (Aries) and Vrsabha (Taurus). As with the *disha* discussed in the introduction, Agni's shining beauty of *Bhanu* wove like threads throughout the underbelly of the Vedic dharma. (RV 10.53.6.)

Bhanu is rightfully compared to sunlight. As sunlight, it is the only reason sentient exist on earth. Without *Bhanu* (sunlight) the material world would be a very different place. Sunlight is the basis of all life on earth, it is the basis for the Vedic astrologer's existence and the reason for the worshiper's spiritual journey. *Bhanu*, sunlight, allows the stage for the worshiper's spiritual journey:

- The Lunar house of Agni, the Sun, the dispenser of the inner secret of *yajna* and divine response through the asterism of Krittika and the zodiacal houses of Mesa (Aries) and Vrsabha (Taurus), shines in the beauty of *Bhanu* comparable to the sunlight of Savitr, and the power of this light lifts Agni high above to the heavens. (RV 4.13.2.)
- The Lunar house of Agni, the Sun, the dispenser of the inner secret of *yajna* and divine response through the asterism of Krittika and the zodiacal houses of Mesa (Aries) and Vrsabha (Taurus), shines with the power of *Bhanu*, and, like the Sun, emits a fiery flame. RV 2.8.4.)

Bhanu is a significant ingredient of the worshiper's life and supports the world in which the worshiper lives and conducts the spiritual journey:

- The Lunar house of Agni, the Sun, the dispenser of the inner secret of *yajna* and divine response through the asterism of Krittika and the zodiacal houses of Mesa (Aries) and Vrsabha (Taurus), fills the heart of the worshiper with the white beauty of *Bhanu*. (RV 10.1.1.)
- The Lunar house of Agni, the Sun, the dispenser of the inner secret of *yajna* and divine response through the asterism of Krittika and the zodiacal houses of Mesa (Aries) and Vrsabha (Taurus), expiates the sins of the worshiper through the beauty of *Bhanu*. (RV 1.92.1, 2.)
- The Lunar house of Agni, the Sun, the dispenser of the inner secret of *yajna* and divine response through the asterism of Krittika and the zodiacal houses of Mesa (Aries) and Vrsabha (Taurus), shines with the purifying beauty of *Bhanu*. (RV 6.15.5.)
- The Lunar house of Agni, the Sun, the dispenser of the inner secret of *yajna* and divine response through the asterism of Krittika and the zodiacal houses of Mesa (Aries) and Vrsabha (Taurus), is the highest hotr (officiating priest) at the sacrifice and is resplendent in *Bhanu*.

The worshiper is not the only beneficiary of the beauty of *Bhanu*. The existential levels of earth, mid-earth and heaven in the Vedic dharma receives the blessings.

- The Lunar house of Agni, the Sun, the dispenser of the inner secret of *yajna* and divine response through the asterism of Krittika and the zodiacal house of Mithuna (Gemini), spreads his light of his *Bhanu* over the three existential levels of earth, mid-earth and heaven. (RV 10.88.3.)

- *Bhanu* indeed is the force of light with which Agni, the Sun, the dispenser of the inner secret of *yajna* and divine response through the asterism of Krittika and the zodiacal houses of Mesa (Aries) and Vrsabha (Taurus), binds Heaven and Earth. (RV 3.22.2.)

- *Bhanu* is radiance itself and Agni, the Sun, the dispenser of the inner secret of *yajna* and divine response through the asterism of Krittika and the zodiacal houses of Mesa (Aries) and Vrsabha (Taurus), invests this light on Heaven and Earth. (RV 4.17.)

In alignment with Agni as the presiding deity of and conveying the spiritual endowments from the asterism of Krittika, in conjunction with the zodiacal houses of Mesa (Aries) and Vrsabha (Taurus), is the power of Usas, a terrestrial manifestation of Agni. These two Lunar houses act together in conveying the spiritual endowments of *Bhanu* to the worshiper.

- The light of the daybreak dawn of Usas kindles Agni, and from there Agni emits its beauty of *Bhanu*. (RV 2.2.8.) This "kindling" of Agni is a term of art. Physical fire is "ignited," but Agni as the Sacrificial Fire is "kindled." There is a plethora of occult and esoteric energies and qualities permeating the cosmos. Kindling imparts all those qualities and energies from the universe and channeled those qualities and energies into the Fire. The Sacrificial Fire plays a central role in the Sacrificial ritual. It is the center of attraction. Once kindled it is beheld by the worshiper, or, as in the Soma Sacrifice, the principal means of producing the Soma juice to be consumed by the worshiper. In all sacrificial settings, the central fire is the means by which the worshiper is transformed spiritually. The Sun is the source of all life. It is the agent which destroys the old life of the worshiper, and like the phoenix rising from the ashes, a new worshiper emerges. Breath in this above passage is prana, the subtle essence of the life force permeating the universe and sustaining the life of the worshiper. In other words, in part, the fire of Agni is powered by and empowers the elements of the Vedic dharma, the natural order (*Rta*).

- The Vedic force of Usas thereby shines the beauty of *Bhanu* to the worshiper at the Sacrifice. (RV 1.48.9.)
- The daybreak dawn of Usas conveys the light (*Bhanu*) of awareness to the worshiper. (RV 6.65.1; 7.7.5; 7.79.1.) "Dawn" should be read with both and literal and figurative meaning. It is both the beginning of each new day and the beginning stage of self-realization, liberation, and salvation, which is the goal of the worshiper's spiritual journey.
- With the effulgence of *Bhanu*, the worshiper opens the doors of heaven. (RV 1.48.15.)

The Lunar house of Agni, the Sun, the dispenser of the inner secret of *yajna* and divine response through the asterism of Krittika and the zodiacal houses of Mesa (Aries) and Vrsabha (Taurus), is asserted in other ways. The Maruts are a manifestation of the Fire of Agni in the Firmament The Vedic forces of the Maruts are utilized to spread the beauty of *Bhanu* to the worshiper. The beauty of *Bhanu* is compared to the brilliance of the Maruts. (RV 5.52.6.) The Maruts are radiant and powerful. (RV 1.19.5.)

The Lunar house of the Asvins also plays a part. The Asvins as the presiding deity of and conveying the spiritual endowments of the asterism Ashvini, in conjunction with the zodiacal house of Mesa (Aries), conveys the benefits of *Bhanu* to the worshiper.

- *Bhanu* is the light of Asvins. (RV 4.45.1.) Through these Vedic forces the beauty of *Bhanu* illumine the divine duality which exists in the Vedic dharma.
- The horses convey the Asvins like the beauty of *Bhanu*. (RV 7.72.4.) The symbol of the Horses contain a diverse collection of meanings. Here, the senses possessed by the worshiper perceive and implement the beauty of *Bhanu*.

The beauty of *Bhanu* is important to open the eyes of the worshiper. Once opened the worshiper's eyes are trained to the spiritual journey. That journey is ruled by "rules of the road." These rules are the subject of the next spiritual teaching of the asterisms.

In their Capacity of Ruling the Magha Asterism, the Pitrs, the Forefathers, Dispense, and the Worshiper Learns, the Spiritual Endowment of *ayana* (Guide to Right Conduct During the Spiritual Journey)

Ayana lies at the very heart of the worshiper's spiritual journey. Monier Williams defines "ayana" as "walking, a road, a path." The Vedic forces which predominate the conveying of spiritual benefits of *ayana* to the worshiper are the ptrs, the forefathers, presiding over and conveying the spiritual endowments from the asterism of Magha, in conjunction with the zodiacal house of Simha (Leo). Ayana therefore is the worshiper's spiritual journey.

There is an entire body of doctrine in the Rg Veda pertaining to "The Path." While relevant to our discussion here about the Nakshatras, The Path plays a much greater role in the planetary movements. This will be discussed at length in a later installment in this series. The spiritual endowment of *ayana*, at least as it pertains to the Prtrs, and as it applies to the powers bestowed upon the Ptrs by the lunar mansion of Magha, has more to do with the Northern and Southern Paths.

The Northern and Southern Paths play a crucial role in the Vedic path to salvation and liberation. The Northern and Southern Paths are intricately tied to the most important aspects of the worshiper's spiritual journey. In fact, it concerns the greatest of all issues — the destination of soul after death whether concerning the Vedic astrologer, the worshiper, or any other person's life — and whether their souls will be reborn or liberated. There are only two places the soul may travel upon — the Northern Path or the Southern Path.

The Northern Path has these properties:

- It is the *devayana*.
- It is the Path of the Gods.
- The destination is the liberation of the worshiper's soul such that the soul does not transmigrate to the material world after death.

The Southern Path has these properties:

• It is the ptryana,
• It is the path of the forefathers.
• After death the worshiper's soul transmigrates to the material world.

While relatively simple in its delineation, the Northern and Southern Paths implicate many aspects to which the Vedic astrologer understands. The Northern and Southern Paths are described in astronomical and astrological terms. The Sun is the vantage point in the soul's progression. The Sun travels south for six months from the Vernal Equinox to the Autumnal Equinox, consisting of the three seasons of spring, summer and the rains (Tilak, *The Orion*, p. 23), reaching the Winter Solstice, and then travels north. (TS 4.5.3; SPB .3.1-3.) In addition, the Vedic zodiac consists of two hemispheres. There is the Southern Hemisphere from where the Lunar house of Indra, as an incarnation of Agni, released the waters to feed into the Northern Hemisphere following the death of Vrtra. (RV 6.32.5.) The Northern Hemisphere consists of the Vernal progression from Spring to Autumn. In its most essential meaning, in a phrase which frequently appears in the Vedas, day to day, signifies that progression between the two equinoxes, the Vernal to Autumn Equinox. This progression is located at the Northern portion of the Vedic zodiac. This is a cryptic reference to the Northern Path, the Path of Gods leading to liberation, and is consistent with the worshiper's travel to heaven, since the terminus on that path is Orion, the gateway to heaven. In truth the expression "Day to day" signifies all these meanings—the progression of one day after another, the Vernal and Autumnal Equinoxes and the progression between these astronomical events. These events are aptly summarized by its interpretation as the Northern Path of the Gods and liberation in the Veda.

The asterisms to watch are those in the Northern and Southern Paths.

After death, the Vedic astrologer's soul will face two choices. The *devayana*, heaven, and similar words do not give the full meaning of ultimate destination of the worshiper's soul. *Devayana*, while literally meaning the path of the gods, in the context of grace and salvation, is the Land of Pure Being. Path of the forefathers, the ptrs, that place where the worshiper's soul transmigrates, is the Land of Becoming. This is the context these terms should be understood for the ultimate choices of the worshiper's soul.

Therefore, at death the worshiper's soul will encounter a fork in the road in the path towards Vedic salvation. At that juncture, the departing soul of the worshiper will take one of two paths. (SPB 1.9.3.2.) One direction leads to the path of the gods, *devayana* (RV 1.183.6; 1.184.6; 3.58.5, 6; 4.37.1; 5.43.6; 7.38.5; YV 19.47; SPB 12.8.1.21; NB 12.525), and the other the path of the forefathers, *pathi a/nu*. (RV 10.88.16; 3.12.7; 3.35.6; 7.7.2; 10.14.2; YV 19.47; SPB 12.8.1.21; NB 12.525.)

The Southern path is that world in which Vedic astrologers live their lives. The Moon is the gate leading to this path. (MB 13.1082; CU, 5.3; SPB 6.6.2.4.) There, the soul's progression during its physical life begins with the path of the forefathers, the ptrs. It is this path in which everything and everyone under heaven and earth are born and created. (RV 4.18.1.) Every living thing and person travels on this path of the forefathers. (RV 10.2.7.) This path, however, is not the preferred route because of the difficulties in erasing the residual karmic impressions and fruit left by the forefathers. (RV 4.18.2.) The preferred path leading to liberation is through the path of the gods. The *devayana*, this is the path which leads to the gods. The Sun is the gate for this path. (MB 13.1082; CU, 5.3; SPB 6.6.2.4.) The Northern Path belongs to the gods and is the path leading to the liberation of the soul.

To give the soul the orientation needed to navigate where and when the *devayana* and ptryana converge and digresses, the Rishis often looked to the asterisms, constellations, and elliptical directions of the sky for direction. The directional distribution of the universe is reflected in these two paths. The divergent paths a soul may take after death are good examples of how the macrocosm and microcosm are inextricably connected.

- When traversing on the path of the gods, the worshiper travels across the regions between heaven and earth. (RV 3.58.5.)
- Eastward of the northern path of the gods is the domain wherein the divine dynamic Vedic force of Awareness (Usas) resides. (RV 7.76.2.) There are two paths between heaven and earth, the Land of Pure Being and that of the Becoming, and these paths converge

in the regions of the universe, where the karmic results are found. (RV 10.88.15.)

The Northern Path is thereby associated with liberation from the endless cycle of rebirth and temporal existence, never to return to this world. (BU, 6.2.15; Kaus.Up., 1.3.) The Southern Path is associated with rebirth, transmigration of soul, an endless cycle of death and rebirth.

These two paths are implicated in the various Lunar houses. The Lunar house of Indra is the Eastward directions. The Lunar house of Agni, the Sun, the dispenser of the inner secret of *yajna* and divine response through the asterism of Krittika and the zodiacal houses of Mesa (Aries) and Vrsabha (Taurus), governs the Westward directions. In the worshiper's ultimate spiritual journey, Agni, the Sun, the Fire of Change, aligned with the Sun, the dispenser of the inner secret of *yajna* and divine response through the asterism of Krittika and the zodiacal houses of Mesa (Aries) and Vrsabha (Taurus), presides over these spiritual paths:

- Path of the gods.
- Northern Path
- Liberation of the Soul.

The Lunar house of Indra, the dispenser of Happiness as a Lunar house ruling Jupiter, the asterism of Jyestra, and the zodiacal house of Vrscika (Scorpio), presides over the Southern Path, which leads to the rebirth and transmigration of Soul.

The Northern and Southern Paths, however, are part of a binary system. Another binary system is the dichotomy of the Left and the Right. The interplay between the left and right movements of sama is esoteric, occult, and unknown to most. (RV 2.27.11.) Vedic astrological traditions assign left and right coordinates to the asterisms. These coordinates were located in the Phalgunis. Purna Phalguni held the right hand and Uttara Phalguni held the left hand. (Komilla, Nakshatras, The Stars Beyond the Zodiac (2014), pp. 114, 121.) These left and right handed motions are a reflection of the powers present in the Lunar houses. They reflect the different subtle spiritual movements as manifested in the material world. The right handed movement displays the expansive expression of protection, and the left handed movement displays the left handed movement of dispensation. They are accordingly represented in the give-and-take exchange in the sacrificial ritual. Some of these movements are revealed in the rcs (mantras) of the Rg Veda and reflected in the divine attributes the asterism under the domain of Indra, the dispenser of Happiness as a Lunar house ruling Jupiter, the asterism of Jyestra, and the zodiacal house of Vrscika (Scorpio):

- The right-handed (expanding) powers of Indra, the dispenser of Happiness as the Lunar house ruling Jupiter, the asterism of Jyestra, and the zodiacal house of Vrscika (Scorpio), protects all humans from the perils of evil. (RV 8.24.6.)
- The left-handed (contracting) powers Indra, the dispenser of Happiness as a Lunar house ruling Jupiter, the asterism of Jyestra, and the zodiacal house of Vrscika (Scorpio), brings spiritual blessings. (RV 8.81.6.)
- The right-handed (expanding) powers of Indra, the dispenser of Happiness as a Lunar house ruling Jupiter, the asterism of Jyestra, and the zodiacal house of Vrscika (Scorpio), protect all with the powers of purification (Soma). (RV 8.4.8.)
- The left-handed (contracting) powers Indra, the dispenser of Happiness as a Lunar house ruling Jupiter, the asterism of Jyestra, and the zodiacal house of Vrscika (Scorpio), bestows spiritual riches after receiving the same. (RV 5.36.4.)

These same left and right handed motions correspond and are expressed differently accordingly to expanding and contracting powers of discernment and blessing respectively.

- The right-handed (expanding) movement of discernment is reflected in and a product of the sacrifice itself, which establishes consciousness, mind and thought. (VYV 4.19; 4.23; TS 1.2.5.6-8.)
- The left-handed (contracting) movement of the blessing is based on the action of giving. (RV 1.4.22; TS 1.4.22; VYS 8.2.)

Day and Night (RV 2.3.6; 6.9.1-3) is another binary system. Of all the phrases in the Veda, there is none so shrouded in obscurity than "day to day," dive-dive. In one level this phrase is simply what it literally means, day to day. What is day, however, but that which shines. The Rishis equated the shining asterism of Orion with the Equinox. On a deeper level, then, day to day signifies the progression between the two equinoctial asterisms, the Vernal to the Autumnal Equinox.

Day and night, *dive-dive*, plays a special part in the travel of the soul to the Northern and Southern Paths. (BU, 6.2.16; CU, 10.5.3.) The gods are etymologically connected to and associated with "day," as they arrive at their deified status as a result of the eight-day rite (PVB 22.11.1), or the fifteen day rite (PVB 23.6.2), and they became gods in the first place by entering heaven, div. (SPB 11.1.6.8; TB 2.3.8.2.) The word for demon, asura, the antithesis of divinity, is derived from "a + surya," or "not light."(SPB 13.4.3.11 (the King of the demons is Asita ("Black")); 11.1.6.8 (after the creation of the demons there was only darkness).) Day thus becomes the Northern Path and night becomes the Southern Path. The soul reaches liberation and release when it travels northward in the path of the gods where there is light (TS 1.1.7) and is condemned to be reborn again and again when it traverses the paths of the forefathers. Thus, Yama, Death, is admonished to go on the path other than the path of the gods so that the worshiper may travel there unmolested. (RV 10.18.1.) This doctrine was later repeated in the Upanishads.

The Vedic forces and energies responsible for providing the northern path of the gods is another example of the interchangeable roles between the divine dynamic Vedic forces. Assigning separate responsibilities to separate divine dynamic Vedic forces is ultimately irrelevant because these dynamic forces collectively forge the paths a worshiper may take. (RV 7.38.5; 7.7.2; SPB 2.9.2.28; 4.4.4.13.) Agni, Indra, the Asvins, and Usas all have a role to play in making the path of the gods available to the worshiper. Agni, the Sun, the dispenser of the inner secret of *yajna* and divine response through the asterism of Krittika and the zodiacal houses of Mesa (Aries) and Vrsabha (Taurus), figures prominently in paving the path of the gods available to the worshiper:

- Agni, the Sun, the dispenser of the inner secret of *yajna* and divine response through the asterism of Krittika and the zodiacal houses of Mesa (Aries) and Vrsabha (Taurus), also leads the worshiper along the path of the gods. (SPB 1.9.2.3; 8.6.3.22.)

- Agni, the Sun, the dispenser of the inner secret of *yajna* and divine response through the asterism of Krittika and the zodiacal houses of Mesa (Aries) and Vrsabha (Taurus), brings the worshiper to the *devayana*, the path of the gods. (RV 5.43.6; 10.51.5.)
- Agni, the Sun, the dispenser of the inner secret of *yajna* and divine response through the asterism of Krittika and the zodiacal houses of Mesa (Aries) and Vrsabha (Taurus), knows all things, including the path between heaven and earth and to the *devayana*, the path of the gods. (RV 1.72.7; 10.98.11.)

The Asvins play an important role:

- The Asvins, through the power of their lunar mansion, Asvini, guide the worshiper across the darkness on the journey along the *devayana*, the path of the gods. (RV 1.183.6; 3.58.5.)

The role of Soma is especially crucial. Soma, the Moon, dispenses the spiritual endowment of Bliss through the power of the asterism of Mrgashirsha in conjunction with the zodiacal houses of Mithuna (Gemini) and Vrsabha (Taurus). Soma provides inspiration from which the *devayana*, the path of the gods, may subsist. The Soma juice produced at the Soma Sacrifice, like Ambrosia, is the beverage fueling the Vedic forces and lunar houses. (RV 9.3.9; 9.6.6; 9.7.6; 9.8.5; 9.13.3; 9.14.3; 9.18.3; 9.20.1; 9.25.1; 9.37.1; 9.38.6; 9.45.2; 9.52.2; 8.78.4; 9.97.1, 27.)

- While there are many paths to follow (RV 9.78.2), the lunar house of Soma, the Moon, dispenses Bliss through the asterism of Mrgashirsha in conjunction with the zodiacal houses of Mithuna (Gemini) and Vrsabha (Taurus), and reveals the right path to heaven. (RV 9.65.13.)
- The Soma juices flow knowing the right path belonging to the gods. (RV 9.101.10.)
- The lunar house of Soma, the Moon, dispenses Bliss through the asterism of Mrgashirsha in conjunction with the zodiacal houses

of Mithuna (Gemini) and Vrsabha (Taurus), and always finds this right and correct path. (RV 9.92.3; 9.95.2; 9.97.16; 9.106.6; 9.107.7.)

- The lunar house of Soma, the Moon, dispenses Bliss through the asterism of Mrgashirsha in conjunction with the zodiacal houses of Mithuna (Gemini) and Vrsabha (Taurus), finds this correct path, not only for the worshiper, but for the Vedic divine dynamic forces, like Bala (Indra), who, like Soma, knows many paths, but, under Soma's guidance, finds the correct path. (RV 9.106.5.)

The role of Usas is equally important. As the Vedic force of Awareness, the worshiper knows of the Land of Pure Being (the fourth existential level of Being) only through that intuition. (RV 7.76.1, 2.)

The lunar house of Indra, the dispenser of Happiness as a Vedic force ruling Jupiter, the asterism of Jyestra, and the zodiacal house of Vrscika (Scorpio), also plays a pivotal role in providing the *devayana*, the path of the gods:

- The lunar house of Indra, the Vedic force ruling Jupiter, the asterism of Jyestra, and the zodiacal house of Vrscika (Scorpio), was born out of the *devayana*, the path of the gods, or at least born from the supranatural process that engendered the two paths. The Veda speaks of Indra being raised by 180 Maruts. (RV 8.96.8.) This is symbolic language to mean Indra represents the two hemispheres, one hemisphere having the duration of one-half of a year, 360 days.
- This explains why the Veda says that the lunar house of Indra, who dispenses Happiness and is the Vedic force ruling Jupiter, the asterism of Jyestra, and the zodiacal house of Vrscika (Scorpio), like Soma, the Moon, dispenses Bliss through the asterism of Mrgashirsha in conjunction with the zodiacal houses of Mithuna (Gemini) and Vrsabha (Taurus), knows many paths. (RV 9.106.5.)
- But even while the lunar house of Indra, the Vedic force ruling Jupiter the asterism of Jyestra, and the zodiacal house of Vrscika (Scorpio), in alignment with The Principle of Change (Agni) both know the *devayana*, the path of the gods (RV 10.98.11), Indra

arrives at the sacrifice from the *devayana*, the path of the gods. (RV 4.37.1.)

This interpretation gives a new understanding to and adds to our knowledge of the Northern Path of the Gods and liberation:

- It is while traveling on the Northern Path of the Gods that the worshiper undergoes spiritual endowments of Agni, which are the secrets of the *yajna* (Sacrifice) and Divine Response. (RV 1.1.3; 4.8.7.)
- Tanunapi, is that terrestrial manifestation of Agni meaning "the summer sun" or "Son of the Body of the aspirant." (RV 1.13.2; 1.142.2.) It is also through this aspect that the worshiper undergoes the spiritual changes wrought by the endowments of Agni, which are the secrets of the *yajna* (Sacrifice) and Divine Response. (RV 3.4.2.) The body must also be honored in the worshiper's Path to salvation.
- It is in the Northern Path of the gods that spiritual Change (Agni) is born. (RV 1.136.3; 2.9.5; 4.15.6.) Agni, the dispenser of the secrets of the *yajna* (Sacrifice) and Divine Response through the rays of the Sun, and through the powers of the asterism of Krittika and the zodiacal houses of Mesa (Aries) and Vrsabha (Taurus), shines and is made resplendent in that area of the progression between the Vernal and Autumnal Equinoxes. (RV 6.15.2.)
- The birth of Agni, the dispenser of the secrets of the *yajna* (Sacrifice) and Divine Response through the rays of the Sun, and through the powers of the asterism of Krittika and the zodiacal houses of Mesa (Aries) and Vrsabha (Taurus), is affected when the spark of the sacrificial fire is kindled at the altar. (RV 3.29.14.)
- That spiritual endowments of Agni, the secrets of the *yajna* (Sacrifice) and Divine Response through the rays of the Sun, are sustained by food which ultimately results in the salvation of the worshiper. (RV 1.31.7.)
- Once the spiritual endowments of Agni, the secrets of the *yajna* (Sacrifice) and Divine Response, are attained, the spiritual change is permanent and remain in force for perpetuity. (RV 1.1.7.)

- Spiritual wealth is obtained through meditation upon the progression of the Vernal Equinox to the Autumnal Equinox. (RV 2.30.11.)
- This is due to the consciousness (rivers) increasing to a higher state (ocean) when meditating on the progression of the Vernal Equinox to the Autumnal Equinox. (RV 2.30.2.)
- The powers of meditation are therefore increased while proceeding along the Northern Path of the Gods. (RV 8.98.8.)
- The Northern Path of the Gods is also the source of purification and divine ecstasy (Soma). (RV 4.54.2; 9.75.4; 9.101.6.)
- The powers of Indra, the dispenser of Happiness as a Lunar house ruling Jupiter, the asterism of Jyestra, and the zodiacal house of Vrscika (Scorpio), are increased in the *devayana*, the path of the gods. (RV 8.12.28; 8.15.6; 8.53.2; 8.45.12.)
- The Northern Path of the gods is an object of veneration and praise. (RV 10.37.7.)
- The worshiper conquers the temptation over evil when traveling on the path to the Northern Path of the gods and is imbued with the spiritual power of Agni. (RV 10.87.22.)

In the months consisting of that portion of the year reserved for the Northern Path of the Sun, the worshiper meets a Purusa who leads the Vedic astrologer to Brahman, the world of the Cosmic Seed, Hiranyagarbha (BU, 6.2.15), and onwards to the realm wherein dwell the Vedic forces, lunar houses, and energies. (BU, 6.2.14; CU, 10.5.2; Kaus.Up., 1.3.) Those worshipers who traverse the Vedic path without this understanding but instead are mindlessly immersed in the minutia of the sacrificial ritual, pass into the smoke of the night of the months of the Southern Path of the Sun and into the night. From there, they move into aimless Space, into the Moon where the Vedic astrologer's soul becomes food for the Vedic dynamic forces, only to find themselves in another cycle of life. (BU, 6.2.16; CU, 10.5.3.)

We said that the Northern and Southern Paths are products of the binary two-dimensional universe. That universe is reflected in the two hemispheres of the ecliptic. In this two-dimensional universe, the world is divided into a binary system. The Northern and Southern Paths are intimately tied to the Asterisms (Nakshatras), Vedic forces (Nak. Kalpa, 27-30), ecliptic seasons, and directional quadrants of the universe. (Nak. Kalpa, 12-17.) Adding to the correspondence formulated in the last chapter, the Northern and Southern Paths are a part of this portion of the universe:

Ecliptic	Nakshatra	Direction	Presiding Vedic Force
Winter Solstice	Krittika	East	Agni (Sun)
Winter Solstice	Rohini	East	Agni (Sun)
Vernal Equinox	Mrgashira	East	Agni (Sun)
Vernal Equinox	Ardra	East	Agni (Sun)
Vernal Equinox	Punarvas	East	Agni (Sun)
Vernal Equinox	Tishya	East	Agni (Sun)
Vernal Equinox	Ashlesha	East	Agni (Sun)
Vernal Equinox	Magha	South	Aditya
Vernal Equinox	Purva Phalguni	South	Aditya
Summer Solstice	Uttara Phalguni	South	Aditya
Summer Solstice	Hasta	South	Aditya
Summer Solstice	Chitra	South	Aditya
Summer Solstice	Svati	South	Aditya

Summer Solstice	Vishakha	South	Aditya
Autumn Equinox	Anurdadh	West	Moon (Soma)
Autumn Equinox	Vrchrtau	West	Moon (Soma)
Autumn Equinox	Ashada	West	Moon (Soma)
Autumn Equinox	Shrona	West	Moon (Soma)
Autumn Equinox	Shravistha	North	Moon (Soma)
Autumn Equinox	Shatabisha	North	Moon (Soma)
Winter Solstice	Purva Prosthapada	North	Moon (Soma)
Winter Solstice	Uttara Prosthapada	North	Moon (Soma)
Winter Solstice	Revati	North	Moon (Soma)
Winter Solstice	Ashvini	North	Moon (Soma)
Winter Solstice	Bharanir	North	Moon (Soma)

The ptrs may not be Vedic deities and they may not be divine. They still offer valuable lessons to the worshiper for the spiritual journey.

In his Capacity of Ruling The Purva Phalguni Asterism, the Lunar house of Aryaman Dispenses, and the Worshiper Learns, the Spiritual Endowment of Good Works

Aryaman is described as the protector of mares, and the Milky Way. Aryaman dispenses the spiritual endowment of Good Works. The Vedic astrologer also knows Aryaman as the dispenser of the spiritual endowment of Good Works, through the asterism of Uttara Phalguni and the zodiacal house of Simha (Leo) and Kanya (Virgo). "Good Works" has an expansive meaning in the case of Aryaman.

The Milky Way in the Rg Veda is called the *aryamnah panthah*. It is said to be his path, the "path of Aryaman." Aryaman passes smoothly like an "excellent cow" (*sugo/ hi/*) along the path of the Milky Way. (RV 2.27.6.) This carries a variety of meanings.

- It could signify how the Milky Way was created, a throw-back or throw-forward to the explanation given by the Ancient Greeks, which held that the Milky Way was created when Hercules was suckling the breast of a mortal woman when Hera, Zeus' wife, pushed Hercules away, spilling the milk across the sky.
- It also carries the general symbolic meaning of "Cow" in the Vedic dharma. Those meanings are contained elsewhere in this book and generally implicates consciousness and knowledge.
- It also implicates the very make-up of the Milky Way, the dazzling collection of stars glistening in the sky, so much so they appeared as the "herds of the sky."

In RV 1.105.6, the "Path of Aryaman," the Milky Way, is equated with the very fundamental purposes of the worshiper's spiritual journey. Those purposes define the parameters of that spiritual journey:

- To support the laws of *Rta*, the inner, essential truths of the Vedic dharma.
- If the worshiper is not acting entirely under the laws of the inner essential truths of the Vedic dharma, how can he travel, so to speak, on the straight and narrow Path of Aryaman?

The Milky Way became a metaphor of finding the right path to travel during the spiritual journey. That the spiritual endowments of Aryaman shine through the brightness of the Milky Way justifies special mention. The "Good Works" of Aryaman thus is anything which supports or fosters the maintenance of *Rta*. Aryaman also is the protector of the mares. This capacity implicates an entirely different aspect of the powers of Aryaman. That aspect implicates Knowledge, which is symbolized by and using metaphors related to the Horse.

The worshiper should understand that in the Vedic path to salvation and liberation, the world will look different, and the world will be perceived in a different way. What does the Vedas teach us about this phenomenon? This Vasistha Samhita, a Hatha Yoga text from the Eleventh Century grounded in the Vedas, provides the elements of sense perception. According to the Vasistha Samhita (Vas. S., 5.8), the process of perception of the material world through the senses consists of five elements:

- Bhokta, the enjoyer.
- Bhogya, the object of enjoyment.
- Bhukti, the enjoyment obtained.
- Bhogayatana, the body.
- Indriya, the sense organs.

On an esoteric level, the elements of sense perception is explained through symbols. One symbol is the Horse. Reference to "horses" in the Vedas has traditionally been interpreted as "energy." There is considerable disagreement among Vedic scholars as to the esoteric meaning of Horses. Throughout his writings and translations, the eminent Vedic scholar and translator Kashyap interprets the horse to symbolize primal energy, prana, and life-force. Singh finds several meanings to the horse, including force and the inception of The Principle of Change (Agni). These interpretations, while valid, ignore the clear understanding of subsequent Vedic Upanishadic scriptures. Principally, the Katha Upanishad (Kath. U., 3.3-10) states:

- Know the Self to be sitting in the chariot, the body to be the chariot, the intellect (Buddhi) the charioteer, and the mind the reins.

- The senses they call the horses, the objects of the senses their roads.
- When he (the Highest Self) is in union with the body, the senses, and the mind, then wise people call him the Enjoyer.
- He who has no understanding and whose mind (the reins) is never firmly held, his senses (horses) are unmanageable, like vicious horses of a charioteer.
- But he who has understanding and whose mind is always firmly held, his senses are under control, like good horses of a charioteer.
- He who has no understanding, who is unmindful and always impure, never reaches that place but enters into the round of births.
- But he who has understanding, who is mindful and always pure, reaches indeed that place, from whence he is not born again.
- But he who has understanding for his charioteer, and who holds the reins of the mind, he reaches the end of his journey at a place that is the highest place of Vishnu.
- Beyond the senses there are the objects, beyond the objects there is the mind, beyond the mind there is the intellect, the Great Self is beyond the intellect.

This highly influential passage accomplishes much to the esoteric understanding of the symbol of the horse and how it relates to other issues of consciousness. It delineates the various elements within which the consciousness resides:

- The Self, the subject, sits with the charioteer.
- The Chariot is the body.
- The intellect (Buddhi) is the charioteer.
- The mind, Manas, is the reins.
- The senses, the indriam, are the horses.
- The object of the senses is the road.
- So is the image of the horse in the Veda.

No one element of this passage takes precedence of another. The better view is that each — the body, the senses, the mind, the Buddhi, and the Universal Self — "each must play its own part" in the spiritual journey. (Tiwari, p. 182.) This passage also emphasizes the consequences of and need to yoke — i.e., restrain, control — the senses. A person of understanding always has the senses in control, has learned to restrain the mind, and is not subject to rebirth. A person without understanding does not have the senses in control and is born time after time. This passage defines the esoteric meaning of horses in the Veda. Horses in the Veda have the metaphorical meaning of the "senses," sight, touch, hear, smell, and feel. Horses represent the senses, the mind's perception of the senses, in all their unbridled glory.

Horses are frequently associated with the Vedic divine dynamic forces:

- The horse is associated with the processes of Agni, the dispenser of the secrets of the *yajna* (Sacrifice) and Divine Response through the rays of the Sun, and through the powers of the asterism of Krittika and the zodiacal houses of Mesa (Aries) and Vrsabha (Taurus). (RV 3.27.14; 3.29.6; 6.3.4; 8.22; 4.2.8; 1.36.8; 1.27.1; 1.6.53; 1.66.2; 1.69.3; 1.73.9, 10; 1.74.7; 1.149.3; 1.58.2; 2.1.16; .2.2.10; 3.2.3; 3.26.3; 4.1.3; 4.2.4.4.39.6; 4.2.11; 4.10.1; 4.15.1; 5.6.3; 5.18.5.)
- Usas, mental and spiritual awareness, is seen mounting the carriage as the charioteer (the Self).(RV 3.61.2.)
- Owing to their extremely concentrated focus, the Maruts move with swift horses (senses) which are easily controlled. (RV 5.55.1; 5.54.1.)

The Horses (sense perceptions) however are ruled and governed by other aspects:

- The senses (horses) are harnessed in accordance with the dynamic force of *Rta*, the inner essence of the Vedic dharma. (RV 4.51.5.)

The horse is primarily used as a metaphor for the senses, consistent with the interpretation given in the Katha Upanishad:

- The Soma plant is ground with the pistol and mortar much like reins are used to tether a horse. (RV 1.24.)
- The mind of the Vedic force of Varuna, who dispenses Greatness through the power of the asterism of Shatabhisha and the zodiacal

house of Kumba (Aquarius) — as well as the worshiper's own mind — are soothed by the praises at the sacrifice like the horses (sense perceptions) are soothed by the reins (mind). (RV 1.25.3.)

• The worshiper accepts the offering as a charioteer (the Self) and accepts the reins (mind) to a horse (senses). (RV 1.144.3.)

These dynamic Vedic forces possessed their own horses which the Brhad-Devata (BD, 4.140, 141) listed as the following:

• The Bay Horses (*Hari*), the horses of the Lunar house of Indra, who dispenses Happiness as a Lunar house ruling Jupiter, the asterism of Jyestra, and the zodiacal house of Vrscika (Scorpio). (Nir., 1.15.1.)

• The Ruddy Ones (*Rohit*), the horses of the Lunar house of Agni, who dispenses the secrets of the *yajna* (Sacrifice) and Divine Response through the rays of the Sun, and through the powers of the asterism of Krittika and the zodiacal houses of Mesa (Aries) and Vrsabha (Taurus).

• Fallows (*Harit*), the horses of the Vedic force of Surya.

• Teams (*Niyut*), the horses of the Lunar house of Vayu, who dispenses of sukha, deep Spiritual Fulfillment, Happiness, through the powers of Svasti, in conjunction with the zodiacal house of Tula (Libra).

• The Ass (*Sahita*), the horses of the Lunar house of Asvins, the dispensers of Bhaga (Enjoyment) through the asterism of Asvini and the zodiacal house of Mesa (Aries).

• The Steeds (*Vajin*), the horses of Pusan, the dispensers of Bhaga Enjoyment) through the asterism of Revati, in conjunction with the zodiacal house of Mina (*Pisces*).

• The Drappled mares (*Prsati*), the horses of the Maruts.

• The Ruddy Cows (*Aruni*), the horses of Usas, Dawn.

Each steed represents a different aspect of the mind-body relation as regards to conscious perception. Hari, for instance, the horses of Indra, is seen as the instrument of achieving divine inspiration, ecstacy and union. In reaching that goal, constant mention is made to "harness the horses" so that they may be "yoked." This is but another way of saying that the mind must be restrained, controlled, and focused to achieve liberation and salvation.

The Lunar house of Indra, the dispenser of Happiness as a Lunar house ruling Jupiter, the asterism of Jyestra, and the zodiacal house of Vrscika (Scorpio), appropriately, plays a crucial role in the management of the horses (sense perceptions):

- The Lunar house of Indra, the dispenser of Happiness as a Lunar house ruling Jupiter, the asterism of Jyestra, and the zodiacal house of Vrscika (Scorpio), appropriately, is called the "Lord of the Bay (Horses), consistent with the need of knowledge to restrain the fluctuations of sense perceptions. (RV 1.3.6; 1.33.6; 1.81.4; 1.145.3; 1.147.1; 1.173.13; 1.174.6; 1.175.1; 3.30.2; 3.32.5; 3.47.4; 3.51.6; 3.52.7;4.16.21; 4.17.21; 4.19.11; 4.20.11; 4.21.11; 4.22.11; 4.23.11; 4.24.11; 4.35.7; 5.31.2; 6.19.6; 6.32.3; 6.41.3; 6.44.10; 7.19.4, 7;7.20.4; 7.21.1; 7.23.4; 7.24.4, 5; 7.29.1; 7.32.12; 7.37.4, 5; 8.2.13; 8.21.6; 8.24.3, 5, 14; 8.40.9; 8.48.10; 8.50.3; 8.55.4; 8.88.2; 10.49.11.)

- The dynamic force of Indra is the "yoker" of the Bay Horses. (RV 1.82.1, 2; 1.61.16; 1.81.3; 1.82.3, 4, 5; 1.83.3; 1.141.6; 3.43.6; 5.40.4; 6.23.1; 6.37.1; 6.47.18, 19; 7.28.1; 8.3.17; 8.33.14; 8.45.39; 8.59.7; 8.79.3, 9; 10.33.5; 10.105.2; 10.122.4.) The meaning of "yoking" the horses are readily apparent. Just as horses are yoked and held back, so are the fluctuations of the mind are restrained to allow entry of *Rta*, the inner essence of the Vedic dharma.

- One rc (mantra) made this metaphor plain and simple. The Lunar house of Indra yokes, or restrains, the fluctuations of the senses. (RV 3.50.2.)

- The movement of the Lunar house of Indra in the chariot (body) thus becomes the seat of discernment. (RV 3.53.6.)

What better work can the worshiper achieve but the proceed with on the spiritual journey with retrained mind trained in austerity and learned in the ways of the Path of Aryaman? This is the import of these members of the stellar population.

In his Capacity of Ruling the Hasta Asterism, the Lunar house of Savitr, in Conjunction with the Zodiacal House of Kanya (Virgo), Dispenses the Spiritual Endowment of Bliss.

Savitr is the Principle of Immortality. He bestows the benefit of immortality to other Vedic forces and to us, mere mortals. He bestows the benefit of immortality to other dynamic Vedic forces and to mortal humans. Savitr is better understood contrasted with his cousin, Surya. Surya is primarily an astronomical body, but Surya's energy has the qualities of measuring the days, prolonging the days of life, driving away sickness, disease and other evils, and the Creator of all. The distinction between him and Savitr, let alone Pusan, remained hazy and at best indefinite. Ancient commentators clarified the relationship of Surya and Savitr. Even the commentators could not agree. Yaksa notes that Savitr appears when the darkness disappears. (Nir. 12.12.) Yet, commenting on RV 5.81.4, Sayana states before its rising the Sun is called Savitr and from the rising of dawn to its setting the Sun is Surya. These two conflicting commentaries are reconciled by the Vedas in the dynamic force inherent in Savitr. Savitr "approaches" or "brings" Surya. (RV 1.35.8.) "Bringing" Surya" implies a similarity but also increase. In the hierarchy of Vedic dynamic forces, Surya is accorded a greater importance.

Yet, Savitri remains the Vedic principle of immortality. These are some of the ways in which Savitri bestows immortality:

- He also bestowed immortality to the Rhbus, who were previously mortal and acquired life immortal by virtue of their fine character. (RV 1.110.1, 2.)
- He bestows immortality to the gods and duration to humans. (RV 4.54.2.)
- After bestowing duration to the life of humans, Savitr conducts the remains of the worshiper's mortal coil, the smoke of the cremated body, upwards to the heavenly world (RV 10.17.4), under the guidance and protection of Pusan (AGS 4.4.7), another Sun deity and member of the Adityas (astrological houses).

The Upanishads are a little more detailed on the mechanics to immortality according to Savitri. A minor Upanishad, the Savitri, outlines the method by which Savitri bestows immortality in the Vedic dharma. The common denominator in this process is Savitri bestowing the endowment of immortality by using *mithuna*, the power of coupling which is the spiritual endowment bestowed by the zodiacal house of the same name. Engaging the elements and other principles present in the Vedic dharma, Savitri bestows the principle of immortality in these couplings:

- Coupling the Fire element, a masculine aspect, with the Earth element, a feminine.
- Coupling the Air element, a masculine aspect, with the Water element, a feminine.
- Coupling yajna, Sacrifice, a masculine aspect, with the Chhandas, mantras from the Yajur Veda, a feminine principle.
- Coupling Thunderclouds, a masculine aspect, with Lightning, a feminine.
- Coupling the Sun, a masculine aspect, with Celestial Space, a feminine.
- Coupling the Moon, a masculine aspect, with the Constellations, a feminine.
- Coupling Manas, the Mind, a masculine aspect, with Speech, a feminine.
- Coupling Purusa, a masculine aspect, with Woman, obviously, a feminine.

Savitr is also the Principle of Creation:

- This principle is the ultimate giver of life. (RV 1.22.7.)
- This principle is responsible for all physical manifestation. (RV 6.71.2.)
- Savitr fosters the lives of successive generations. (RV 4.54.2.)
- Savitr establishes the fullness of being. (RV 7.45.11.)
- With these attributes, this principle creates the entire work of creation. (RV 2.38.1, 2.)

In its many regenerative properties, Savitr representing the astral symbol of the creative, generative power in the Vedic dharma, and Agni and the Maruts, whose active principles are several, are responsible for *arkam*, which Sayana interprets as the luminous nature of Indra and Light emitted from the descending waters. (RV 1.19.4.) The two sides of the divine force of Savitr are complimentary. The work of creation itself is a perpetual process; the soul, as the world, is eternal. (RV 2.38.1.) Those powers are harmonized in a sacrificial context by the Golden Man, Purusa. (SPB 7.4.1.25, 32, 43; 7.4.3.1, 14, 17, 19; 7.5.2.11; 8.1.4.11; 10.5.2.6, 7, 8; 10.5.4.14, 15.)

Thus, there are two powers at work. On a physical level Surya implicates the process of evaporation, and the other Savitr is the continual power inherent in that natural process. One level of interpretation of 1.164.7 invokes Surya and is scientific, asking those who understand the physics of water evaporation to explain those dynamics. On a deeper mystical level Savitr is invoked and is a commentary of the principle of regeneration. The rain originates from water evaporated by the Sun; once deposited in the clouds, the water droplets return to the earth as rain, only to return to the clouds in order to fall as rain. It is an eco-system taught in high school science class, but also emblematic of the regeneration and rejuvenation of the natural system.

The golden element of Savitr augments this interpretation. Surya's characteristic as the Principle of Energy gives this dynamic an added dimension. When the Rishii is requesting those who "knows the dynamics of Energy," with the interposition of Savitr as the Principle of Immortality, the Rishii appears to articulate his version of the scientific principle of the Conservation of Energy, that energy itself never dissipates or is lost but merely changes into a different form.

There is a deeper, more occult and symbolic meaning to this rc (mantra), RV 1.164.7. According to this meaning Fire and Water contain the same essential nature and origin. The essential equivalence of fire and water is reflected in the elements found in the sacrifice, the sacrificial grass, fire and water.

- The sacrificial grass is considered to be the cosmic, primeval, Water. (Gonda, *The Ritual Functions and Significance of Grasses in the Religion of the Veda*, (1985), p. 36.)
- Fire (Agne) is produced out of the water from which the grass is represented. (SPB 2.2.3.1; 1.2.3.9; BSS 5.19.8.)
- The sacrificial Agni fires are established in the rainy season.
- This is how the Fire of Agni is kindled (idhyase): in the waters. (RV 3.25.5.)

The sum total of all these attributes is comprise the spiritual endowment of Bliss. Savitr is not the only Lunar house to dispense Bliss.

- The Lunar house of Soma dispenses Bliss through the Moon, Mrgashirsha, and Mithuna (Gemini)
- The combined Lunar house of Indra and energy of Tvastr are supplicants for the Lunar house of Agni. Indra, the Lord of the Mid-World, is the incarnation of Agni both generally (RV 2.1.3) when battling Vrtra. (RV 3.14.7; 10.80.2; Mikhailov, (2001) RgVedic Studies, p. 14.) is the incarnation of Agni Vasivanara when battling the "enemies." (RV 1.59.6.) Tvastr is the Architect, "Fashioner of Forms," (BD 1.84) of the Universe. Tvastr is a manifestation of the terrestrial fire of Agni. (BD, 1.108.) Together these supplicants of Agni dispense Bliss to the worshiper through the asterism of Chitra and in conjunction with the zodiacal houses of Kanya (Virgo) and Tula (Libra).

The precise framework within which Savitr dispenses Bliss differs from these other Lunar houses. In its many regenerative properties, Savitr representing the astral symbol of the creative, generative power in the Vedic dharma, and, with its generative powers and the powers of Hasta, in conjunction with the zodiacal house of Kanya (Virgo), is responsible for the existence of oppositions. The Lunar house of Agni, the principle of Change and Transformation, and Agni, the Sun, the dispenser of the inner secrets of the *yajna* and divine response, via the power of the asterism of Krittika, in conjunction with the zodiacal houses of Mesa (Aries) and Vrsabha (Taurus), supply the active principles containing the qualities of combustibility and fluidity found in Fire and Water. Thereupon, This is the mystery of *Rta* that the Rishii appears to convey: That the cosmic order in the Vedic dharma is a collective symbiotic vortex of unreconciled opposites, one complementing the other, yet equally opposed, until they are conjoined by the uniting powers of the asterism of Ardra. Then, once united, these opposites experience the Bliss of their congress in the powers of the asterism Hasta. This mystery is reflected in simple physical processes, from the minutest workings of the cosmos, to the broadest expanse of the Vedic dharma (*Rta*).

The Vedic astrologer knows Savitr in this light. Savitr is the dispenser of the spiritual endowment of Bliss through the asterism of Hasta and the zodiacal house of Kanya (Virgo). In his dispensation of Bliss, Savitr furthers his traditional, Vedic, nature (svadha). All stages of the worshiper's spiritual journey is important but Bliss is the stage which prepares the worshiper's being to fully appreciate the pleasures of salvation and liberation.

In his Capacity of Ruling the Chitra Asterism, and in Conjunction with the Zodiacal Houses of Kanya (Virgo) and Tula (Libra), the Lunar house of Indra (Tvastr) Dispenses, and the Worshiper Learns, the Spiritual Endowment Of Bliss.

The combined Lunar houses and energies of Indra and Tvastr present a unique instance of dispensation. Note, this is not simply the lunar house of Indra alone, but Indra with Tvastr. This force and energy dispenses Bliss, as Soma, the Moon, via Mrgashirsha, and Vrsabha (Taurus) and Mithuna (Gemini) and Savitr through the asterism of Hasta and the zodiacal house of Kanya (Virgo).

- The Lunar house of Soma dispenses Bliss through the Moon, Mrgashirsha, and Vrsabha (Taurus) and Mithuna (Gemini)
- The Lunar house of Savitr is the dispenser of the spiritual endowment of Bliss through the asterism of Hasta and the zodiacal house of Kanya (Virgo).

The magnitude of these Lunar houses combined are formidable and transformative. The lunar house of Indra, the incarnation of the fire of Agni, is instrumental is conveying knowledge obtained, derived, and learned from the stellar population:

- The lunar house of Indra, the Lord of the Mid-World, is the incarnation of Agni both generally (RV 2.1.3) and when battling Vrtra. (RV 3.14.7; 10.80.2; Mikhailov, (2001) *RgVedic Studies*, p. 14.) Indra is the incarnation of Agni Vasivanara when battling the "enemies." (RV 1.59.6.)
- RV 1.7.3: So, in a Sukta in which Indra, as the incarnation of the fire of Agni, presides, the lunar house of Indra destroys the mountain, releasing the cattle, *gobhir,* which, in the fire of the zodiacal house of Vrscika (Scorpio), release not simply cattle, but happiness and bliss.
- RV 1.16.9: For those same reasons, Indra, as the incarnation of the fire of the lunar house of Agni, provides happiness and bliss to the worshiper.

- RV 1.53.4: The lunar house of Indra, as the incarnation of the fire of Agni, in conjunction with the fire of the zodiacal houses of Vrscika (Scorpio), releases happiness and bliss held by Vrtra.
- RV 1.62.5: Indra, as the incarnation of the fire of Agni, dispels the darkness with the light shining from the planet of Jupiter and the asterisms of Anuradha Jyestra.

Tvastr is also well suited, and, like Indra, an incarnation and terrestrial manifestation of Agni, to do battle with Vrtra.

Tvastr is the Architect, "Fashioner of Forms," (BD 1.84) of the Universe. Tvastr is a manifestation of the terrestrial fire of Agni. (BD, 1.108.) Tvastr is the fire which gives shape to the manifold appearance of Creation. From a material standpoint Tvastr supplies the fire of the material world. Tvastr is also known as Tvasta. (RV 3.4.9, 5.5.9, 7.2.9, 10.70.9.) Tvastr makes many appearances in the Veda.

- Tvstr is the author of all forms. (RV 1.13.10.)
- Tvastr is the maker of forms and all types of beings in the universe. (RV 3.55.19.)

Tvastr is the great victor over the enemies of the world and is terrestrial fires power the internal subtle bodies of the Vedic forces and energies. (RV 2.31.4.)

- Tvastr is the possessor of light and the possessor of the essence of the Vedic dharma (*Rta*) and establishes in the worshiper all that is needed for spiritual increase and protection. (RV 3.54.12.)
- More importantly for this discussion, Tvastr made the weapon Indra used to slay Vrtra, Vayra. (RV 1.92.2.)

Together, the lunar house of Indra and Tvastr battle Vrtra with the powers bestowed upon them by the asterism of Chitra and in conjunction with the zodiacal houses of Kanya (Virgo) and Tula (Libra). If the practical results of the slaying of Vrtra can be categorized in any cogent manner, Indra overcoming Vrtra are placed in four general consequences.

- One, Vrtra's fall results in the establishment of the inner essence of the Vedic dharma, the Waters, which thereafter begin to evolve.
- Two, Vrtra's fall results in the supports the advancement of consciousness.
- Three, Vrtra's death Supports the Vedic Dharma.
- Four, once so established, the downfall of Vrtra released the Light, which contains the wisdom of the Stellar Population.

So this is what happens when Vrtra is killed by Indra:

Releases of the Waters, the Inner Essence of the Vedic dharma

In the beginning this element of cosmic order was inert physical matter. Samkhya Karika 1.20 teaches us that consciousness appears in the world when Purusa, the universal consciousness, makes contact, "conjoins," with Prakrti, primordial, inert, matter. In the Veda this conjoining is symbolized in the battle between Indra and Vrtra.

When the lunar house of Indra initiates contact with the inert matter present there was nothing but this indiscriminate mass of undefined matter pervading the cosmos. There had not been present a Vedic dharma at that time — just a mass of dead matter. RV 6.24.5 describes this state as the world was converted from that which is to "that which is" prior to the evolution of cycles of universes in the Vedic dharma, indeed, prior to the presence of that indiscriminate mass itself.

The simile used is that Vrtra retained the waters. (RV 1.15.4; 1.49.3; 1.84.18; 1.95.3; 1.162.19; 3.47.2; 4.34.2; 5.32.2; 10.2.1; 10.7.6; 10.18.5; 10.26.1; 10.85.18; 1.55.5; 1.57.6; 5.32.2; 5.33.1.) The lunar house of Indra is *apsuji*, the beloved conqueror of the waters. (RV 8.13.2; 8.36.1-6; 8.43.28; 9.106.3.) As the conqueror of the waters, the lunar house of Indra is victorious over Vrtra. The simile used to signify the beginning of the process which would be the Vedic dharma is that Indra "releases the waters." (RV 1.51.1; 1.5.2; 1.5.3. 1.5.4; 1.15.5; 1.15.6 1.15.9; 1.15.10; 1.15.11; 1.15.20; 1.32.1, 2; 1.33.11, 12; 1.49.3; 1.51.11; 1.52.2, 6, 8, 10, 14; 1.54.4; 1.57.2, 6; 1.59.6; 1.61.10, 12; 1.80.2, 5, 10; 1.125.5; 1.130.3; 1.131.4; 1.169.8; 1.174.2, 4; 2.37.6; 1.84.18; 1.95.4; 1.162.4; 1.33.13; 1.51.11; 1.80.10; 2.28.4; 3.31.11, 16; 4.18.7; 4.19.8; 5.30.10; 6.20.2; 2.11.5;

2.20.7; 2.30.1; 3.30.9, 10; 3.31.20; 3.32.5, 6, 11; 3.33.6; 3.38.5; 3.45.2; 3.51.9; 5.30.5; 5.31.6; 5.33.6.) The phraseology is purposeful. The Waters signify the fundamental, inner essence of the Vedic dharma. Further, on a spiritual level the Waters are that aspect of the divine dynamic cosmic order symbolizing the forces of creation, purification and life; on a subtle and material level, the Waters represent the Vedic field. Thereafter, once the lunar house of Indra makes contact with *adya* ("What is") and the other *anya/d* ("What is not"), he transforms the latter into the former, beginning the evolution of the Vedic dharma. The asterisms are eventually formed in the process described earlier. Indra and Tvastr are associated with the powers of Chitra and the zodiacal houses of Kanya (Virgo) and Tula (Libra). The specific purpose of this association is to battle Vrtra. That battle is expressed in many places and in many ways.

- The lunar house of Indra with the weapon created by Tvastr and with the power of Chitra in conjunction with the zodiacal houses of Kanya (Virgo) and Tula (Libra) releases the waters. (RV 2.11.2; 2.22.4.)
- The waters arrested by Vala are freed by the lunar house of Indra with the weapon created by Tvastr and with the power of Chitra in conjunction with the zodiacal houses of Kanya (Virgo) and Tula (Libra). (RV 4.17.1.)
- The lunar house of Indra frees the rivers and the waters with the weapon created by Tvastr and with the power of Chitra in conjunction with the zodiacal houses of Kanya (Virgo) and Tula (Libra). (RV 6.17.12.)
- Under the influence of Soma, the lunar house of Indra with the weapon created by Tvastr and with the power of Chitra in conjunction with the zodiacal house of Vrscika releases the waters after killing Vrtra with a rock. (RV 1.56.6.)
- The lunar house of Indra releases the nourishing waters with the weapon created by Tvastr and with the power of Chitra in conjunction with the zodiacal house of Vrscika. (RV 1.61.10.)
- The lunar house of Indra with the weapon created by Tvastr and with the power of Chitra in conjunction with the zodiacal house

of Vrscika smites Vrtra with Vayra, impelling the waters to flow. (RV 1.80.5.)

- The lunar house of Indra slays Vrtra and releases the waters with the weapon created by Tvastr and with the power of Chitra in conjunction with the zodiacal house of Vrscika. (RV 1.54.10.)
- The lunar house of Indra releases waters concealed by Vrtra with the weapon created by Tvastr and with the power of Chitra in conjunction with the zodiacal house of Vrscika. (RV 1.80.4.)
- The lunar house of Indra releases the waters concealed in darkness with the weapon created by Tvastr and with the power of Chitra in conjunction with the zodiacal house of Vrscika. (RV 1.32.10, 11; 3.33.7.)
- The waters are set free by the lunar house of Indra with the weapon created by Tvastr and in alignment with the power of Chitra in conjunction with the zodiacal house of Vrscika. (RV 1.23.5; 1.32.4; 1.133.1; 1.152.1; 1.185.6; 2.27.8; 3.4.5; 3.5.3; 3.31.9. 21; 4.3.9, 10; 4.23.9; 4.42.4; 5.1.7; 5.12.3; 5.15.2; 5.62.1; 5.63.7; 5.68.4; 5.80.1; 6.68.2; 7.34.7.56.12; 7.8.86.5; 9.80.8; 9.108.8; 10.12.1, 2; 19,62.2, 3; 10.108.11; 10.109.1; 10.123.4, 5; 10.139.4.)

This is probably the most important meaning of the struggle with Vrtra. By Vrtra's downfall, Indra, with the weapon fashioned by Tvastr, Vayra, subdued Vrtr, with the additional assistance of the asterism of Chitra and in conjunction with the zodiacal house of Vrscika (Libra). As a result the inner essence of the Vedic dharma, the Waters, were released. The beauty of symbol, however, is its variation. And the downfall of Vrtra has other meanings.

Awakens and Supports Consciousness

There are variations of this theme. Those variations make use of other symbols and those symbols signify additional meanings. For example, Vrtra is sometimes likened to a mountain, and the mountain is taken as the symbol of ignorance. In this instance, the result is the same:

- The lunar house of Indra cleaves the mountain which releases the waters Indra with the weapon created by Tvastr and with the power of Chitra in conjunction with the zodiacal house of Vrscika. (RV 1.55.5; 1.57.6; 5.32.2; 5.33.1.)
- The lunar house of Indra shatters the mountain of Vrtra with Vrtra, releasing the waters with the weapon created by Tvastr and with the power of Chitra in conjunction with the zodiacal house of Vrscika. (RV 4.17.3.)

The release of water or the streams on an individual level means the flow of consciousness:

- The lunar house of Indra releases the rivers with the weapon created by Tvastr and with the power of Chitra in conjunction with the zodiacal house of Vrscika. (RV 1.32.1 1-15; 2.13.5; 4.19.5, 8; 4.28.1; 6.17.12; 10.67.12.) "Rivers" has a broad application and meaning. Meaning both individual and macrocosmic consciousness activity, the Rivers can also signify individual existential levels in the Vedic dharma.
- The lunar house of Indra with the weapon created by Tvastr and with the power of Chitra in conjunction with the zodiacal house of Vrscika releases the streams after slaying Vrtra. (RV 1.33.13, 1.51.11, 1.80.10, 2.28.4, 3.31.11, 16, 4.18.7, 4.19.8, 5.30.10.) In the language of the Veda," streams" signify the worshiper's individual consciousness.

When individual rivers are implicated, the import is the same. When Vrtra is subdued the worshiper's individual consciousness is activated. The lunar house of Indra releases the Vipas and Sutudri Rivers with the weapon created by Tvastr and with the power of Chitra in conjunction with the zodiacal house of Vrscika. (RV 1.61.10; 3.31.1.) The simile is extended in other ways to indicate higher states of being and consciousness.

- The lunar house of Indra releases the waters to the ocean with the weapon created by Tvastr and with the power of Chitra in conjunction with the zodiacal house of Vrscika. (RV 5.29.3; 1.52.8; 1.61.10; 1.32.2; 2.19.2; 6.17.12.) The additional symbol here, the Ocean, refers to that feature in Vedic cosmology for the upper existential levels, essentially, Heaven, the Five-and Seven Dimensional Universes. By subduing Vrtra and releasing the waters to the Ocean, Indra established Heaven and the Five-and Seven Dimensional Universes.

- The lunar house of Indra releases or is the giver of the seven rivers (Seven eternal laws) Indra with the weapon created by Tvastr and with the power of Chitra in conjunction with the zodiacal house of Vrscika. (See RV 1.32.6; 1.32.12; 2.12.3, 12; 4.8.7.) The "river" refers here pertain to the specific existential level, here the Seven-Dimensional Universe. This is simply another name for Heaven, which is established when Vrtra is vanquished.

- The lunar house of Indra with the weapon created by Tvastr and with the power of Chitra in conjunction with the zodiacal house of Vrscika releases of the waters which give birth to the *hiranyabarbha*, the cosmic egg. (RV 10.121.7, 8.) This is another significant event in the establishment of the Vedic dharma. The death of Vrtra allowed the emergence of the Cosmic Egg, the Seed containing the potentiality of what will become the Vedic dharma.

- The lunar house of Indra with the weapon created by Tvastr and with the power of Chitra in conjunction with the zodiacal house of Vrscika releases or is the giver of the ordinary rivers, symbolic for the stream of individual mental consciousness present in perceptive awareness and possessed of the worshiper and all sentient beings. (RV 2.12.3; 1.33.11; 1.62.6; 1.83.1; 1.102.2; 1.174.9; 1.181.6; 4.17.1; 4.19.2, 6, 7, 8; 4.22.6.) For the worshiper this means the unveiling of ignorance as the concealment of Vrtra to the inner essence of the Vedic dharma is terminates on the death of Vrtra.

- The lunar house of Indra uses a weapon created by Tvastr and with the power of Chitra in conjunction with the zodiacal house of Vrscika releases or is the giver of the dawn (mental understanding and awareness) and the rivers. (RV 4.19.8; 7.21.3.) Dawn, uSa/saH, is both the physical beginning of a new day and the birth of awareness in the worshiper. Both events are the result of the downfall of Vrtra.

- The lunar house of Indra gives birth to the universal streams and allowed the waters to flow with the weapon created by Tvastr and with the power of Chitra in conjunction with the zodiacal house of Vrscika. (RV 4.19.6.) This simile actually refers to two different phenomena. The flowing of the "universal streams" is the application of consciousness to a macrocosmic level, not applied to the worshiper individually but to the Absolute Self, Atman. The application to the worshiper individually is implicated generally in the allowance of the "waters to flow," which is the energization of mental activity and acuity. Both phenomena result from the downfall of Vrtra.

Supports the Subtle Foundation of the Vedic Dharma

The Panis are kindred to Vrtra and restrained *ghrta*. The Panis and Vrtra are functionally the same. *Ghrta* is derived from the Sanskrit root, *gh*, meaning, to go, to hasten towards, + *Rta*. *Ghrta*, ghee, is "that which hastens towards or go to *Rta*," anything which supports the Vedic dharma. That which supports the Vedic dharma supports the sentient beings which inhabit the dharma. *Ghrta* implicates mental acuity, clarity and brilliance. In this state the mind is receptive; in its cloudy state, blocked in its own cloudy fog. The cloudy fog is created by Vrtra, the clear brilliant state of mental acuity and consciousness is removed by Indra, who with Tvastr, grants the Bliss which accompanies this state of consciousness through the power of the asterism of Chitra in conjunction with the zodiac house of Vrscika (Libra). This is also reflected in the following rcs (mantras):

- The lunar house of Indra releases or removes the clouds (mental doubt or anguish) with the weapon created by Tvastr and with the power of Chitra in conjunction with the zodiacal house of Vrscika. (RV 1.7.6; 2.17.1; 8.7.23 (releases the "mountain mists.") The esoteric meaning of "clouds" according to Sri Aurobindo is the active movements of the mind which cover the inner light, analogous to the vrittis clouding.
- The lunar house of Indra releases the Light, Starlight, the Wisdom of the Stellar Population.

As a result of emerging victorious over Vrtra, Indra recovers the "Light." There are specific types of Light that we encountered earlier. Two of the most prominent are *go* or *gobhir,* the "rays of light," and *jyotir,* the light of the divine principle of life. Both are recovered from Vrtra, who had kept them covered. Ghrta is the Light of Knowledge. The Vedic scholar Kashyap renders *go* or *gobhir* as "rays of light." Indeed, in most situations they are. This is exactly the conventional interpretation of *go* or *gobhir.* Kashyap and other scholars follow this meaning first ascribed by Sri Aurobindo, and render *go* or *gobhir* "ray-cow," "rays of intuition," "rays of knowledge," or the like. Monier Williams offers a more specific definition. Monier Williams, the authoritative dictionary of Sanskrit, defines *go* or *gobhir* as "herds of the sky," or skylight or the light from the collective stellar population, from stars, planets, or other apparent astronomical phenomena or events. In reality, *go* or *gobhir* are all of these. They are indeed the flickers of light we see in the evening sky, but those white dots transmit the wisdom of the collective stellar population, wisdom in which gives the worshiper the "rays of intuition," "rays of knowledge," needed for the spiritual journey. It is exactly this knowledge, wisdom, and intuition which is obstructed by Vrtra and which Indra and Tvastr release for the worshiper.

The lunar house of Indra with the weapon created by Tvastr and with the power of Chitra in conjunction with the zodiacal house of Vrscika is the Lord of the Cattle, metaphoric language for Knowledge or the Mind. (RV 1.101.4; 3.21.4; 4.24.1; 7.86.6; 10.108.3.)

- The lunar house of Indra with the weapon created by Tvastr and with the power
- of Chitra in conjunction with the zodiacal house of Vrscika collects all the cows. (RV 3.54.15.)
- The lunar house of Indra with the weapon created by Tvastr and with the power of Chitra in conjunction with the zodiacal house of Vrscika wins the cows, the Sun, and the Horses. (RV 3.34.9.)
- The lunar house of Indra with the weapon created by Tvastr and with the power of Chitra in conjunction with the zodiacal house of Vrscika shows the cows to the worshiper. (RV 3.31.21.)

- The lunar house of Indra with the weapon created by Tvastr and with the power of Chitra in conjunction with the zodiacal house of Vrscika breaks open the pens which restrained the cows. (RV 4.16.8.)
- The lunar house of Indra uses the weapon created by Tvastr and with the power of Chitra in conjunction with the zodiacal house of Vrscika to uncover the hidden ray-cows. (RV 8.63.3.)
- The lunar house of Indra with the weapon created by Tvastr and with the power of Chitra in conjunction with the zodiacal house of Vrscika releases or is the giver of the cows (knowledge or the light of consciousness). (RV 2.12.3; 2.14.3; 2.19.3; 2.20.5; 2.24.3, 6; 2.30.7; 3.30.14, 20, 21; 3.31.8; 3.44.5; 3..47.4; 3.38.7; 3.39.6; 3.50.3; 4.9.7;4.17.10, 11; 4.20.8; 4.22.5; 4.24.1; 5.45.1; 5.86.4; 8.45.19 6.17.3; 1.32.1-15 (released the ray-cows and waters).)
- The lunar house of Indra, with the weapon created by Tvastr and with the power of Chitra in conjunction with the zodiacal house of Vrscika, releases or is the giver of light (Truth). (RV 1.42.2; 1.100.8; 2.12.3; 2.11.18; 2.14.3; 2.21.4; 2.24.3, 6; 3.30.14, 20, 21; 3.34.4.; 3.38.7; 3.39.7; 4.19.7; 4.22.5, 10..)

Monier Williams assigns the following meanings to the light of *jyotir*:

- Moonlight.
- The light representing the divine principle of life or intelligence and/or the source of intelligence.

The import of Vrtra to *jyotir* is similarly profound and far-reaching. Vrtra is a concealer; it obstructs and obfuscates the inner truth from within. Once Vrtra is overtaken that inner truth of *jyotir* is revealed. The light of *jyotir* was released when Indra slew Vrtra with the weapon created by Tvastr and with the power of Chitra in conjunction with the zodiacal house of Vrscika. (RV 2.11.8.)

- With the dual Vedic forces of Agni-Soma, when Vrtra was slain, the divine light of *jyotir* was created for the benefit of all sentient beings. (RV 1.93.4.)

- The Vedic force of Indra is the winner of light (*jyotir*) as a result of being victorious over Vrtra. (RV 3.34.34.)

Other passages reveal that the light of *jyotir* resulted from the death of Vrtra at the hands of Surya. (RV 10.170.2.) According to this rc (mantra) the struggle with Vrtra was very much seen as a struggle between two forces — *Rta*, the inner essence of the truth of the Vedic dharma and Vrtra, which, because he is in reality that which covers or obscures *Rta*, the inner essence of the Vedic dharma, that which is diametrically the opposite of the inner essence of the truth of the Vedic dharma. In other passages, Indra, through *Tapas*, the intense and austere practice of meditative contemplation, creates the framework for the Vedic dharma:

- The *Tapas* of the lunar house of Indra with the weapon created by Tvastr and with the power of Chitra in conjunction with the zodiacal house of Vrscika destroys Vrtra. (RV 1.55.1.)
- *Rta* is born at the request of the lunar house of Varuna (Lord Protector of the Dynamic Cosmic Order). (RV1 .105.15.) This means Indra was instrumental in creating the Vedic dharma.
- Through the *Tapas* of Indra with the weapon created by Tvastr and with the power of Chitra in conjunction with the zodiacal house of Vrscika, he establishes the Svar. (RV 3.34.4.)
- The *Tapas* of the lunar house of Indra with the weapon created by Tvastr and with the power of Chitra in conjunction with the zodiacal house of Vrscika creates the Sky (i.e., the Mid-World) after Vrtra's death. (RV 10.167.1.)

When Vrtra is overcome by the lunar house of Indra and Tvastr, Bliss is the ultimate reward. It is a Bliss born from the inner recesses of the Vedic dharma, conveyed to the worshiper, and used in the spiritual journey towards ultimate salvation and liberation.

With the Power of the Svasti Asterism, the Lunar house of Vayu Dispenses the Spiritual Endowment of Sukha, Profound Spiritual Fulfillment and Happiness, in Conjunction with the Zodiacal House of Tula (Libra)

Vayu is traditionally known in the Vedic dharma as the deity of prana, breath, life force. Vayu represents the Vedic element of Air. Vayu is ruled by Rudra, who is a manifestation of the Fire of Agni in the firmament. The Vedic astrologer knows Vayu as the dispenser of sukha, which is deep Spiritual Fulfillment, Happiness. Vayu dispenses Sukha through the zodiacal house of Tula (Virgo), and the lunar house of Svasti (Srati).

There is no mystery to this spiritual endowment. In addition to being the seat of deep spiritual fulfillment and happiness, Sukha has an element of speed, lightness and brightness which endows sentient and non-sentient beings the glow of the divine fulfillment the name implies. The worshiper acquires this contentment.

Vayu is the Vedic force of the prana, the principle of life. Vayu, with the power from Svasti and in conjunction with the zodiacal house of Vrscika, endows also to non-sentient objects and natural phenomena in the Vedic dharma. Thus,

- while the Lunar house of Vayu endows *sukha* to the worshiper with the power of Svasti and in conjunction with the zodiacal house of Tula (Virgo), Rbhus, who dwells in the Sun's radius (AB, 3.30), fashioned the fast-speeding chariot for the Asvins. (RV 1.92.10.) The Vedic astrologer interprets this to mean that the Rbhus is responsible for creating the Asvini asterism and the power inherent in it.
- Similarly, Dawn is said to ride on its bright chariot. The "bright chariot" is the new day which Dawn awakens.

The next asterism provides the principle which governs the dispensation of spiritual endowments to the worshiper and non-sentient objects and natural phenomena in the Vedic dharma.

In his Capacity of Ruling the Vasakra Asterism, the Lunar house of India/Agni Dispenses, and the Worshiper Learns, the Spiritual Endowment of *Radha* (Spiritual Increase, Great Achievements)

The Vasakra asterism is the combination of formidable and complex Vedic powers, Agni and Indra. Agni is the God of Fire and the presiding force behind the Principle of Transformation, and Indra is Lunar house powering the Principle of Increase; Agni represents the Vedic element of Fire, and Indra with Soma represents the Vedic element of Akasha. These Vedic elements represent tremendous physical and subtle forces.

- The Sun, Agni, in alignment with Indra, dispenses the spiritual endowment of radha (Spiritual Increase, Great Achievements). Agni dispenses these endowments through the agencies of the Sun, the zodiacal houses of Mesa (Aries) and Vrsabha (Taurus).
- Indra gives the spark of existence to dead, inert matter. Once enlivened, the fields operate to sustain all dimensions in the cosmos. Indra, in his capacity as the presiding deity of the planet Jupiter, the zodiacal houses of Dhanus (Saggitarius), and the lunar house of asterism of Jyestra.
- Indra, with Tvastr, slays Vrtra to release the Vedic fields from time-space. This is done through the power of the asterism of Chitra and zodiacal house of Tula (Virgo).

There is a synergy among these three cosmic forces.

- Both Indra and Tvastr are supplicants of Agni. Tvastr, a terrestrial manifestation of Agni and fabricated Vayra, Indra's weapon which killed Vrtra. When Indra slew Vrtra, he acted as an incarnation of Agni. The release of these Vedic fields is accomplished by Indra as an incarnation of Agni, taken together, provide the medium wherefrom radha (Spiritual Increase, Great Achievements) is dispensed.

The Lunar house of Agni represents in the broadest possible terms the Vedic principle of Change and Transformation. Agni is the Fire of Change and Transformation. Related to the Vedic concept of Change and Transformation is Increase. Increase is an esoteric, yet important, element in the Vedic dharma. Increase is what it is all about. There can be no development — upward movement, downward movement, spiritual or otherwise — without Increase. Increase is the practical means of the worshiper to gain the spiritual endowments provided in the Vedas. More generally the only means by which the fire of Change and Transformation may occur. Agni is the guiding force for the power of Increase.

The idea of increase is expressed in the fact that the spiritual development of the worshiper admits to the addition of qualities not present before of characteristics not previously exhibited. In many cases, previous views are modified, some are outright discarded. It is the very essence of sacrifice. Sacrifice is basically a giving and taking.

The fire of giving and taking is grounded in the Two-Dimensional Universe which serves as the basis for the material world. The rising of the Sun gives rise to the appearance of the Moon, Day rises to bring in the night, Hot is the flip side of Cold. This dynamic was not unknown in Vedic literature. The Chandogya Upanishad recognizes the dichotomy of pleasant and unpleasant smells, Truth and Falsity, pleasant and unpleasant sounds, and even pleasant and unpleasant thoughts. This dichotomy is grounded on the existence of Good and Evil. But even with these polar opposites there comes a point where there is unification. This is the purpose of Increase and implies the importance of Soma in the resolution of this push and pull. The chaotic Two-Dimensional universe is resolved with the worshiper's spiritual awakening. In the process of spiritual awakening, the world and its perception are different because the worshiper is different. The old worshiper is discharged in exchange of the new. The sacrifice of the higher element produces an increase of the lower is called an out-and-out increase: it indicates the spirit that alone has power to help the world. Sacrifice thus becomes a prominent feature of increase, because it is a product of a give and take process.

As Richard Wilhelm, commenting on the I-Ching, once observed, "Sacrifice on the part of those above for the increase of those below fills the people with a sense of joy and gratitude that is extremely valuable for the flowering of the commonwealth. When people are thus devoted to their leaders, undertakings are possible, and even difficult and dangerous enterprises will succeed. Therefore in such times of progress and successful development it is necessary to work and make the best use of time. This time resembles that of the marriage of heaven and earth, when the earth partakes of the creative power of heaven, forming and bringing forth living beings. The time of increase does not endure; therefore it must be utilized while it lasts."

Here however is where the I-Ching and Vedas depart. Where the I-Ching credits the worshiper for this increase, in the Vedic dharma, Agni is the agent for increase. (RV 5.16.7, 5.17.5.) Thus, it is said that

- Agni obtains his powers of Increase from the Waters, from the foundation of the Vedic dharma itself. (RV 1.95.5.)
- The Lunar house and Vedic force of Agni supplies the means of increase in every aspect of the worshiper's life. (RV 5.10.3.)
- We will soon meet Parjanya, the Fire of Regeneration. Parjanya's Fire of Regeneration increases the spiritual fire of Agni. (RV 7.101.3.)
- The Lunar house and Vedic force of Agni in its manifestation as the Bull increases the life of the worshiper. As the Bull, the change and transformation effected by Agni is accomplished through regeneration, which the Bull symbolizes. (RV 1.31.5.)
- The lunar house of Agni's supplies the source and capacity of Increase in the worshiper from the brilliance of his light. (RV 1.71.8.) It seems rather self-evident that there should be some correspondence between fire, flames and light. There is another aspect in the symbolic meaning of Light. Light is associated with Illumination and Consciousness, and Agni is considered the Light of Consciousness.
- The divine force and energy of Agni, in its manifestation as Jatavedas, is the source of Increase for the Vedic dharma as a whole. (RV 1.87.5.)

The Veda states that the Increase of Agni will "prosper" the worshiper, be a source of wealth. (RV 1.92.11.) We need to be clear on what is meant by "wealth." The Veda speaks of "benefits," and "riches." These references are not to taken literally to mean material wealth. There is a symbolic meaning to "wealth," "benefits," and "riches." The goal of the worshiper's spiritual journey is to obtain those spiritual benefits which enrich the worshiper's soul. Ostensibly, the Lunar house of Agni, in his aspect as the Sacrificial Fire, provides these spiritual endowments and entitlements to the worshiper. (RV 7.10.3.) The worshiper receives these riches once the worshiper stands before the Sacrificial Fire (RV 8. 44.15), laying bare the worshiper's soul for renewal. These riches are interpreted to mean the specific characteristics of the spiritual increase personally experienced by the worshiper. The Spiritual Fire of Agni creates and instills in the worshiper the desire to seek the same during the spiritual journey. (RV 6.1.3.) The Spiritual Fire of Agni casts a light on the path the worshiper should tread to achieve these riches, (RV 6.1.3), although not completely. In a manner of speech relatively common in the Rg Veda, these spiritual endowments are the "treasures" obtained by Agni in his manifestation of the Sacrificial Fire. The spiritual endowments and benefits — the worshiper's prosperity — is made possible through the process of Increase.

In his Capacity of Ruling the Anuradha Asterism, the Lunar house of Mitra Dispenses, and the Worshiper Learns, the Spiritual Endowment of Response.

Mitra has essentially the same attributes as his counterpart, Varuna, as the principal guardian of the inner essence of the Vedic dharma, *Rta*, the breaches of which are punished. (*https://en.wikipedia.org/wiki/Mitra_(Vedic)*.) The Vedic astrologer knows Mitra as the dispenser of Response, through the asterism of Anuradha and in conjunction with the zodiacal house of Vrscika (Scorpio). Mitra dispenses this spiritual endowment additionally with the assistance of Indra in his capacity as the presiding deity of the planet Jupiter.

The name of the asterism aligned with Mitra — "Anuradha" — consists of two different roots, *"anu"* + *"radha."* The authoritative Monier Williams dictionary of Sanskrit has this to say about "Anu": Anu: "is a prefix to verbs and nouns, expresses) after, along, alongside, lengthwise, near to, under, subordinate to, with. (When prefixed to nouns, especially in adverbial compounds), according to, severally, each by each, orderly, methodically, one after another, repeatedly." "Radha" as employed by the Vedic astrologer is Increase, generally, and Spiritual Increase as applied to the worshiper. Anuradha accordingly means that which is consistently associated with Increase or spiritual increase. The Lunar house of Mitra, through its asterism Anuradha responds to the worshiper with Increase of any kind to the worshiper.

The spiritual endowment dispensed by Mitra through the asterism of Anuradha is Response. It is a Response which informs the quality of Increase. This is related to the spiritual endowments dispensed by Agni, the Sun, through the power of the asterism of Krittika, through the zodiacal houses of Mesa (Aries) and Vrsabha (Taurus), and Prajapati, through the asterism of Rohini, through the zodiacal house of Vrsabha (Taurus).

In his Capacity of Ruling the Jyestra Asterism, the Lunar house of Indra Dispenses, and the Worshiper Learns, the Spiritual Endowment of Happiness.

Indra, a prominent Vedic deity, gives the spark of existence to dead, inert matter. Once enlivened, the Vedic fields operate to sustain all dimensions in the cosmos. Once enlivened, these fields operate to sustain all dimensions in the cosmos. Indra, in his capacity as the presiding deity of the planet Jupiter, in the zodiacal houses of Vrscika (Scorpio) and the lunar house of asterism of Jyestra, slays Vrtra to release the Vedic fields from confines of physical time-space. For this reason, with Soma Indra represents the Vedic element of Akasha, the vast expanse of the aether pervading the Vedic dharma, the physical foundation of the Vedic fields. The release of these Vedic fields is accomplished by Indra as an incarnation of Agni. The Vedic astrologer knows Indra as the dispenser of Happiness. Indra dispenses this spiritual endowment additionally in his capacity as the presiding deity of the planet Jupiter.

Indra is a complex amalgamation of Vedic forces. The lunar house of Indra is an extremely diverse complex Vedic divine force:

- Whereas the lunar house of Agni the Sun, through the power of the asterism of Krittika, is consciousness itself, Indra bestows that consciousness to the worshiper in the form of knowledge.
- If the lunar house of Agni is the personification of the Eternal Fire of Change, which partially subsumes consciousness, the lunar house of Indra is the personification of the force of that consciousness, translated into intelligence, knowledge, discernment, and further the agent of the product of these attributes, divine grace.
- If the lunar house of Agni is the personification of the Vital Life force and the force of the light of consciousness, then Indra is simply the personification of the strength and power through his attributes.
- If the lunar house of Agni expiates the sins of the worshiper, the lunar house of Indra inheres in the principle of the strength of intelligence and grace.

- If the lunar house of Agni expiates the sins of the worshiper, the lunar house of Indra is the over-arching symbol of Divine Grace.

For all these reasons, the essence of Indra is known as *Bala* (RV 1.37.12; 1.80.8; 1.179.6; 3.53.18; 5.57.6; 6.47.30; 7.82.3; 9.113.1; 10.116.5; 10.133.5), the dynamic force that unifies and intensifies the powers intelligence, knowledge, discernment, and divine grace. These qualities work to create a complex fabric of cosmic forces meandering across the expanse of the Vedic dharma. These qualities of strength and resilience are reflected in the role of Indra in the worshiper's spiritual journey.

- The power of Indra, through the Nakshatra of Jyestra and the zodiacal house of Vrscika (Scorpio), works in alignment with Soma, whose power is obtained from Mrgashirsha and the zodiacal houses of Mithuna (Gemini) and Vrsabha (Taurus), defines the path to *Rta*, the inner essence of the Vedic dharma. (RV 6.44.8.)
- This power of Indra, through the Nakshatra of Jyestra and the zodiacal house of Vrscika (Scorpio), leads the worshiper during the spiritual journey. (RV 10.133.6.)

The scope and powers of Indra are defined from the etymological derivations obtained from the name of Indra. For instance, these attributes are realized in:

- *Indriyam.* (RV 1.55.4; 1.84.1; 1.85.2; 1.103.1; 2.16.3; 4.24.5; 4.30.23; 6.27.3, 4; 8.3.13; 8.12.8; 8.15.7; 8.52.7; 8.59.5; 8.93.27; 9.23.5; 9.30.2; 9.48.5; 9.92.1; 10.36.8; 10.65.10; 10.113.3; 10.124.8.) This is the root signifying the sensory organs, the human organs responsible for hearing, seeing, feeling, etc. In the language of the Vedas, the worshiper's knowledge of the outside world is obtained through the information acquired through the senses. Under this aspect of its divine force, Indra is the energy powering the force of sensory knowledge.
- *Indhate.* (RV 1.22.21; 1.36.4, 7; 1.170.4; 2.35.11; 3.10.1, 9; 3.13.5; 3.27.11; 4.8.5; 5.7.2; 6.2.3; 6.16.48; 7.16.4; 8.43.27; 8.45.1; 8.60.15; 10.69.1.) To kindle, to start the fire. Before the worshiper

may become a knowing subject, it must first have the capacity of spiritual awareness and consciousness. This aspect is implicated in Indra. *Indhate* is the aspect of *Bala* (Indra) which simulates that awareness and consciousness. This is the root for the verb "kindle." The kindling refers to that which ignites the Sacrificial Fire. The Sacrificial Fire is symbolic of the light of consciousness obtained through knowledge. The kindling is the spark that ignites the force of consciousness. Indra represents the spark of this energy of consciousness.

- *Indha.* (RV 7.1.16; 7.8.1.) Embers — an etymological cognate for Bala (Indra) — are the heated coals after the fire has subsided, and these embers remain after the Sacrificial Fire has been ignited. If the Sacrificial Fire represents knowledge, the embers represent the irreducible essence of that fire. Indra represents the essence of this aspect of the sacrifice and resultant knowledge.

- *Indo.* (RV 8.92.4; 9.1.5; 9.2.1; 9.8.7; 9.23.6; 9.24.5; 9.31.6; 9.35.2; 9.43.4; 9.45.6; 9.55.2; 9.59.4; 9.63.30; 9.64.13, 25; 9.66.14; 9.67.31; 9.86.18, 4; 9.90.6; 9.97.29; 9.98.1, 4; 9.104.5; 9.105.5; 9.106.7; 9.114.1.) *Indo* is most commonly associated with Soma, the dynamic force of Purification and Divine Union. Indu is an epithet for the Soma juice, literally a "drop" of Soma juice to induce the divine union of the worshiper. The conjunction of this dynamic force with that of the energy of consciousness and knowledge results in a transcendental knowledge which inheres in *indu.* In this aspect of Indra represents the Divine Mind.

- *Indrasha* (RV 1.2.5, 6; 1.18.5; 1.32.6, 10, 13; 1.135.4, 6, 13; 1.164.19; 1.166.12; 2.5.2-9; 2.41.11; 3.25.4; 4.28.4; 4.37.6; 4.47.2, 3; 4.49.3; 4.50.10; 5.51.6, 14; 6.69.8; 7.97.10; 7.98.7; 8.6.5; 8.33.17; 8.34.16; 8.62.9; 8.34.16; 8.33.1; 8.34.16; 8.62.9; 8.69.7; 9.19.2;9;95.5; 10.89.3;10.90.13; 10.105.4; 10.173.5), the vital principle that conjoins the active attributes of *Bala* (Indra) and Vayu (Breath).

- *Indrasya.* The simple possessive of *Bala* (Indra), those attributes which are possessed of *Bala* (Indra).

- *Indram.* That which pertains to or is manifested in *Bala* (Indra), prana, the life-force regulating the in-breath and out-breath.

- *Indrena.* (RV 1.6.7; 1.14.10; 1.23.9; 1.53.4; 1.84.10; 1.101.11; 2.18.8; 2.23.18; 3.4.11; 3.60.4; 4.34.11; 5.11.2; 5.51.10; 6.44.22; 6.47.29; 7.2.11; 7.1815; 7.32.6; 7.48.2; 8.9.12; 8.14.19; 8.40.6; 8.76.4; 8.9.4; 8.96.6; 9.11.9; 9.87.9; 9.103.5; 10.15.10; 10.62.7; 10.103.2; 10.108.4.) That which is accomplished according to the attributes or contains the qualities of *Bala* (Indra).
- *Indro.* The quintessence, sum total, of the attributes of *Bala* (Indra).
- *Indram.* That which pertains to or is manifested in *Bala* (Indra), prana, the life-force regulating the in-breath and out-breath.
- *Indrena.* (RV 1.6.7; 1.14.10; 1.23.9; 1.53.4; 1.84.10; 1.101.11; 2.18.8; 2.23.18; 3.4.11; 3.60.4; 4.34.11; 5.11.2; 5.51.10; 6.44.22; 6.47.29; 7.2.11; 7.1815; 7.32.6; 7.48.2; 8.9.12; 8.14.19; 8.40.6; 8.76.4; 8.9.4; 8.96.6; 9.11.9; 9.87.9; 9.103.5; 10.15.10; 10.62.7; 10.103.2; 10.108.4.) That which is accomplished according to the attributes or contains the qualities of *Bala* (Indra).
- *Indro.* The quintessence, sum total, of the attributes of *Bala* (Indra).

The asterism Jyestra bestows several astral powers to the Vedic force of Indra:

- On the one hand, Indra represents the Sun. (RV 4.31.5-6, 15.)
- On the other hand, Indra represents the many faces of the Moon, either as the Bright Moon (RV 1.52.9), the Full Moon (RV 1.53.2), the Waning Moon (RV 8.96.1, 4), or the Moon proper. (RV 8.81.9; 9.93.5; 10.134.3.)

Indra acts in alignment with the lunar mansion of Soma, Mrgashirsha, to bestow the spiritual endowments to the worshiper. The endowment dispensed by the lunar mansion of Indra, Jyestra, is Happiness, which is increased by the lunar mansion of Soma, which dispenses Bliss. This is as much to do with the phases of the Moon actually undertaken by the Vedic force of Indra. (Mikhailov, *RgVedic Studies* (2001), p. 21.) In these movements:

- Indra represents the waning of the Moon phases. (RV 8.96.1.) The waning of the Moon is accomplished with the assistance of Usas, the Dawn. In this rc (mantra) it is revealed that opens the night to make way for Indra.

- Indra represents the waxing of the Moon phases. (RV 8.96.4.) In this respect, Indra represents Cyavana, the Waxing Moon.

The waning and waxing of the Moon are coalesced in the Moon, Soma, whose lunar mansion, Mrgashirsha, confers Bliss to the worshiper. The Lunar house of Indra is the "Showerer of gifts." (*vRSabha/*). (RV 3.47.5.) These are the spiritual gifts dispensed by the Lunar house of Indra as a consequence of overcoming Vrtra. These spiritual riches are dispensed with the power of Jyestra asterism and the zodiacal house of Vrscika (Scorpio). These spiritual riches produce Happiness, the spiritual endowment dispensed by Indra. The best spiritual gift is yet to come in the next lunar house.

In his Capacity of Ruling the Mula Asterism, the Lunar house of Nirrti Dispenses, and the Worshiper Learns, the Spiritual Endowment of *Amrtra* (The Eternal, Undying Principle)

Nirrti is a nebulous Vedic force, one of the many from which the worshiper seeks protection. The nature of Nirrti's protection is in the form of its spiritual endowment, *amrtra*, which is sometimes known as "Ambrosia," but is better understood as "the Eternal, Undying Principle." *Amrta* is made up of two components. Monier Williams notes that *"am"* is an interjection of assent or recollection + *Rta* ("the essence of the inner truth of the Vedic dharma"). *Amrtra* thus connotes anything that encourages or supports action towards the inner essence of the Vedic dharma. It becomes the assurance the worshiper has in the spiritual journey; namely, a journey properly and successfully done yields the discovery of the inner essence of the Vedic dharma. It constitutes protection on the salvation and liberation of the worshiper's soul. It is, of sorts, a form of insurance policy. This is far from the checkered reputation Nirrti has in the Veda, where she is known as the deity of Bad Luck. (RV 7.104.11.) The Vedic astrologer, however, knows that this protection is endowed to the worshiper from the power emitted from the Mula asterism and conveyed in conjunction with the zodiacal house of Dhanus (Saggitarius) and with the additional assistance of Yama as the presiding deity of Saturn.

Considered together, *amrta*, rendered as "immortality" or "ambrosia" becomes

- That which serves, pertains to, concerns, the Vedic dharma.
- The essence of the Vedic dharma, immortality and ambrosia being a part of that essence.

Amrta is the essence of *Rta and* gives a greater and deeper meaning not only to the concept of Rta but to the entire Veda. To be clear, *amrta* in certain rcs (mantras) legitimately conveys the meaning of "immortality" or "ambrosia." Ambrosia as the essence of the Rta is illustrated in instances where that essence is consumed by the dynamic Vedic energies. The prominent consumers are:

- Agni, the Fire of Change, the Sun, the dispenser of the inner secret of yajna and Divine Response by the power of the asterism of Krittika, in conjunction with the zodiacal houses of Mesa (Aries) and Vrsabha (Taurus). (RV 5.3.4.)
- Indra, the presiding deity of Jupiter, the dispenser of Happiness by the power of the asterism of Jyestra, in conjunction with the zodiacal house of Vrscika (Scorpio). (RV 6.37.3.)
- The Maruts. (RV 5.57.5.) Famously, the Maruts are the helpers to the Vedic force of Indra. They are also a manifestation of Agni, one of the Fires of the Firmament.

The Vedic astrologer knows that *amrta*, the essence of the dynamic Vedic dharma, consists of divine matter. That essence is centered on Soma, the Moon, who dispenses Bliss through the power of the asterism of Mrgashirsha in conjunction with the zodiacal houses of Mithuna (Gemini) and Vrsabha (Taurus). In later yoga traditions *amrta* became associated with the highest states of Consciousness, usually acquired after prolonged *Tapas* and yogic austerities. These later traditions hail directly from the Vedas and are the offspring of the spiritual endowments of the Nakshatras:

- When the Soma plant is effused, distilled and purified, it becomes ambrosia, the essence of the dynamic cosmic order. (RV 6..44.23.)
- Once purified, Soma becomes the essence of the dynamic cosmic order. (RV 8.74.5; 9.74.6.)
- Madhu, that aspect of Soma which refers to divine ecstacy, confers the essence of the dynamic cosmic order to the worshiper at the sacrifice. (RV 9.113.11.)
- Soma, the Moon, the dispenser of Bliss through the power of the asterism of Mrgashirsha in conjunction with the zodiacal houses of Mithuna (Gemini) and Vrsabha (Taurus) is the *dha/rmann Rta/ sya,*—"the support of Rta—signifying that it provides the support and sustenance of the cosmic order. (RV 9.7.1; 9.110.4.)
- Soma, the Moon, the dispenser of Bliss through the power of the asterism of Mrgashirsha in conjunction with the zodiacal houses of Mithuna (Gemini) and Vrsabha (Taurus) is created for the dharma (support) of Rta (the cosmic order). RV 9.110.4

reveals that Soma, the Moon, the dispenser of Bliss through the power of the asterism of Mrgashirsha in conjunction with the zodiacal houses of Mithuna (Gemini) and Vrsabha (Taurus) is the supporter of *amrta*, ambrosia, the elixir that confers immortality.

- Soma, the Moon, the dispenser of Bliss through the power of the asterism of Mrgashirsha in conjunction with the zodiacal houses of Mithuna (Gemini) and Vrsabha (Taurus) is responsible for the production of ambrosia (*amrta*), the liquid which confers divination. (RV 9.70.4.)

The logical byproduct of these spiritual endowments are fully described in the next lunar mansion.

In his Capacity of Ruling the Purva Ashada Asterism, the Lunar house of Apas Dispenses, and the Worshiper Learns, the Spiritual Endowment of *Anna* (Food).

Apas is the deification of the essence of the Vedic dharma, the Waters. Apas represents the Vedic element of Water. The Waters make a frequent appearance in this book and constitute the very nature of the Vedic dharma, which is fluidity and flow. Just as the primordial presence of the cosmic waters provided the fodder for the indeterminate, indiscriminate, mass of darkness which pervaded the evolution of the Vedic dharma and all that followed thereafter, the spiritual endowment dispensed by Apas is *anna*, food.

You, Dear Reader, should know by now that the Rg Veda is a scripture written in symbols. Those symbols are the result of the great antiquity of the Veda, the attempt of the Rishiis to reveal the secrets of the Vedic dharma in recognizable language, and the ability of simple wording to carry multiple meanings. *Anna* is one good example. *Anna*, food, carries with it a highly symbolic meaning. In the Rg Veda, food is takes several forms.

- Food is associated with sustenance. (RV 5.70.2.)
- Food is life. (RV 8.3.24.)
- Soma is food. (RV 9.55.2, 9.41.4, 9.61.1, 3, 9.9.63.2, 9.64.13, 9.65.13, 9.66.4, 23, 31, 9.71.8, 9.74.2, 3, 9.85.3, 9.91.5, 9.97.5, 9.99.2, 9.101.11, 9.104. (Soma food of the gods), 10.94.6.)
- Food is associated with wealth. (RV 8.5.36.)
- Food is also associated with progeny (RV 7.96.6, 9.8.9, 9.13.3, 9.65.21), which, because a person can expect to live on after death through his or her issue, is representative of immortality.
- Water or the waters are considered food. (RV 1.30.1, 1.33.11, 1.52.2, 1.63.8, 1.100.5, 2.34.5, 2.35.1, 11, 2.41.18, 3.4.7, SPB 2.1.1.3, 13.8.1.4, 13.)

Food is important to the sacrifice. In the Veda references to food abound. Entreaties for food are ubiquitous. The request for food is another example of coded language signifying a much deeper meaning. The Vedic divine force of death was not Yama but Mrtyu. (Merh, Yama, *The Glorious Lord of the Other World*, p. 62.) Mrtyu, was seen as the lord over humanity, the personification of death, the Grim Reaper. Mrtyu was the consumer of mortal being or mortal beings. (SPB 10.1.3.1.) Hunger, indeed, was death. (SPB 10.6.5.1.) If hunger is death, food is life, and life of a god is eternal. Considering that the ruling deity is Apas, it is not surprising that the spiritual endowment for the Purva Ashada asterism is Food. Food is the coded language of the Veda, representing:

- The immortal life, or the request for the life divine,
- Salvation, or the request for salvation,
- Liberation, or the request for liberation, moksa,
- The divine, eternal energy which fuels liberation, salvation or the life divine.

Food is the by-product of these Vedic forces. In fact, the entire natural order, the Vedic dharma, is divided into two parts, the eater and the eaten. (SPB 10.6.2.1.) In the coded language of the Veda, to say something is food is to refer to the entire universe and all that exist in it. (BU 1.5.1.) Sankara, in his Commentary of this portion of the Brhadaranyakaupanishad, states that this is tantamount to saying that Food is the Object.

Agni, the Sun, the dispenser of the inner secrets of *yajna* and Divine Response through the power of Krittika, is the Eater of Food, both in his physical aspect of fire and in the sacrificial aspect as the fire altar. (SPB 10.6.2.2.) In all aspects, Agni, the Sun, the dispenser of the inner secrets of *yajna* and Divine Response through the power of Krittika, is the Eater of Food. (SPB 2.1.4.28, 2.2.1.1, 2.4.4.1, 8.6.3.5, 10.4.1.11, 11.1.6.9.) As we have seen, the "Eater" can mean anything from the dissolving entity of the Vedic dharma, to the Vedic force which superimposes the material universe, to obtaining knowledge, enlightenment, or consciousness. As the Eater, Agni, the Sun, the dispenser of the inner secrets of *yajna* and Divine Response through the power of Krittika, produces food again and again. In the fire of producing food again and again, the entire natural order is created, recycled and re-created.

This is not a power reserved only to Vedic deities. The worshiper is included as well. All the talk about "conquering death" or "becoming immortal" is coded language signifying that Agni, the Sun, the dispenser of the inner secrets of *yajna* and Divine Response through the power of Krittika, transforms the worshiper, ordinarily an object in the natural order, to the Subject. Taking food to this deeper level of meaning, once transformed into the Eater of food the worshiper is transformed:

- Is complete in Speech (SPB 3.9.1.9), meaning the worshiper is endowed with *logos*, the wisdom of the Vedic dharma.
- Stands in the midst of cattle (i.e., gains Knowledge, or food). (SPB 7.5.2.14.)

The "Eater" can mean anything from the dissolving entity of the Vedic dharma, to the Vedic force which superimposes the material universe, to obtaining knowledge, enlightenment, or consciousness. In effect, this is coded language of the Subject or the Absolute Self. That the Waters — the inner essence of the Vedic dharma — is the food itself implies a self-sacrifice presenting another instance of the give-and-take of the Vedic sacrifice ritual. The Vedic astrologer knows that this protection is endowed to the worshiper from the power emitted from the asterism of Purva Ashada and conveyed in conjunction with the zodiacal house of Dhanus (Saggitarius) and with the additional assistance of Yamas the presiding deity of Saturn.

In his Capacity of Ruling The Uttara Ashada Asterism, the Lunar house of Visvedevas Dispenses, and The Worshiper Learns, the Spiritual Endowment of Strength.

Visvedevas are the Vedic gods taken together as a whole group. (*https:// en. wikipedia.org/wiki/Visvedevas.*) The spiritual endowment dispensed by the Visvedevas is Strength, an appropriate endowment given that these Vedic forces taken together are indeed a formidable force to be reckoned. The Vedic astrologer knows the Visvedevas as dispensing this spiritual gift through the power emitted from the asterism of Uttara Ashada, the zodiacal house of Dhanus (Saggitarius); and with the additional assistance of Yama as the presiding deity of Saturn.

There is strength in numbers, and this is the source of the spiritual endowments offered by the Visvedevas. There is no great mystery about the spiritual endowment dispensed here. The only mystery is how the strength of this asterism is sought. The next lunar house attempts to answer that question.

In his Capacity of Ruling The Abhijit Asterism, the Lunar house of Brahma Dispenses, and the Worshiper Learns, the Spiritual Endowment of *Punya* (Offering to the Divine).

Brahma dispenses the punya, offerings made to the Divine. *Punya* is an essential element of the give-and-take of the sacrificial process. *Punya* is the representation of the "give" element of the give-and-take exchange. While modernly *punya* has been reduced to offerings of material objects, in the times of the Vedic astrologer *punya* was originally intended to be something more substantial. In those times, the worshiper offered the body, heart and soul at the sacrifice in the hopes of becoming born again. Brahma provides the framework for this exchange. This exchange is conducted through the power provided by the asterism Abhijit, in conjunction with the zodiacal house of Dhanus (Saggitarius), and with the additional assistance of Yama as the presiding deity of Saturn.

This Nakshatra encapsulates the essence of Vedic sacrifice. At its heart, Vedic sacrifice is all about the willing and voluntary sacrifice of the worshiper's body, mind, and spirit to god with the goal of experiencing the re-birth thereof. It is here in this self-surrender that the worshiper finds the spiritual basis from which spring the living of the worshiper's life in accordance with the Vedic dharma. It is here that the worshiper sits before the Fire Altar and opens the mind and heart to allow the consecrating Vedic forces and energies take possession of the Soul and mold it to their liking. It is here that spiritual renewal is situated, and it is under these circumstances that the worshiper is reborn. This is where the worshiper's spiritual journey begins. The worshiper places complete trust in the Vedic forces and energies. The worshiper's soul and body is like putty, the Vedic forces and energies are the artisan, and the finished product is the reborn Soul of the worshiper. Thereafter, as far as the worshiper is able, the worshiper lives consistent with the Vedic forces and energies and according to the Vedic dharma. This is the fire of self-surrender.

There is no mystery to self-surrender. An entire Sukta is devoted to the basic requirements for the worshiper to surrender to the Lunar house or energy. RV 1.57 lists those requirements. While the presiding deity of this Sukta is Indra, the incarnation of Agni, the mechanics of self-surrender can be applied to any Lunar house or energy.

- The worshiper meditates deep in the mind to offers the inner Speech to the Vedic force. (RV 1.77.1.)
- The worshiper's thoughts are clouded, the concentration is weak, there are dark thoughts. Indra, however, will take the golden Vayra to shatter the mountain — symbolic speech that represents the apparent size of these barriers — to cast these impediments away. (RV 1.57.2.)
- The worshiper brings offerings to the sacrifice. Those offerings are the worshiper, mind, body and soul. The worshiper belongs to the Vedic force. (RV 1.57.5.)

The first step of the Sacrifice is self-surrender, the giving of the worshiper's mind, heart and soul. There is an intricate exchange involved when the worshiper surrenders to the Vedic forces and energies. Self-Surrender arises from the very nature of worship. Whenever the worship invokes a Vedic force or energy, the worshiper goes to that Vedic force or energy which is channeled to the worshiper. (BG, 7.23.)

This was the original *punya* — offering the entire being of the worshiper. Over time that punya became an active object of desire on the part of the worshiper. In exchange for offering the worshiper's mind, body and soul, the worshiper sought the spiritual endowments offered by the Nakshatras. The worshiper seeks other spiritual benefits from this meditation. They are the following spiritual endowments revealed in this book by the Rishiis in AV 19.7.2-5:

- From Krittikas and Rohini the worshiper seeks to learn the secret of yajna and receive Divine Response.
- From Mrgashira the worshiper seeks bliss.
- From Ardra the worshiper seeks *sam*, union or conjunction.
- From Purnavasu the worshiper seeks to learn *sunrta*, or "true speech," which is any articulation which contributes to an understanding of the Vedic dharma (*Rta*).
- From Pushya the worshiper seeks beauty.
- From Ashlesha the worshiper seeks *bhanu*, the shining rays of light from the Nakshatras.

- From Magha the worshiper seeks assistance in understanding of *ayana*, or the guide to right conduct during the spiritual journey
- From the Phalgunis the worshiper seeks Good Works, or the assistance in correct action.
- From Hasta and Chitta the worshiper seeks bliss.
- From Svati the worshiper seeks *sukha*, or the profound and abiding Spiritual Fulfillment and Happiness.
- From Vishakha the worshiper seeks *radha*, or the concept and practice of Spiritual Increase, Great Achievements.
- From Anuradha the worshiper seeks a response.
- From Jyeshtha the worshiper seeks happiness.
- From Moola the worshiper seeks *amrta*, or that which is eternal and undying.
- From Purva Ashadha the worshiper seeks *anna*, or food.
- From Uttara Ashadha the worshiper seeks strength.
- From Abhijit the worshiper seeks *punya*, the offering.
- From Shravana and Shravishtha the worshiper seeks nourishment.
- From the two Proshthapada the worshiper seeks protection.
- From Revati and Ashvayuja the worshiper seeks *Bhaga*, or enjoyment.
- From Bharani the worshiper seeks spiritual riches.

Most of all the worshiper seeks to have these qualities incorporated in the worshiper's life through an intricate procedure of self-surrender and sacrifice. That offering was presented to Brahman and the power of the spiritual endowment of *punya* was furnished by the asterism Abhijit. Brahman, of course, appeared millennia after the Vedic times, and although mentioned in the Rg Veda, did not always occupy a significant role in the Vedic theogony. There is disagreement on this point among academic circles, but the Vedic astrologer believes that Brahman is simply relatively recent usurper for the duties of Agni. Not that this really matters. The Vedic astrologer recognizes that the wise speak of many separate deities, but they all refer to the one and only God, *Ekam*. (RV 1.164.46.) This applies with equal force in the Nakshatras, the asterisms in the Vedic dharma.

In his Capacity of Ruling the Sravana Asterism, the Lunar house of Vishnu Dispenses, and the Worshiper Learns, the Spiritual Endowment of Nourishment.

Visnu provides nourishment. This spiritual endowment is conveyed to the worshiper through the power provided by the asterism Sravana, in conjunction with the zodiacal house of Makara (Capricorn) with the additional assistance of Yama as the presiding deity of Saturn.

To enable Visnu to dispense the spiritual endowment of nourishment, the worshiper must actively seek nourishment. There are many entreaties in the Rg Veda from the worshiper for nourishment.

- The Veda generally cites many examples where the worshiper seeks nourishment, *pousti*. (RV 1.18.2; 1.31.5; 1.65.5; 1.77.5; 1.91.2; 1.122.7; 1.166.8; 2.4.4; 1.12.5; 1.13.4; 3.13.7; 4.3.7; 4.16.15; 4.33.2; 5.10.2; 6.2.1; 6.63.6; 7.59.12; 8.48.6; 8.59.7; 10.26.7; 10.86.5.)
- The Waters, the inner essence of the Vedic dharma, provides nourishment to the worshiper in the form of *pibanti*. (RV 1.23.18; 4.28.7; 8.94.5; 9.64.24 (as rasa); RV 10.85.5.)
- This is because the Waters is the Protector, *pita*, of the worshiper. (RV 1.46.4; 1.185.10; 4.17.17; 5.43.2; 5.83.6; 6.83.1; 6.75.5; 7.32.26; 10.22.3.)
- The Cows, *go* and *gobhir*, which symbolize the light of the Nakshatras, are also providers of nourishment. (RV 3.45.3.)

There are frequent references of the worshiper seeking "prosperity." Prosperity is spiritual endowment specifically conferred to the worshiper from the power of Mrgashirsha with the zodiacal houses of Mithuna (Gemini) and Vrsabha (Taurus) by Soma, the Moon. (RV 9.4.2; 9.55.1; 9.62.1; 9.67.5; 9.95.5; 9.97.5.) These requests and entreaties are not materialistically based; these are not demands for material prosperity, nourishment, or riches. Srisa Chandra Vasu remarks that wealth is used to connote "Knowledge" or "Thought," and is closely related to the "Vedas." (Vasu, *Daily Practices of the Hindus* (2000), pp. 180, 181.) Essentially they are requests for receiving spiritual nourishment, spiritual wealth and riches obtained from the knowledge and insights found in the Vedas to achieve spiritual prosperity. These are spiritual requests to achieve union with God, the divine, in the hopes of receiving spiritual prosperity, riches and nourishment. And so it for the Nakshatras. These spiritual endowments are part of the nourishment the worshiper needs for the spiritual journey.

In his Capacity of Ruling the Shatabhisha Asterism, the Lunar house of Varuna Dispenses, and the Worshiper Learns, the Spiritual Endowment of Greatness.

Varuna is the Vedic force administering of *Rta*, the over-arching principle of the Vedic dharma. The Vedic astrologer knows Varuna to be the dispenser of the spiritual endowment of Greatness, for once understood the worshiper indeed becomes "great." Varuna dispenses this spiritual endowment with the assistance of the planet Jupiter which itself is ruled by Indra. Varuna also dispenses Greatness to the worshiper through the lunar house or asterism Shatabhisha and the zodiacal house of Kumbha (Aquarius).

You also might guess, Dear Reader, that the cosmic struggle with Vrtr was far-reaching. The end of Vrtra touched many areas of the Vedic dharma. There were three specific events which impacted the Vedic dharma. Indeed, the Veda reveals that as the result of the slaying of Vrtra:

- Rta, the inner essence of the Vedic dharma, was born. (RV 1.105.15.)
- Varuna is installed as the Lord Protector of *Rta*, the inner essence of the Vedic dharma. (RV 10.124.5.)
- Varuna, Lord Protector of the Vedic dharma, and *Bala* (Indra) become rulers over the newly established world. (RV 3.30; 4.42.)

The laws of Rta are established by the dynamic Vedic energies inherent in Varuna. (RV 1.25.6, 8, 10; 8.27.3; 10.66.5, 8.) In implementing these established laws of Rta, and the other incidents of Rta, Varuna

- Varuna established the present system whereby the Nakshatras appear at night, do not appear during daylight, and are run with the phases of the Moon. (RV 1.24.10.) Indeed, Varuna, and other Vedic forces and energies, are identified with the moon. (RV 1.24.10; 1.27.6, 11, 12; 1.74.6; 5.101.4; 4.2.12; 4.16.19; 5.6.5; 3.25.3; 5.8.1; 1.6.5, 6; 5.10.4; 5.11.1; 5.61.16.)
- Establishes the paths of the planets, stars and constellations. (RV 1.24.8.)

- Establishes the two-dimensional universe of Heaven and Earth. (RV 6.70.1; 7.86.1.) The laws regulating this dimension of the universe is also implemented by Mitra-Varuna. (RV 5.13.7.)
- Establishes the three-dimensional universe of the earth, mid-earth and heavens. (RV 7.87.5.)
- Regulates the laws, with Mitra, regarding the dimension of the Three-Dimensional Universe. (RV 5.62.3.)
- Provides the support of the earth. (RV 5.3.7; 7.61.4.)

Varuna's involvement with the inner workings of the Vedic dharma has bearing on the spiritual gift dispensed in through this Lunar house. The greatness implicated in this Lunar house has everything to do with the majesty of the Vedic dharma itself. Through the lessons learned with and from this Lunar house the worshiper learns the path that must be tread in the spiritual journey and becomes adept at traversing through the existential levels of the Vedic dharma. This journey requires some protection, which is dispensed in the next Lunar house.

In his Capacity of Ruling the Purva Bhadrapada Asterism, the Lunar house of Ajikapada Dispenses, and the Worshiper Learns, the Spiritual Endowment of Protection.

Ajikapada is an ancient fire dragon. It stands for purification and penance. (*https://www.hindutsav.com/nakshatras/*.) It also is viewed as a form of Shiva, and a vehicle for the transport of Agni, the Sun, representing the cleansing spiritual power of fire. (*http:// www. bhavans.info/jyotisha/ nakshatra_purvabhadrapda. pdf*.) Purification, thus, is high in Ajikapada's estimation. The Vedic astrologer knows Ajikapada as the dispenser of Protection, through the astral offices of the asterism Purva Bhadrapada and zodiacal houses of Kumba (Aquarius) and Mina (Pisces). The protection offered by is in this form — purification. Ajikapada works closely with Agni, the Sun, and through the power of the asterism Krittika, disperse the spiritual endowments of protection/purification. To the Nakshatras protection is purification. The Vedic astrologer counts five methods of purification in the Vedas, principally taken from RV 1.140.2.

The Five Methods of Purification

There are some Suktas in the Rg Veda that stand out and communicate, collectively, the message of the Vedas. RV 1.140 is one such Sukta. The meaning of RV 1.140.2 pertains to the powers of Agni's force and energy to purify and cleanse. In a scripture amenable to interpretation and clothed in symbols such as the Rg Veda, one rc, RV 1.140.2, is more prone to multiple interpretation than most. The levels of meaning of this rc (mantra) (mantra) are legion. They include interpretations based on astronomical and alchemical meanings. The Tattiriya Brahmana says that there are five forms to Agni. (TB, 1.2.1.70.) In the same way, the Lunar house of Agni, the close supervisor and associate of Ajikapada, purifies in five different ways.

The purification powers of Agni, the Sun, with the power of Krittika, are foundational and self-originate from his own powers to blacken the forests. (RV 6.60.10.) This rc (mantra) (mantra) emphasizes how the reduction to ash is above all an act of purification, a final reduction to the most essential elements. The stages of purification can be seen in RV

1.140.2. This rc (mantra) implicates five methods of purification. The number is significant The number Five, a cardinal number in the Vedic dharma, resonates in the Five-Dimensional Universe. This existential plane is imbued with a higher level of subtlety than the Third-Dimensional Universe but does not rise to the subtlety of the Seven-Level Universe. RV 1.140.2 states that Agni, the Sun, the Fire of Change, is a "two-fold generated, devours the triple (sacrificial) food, and when the year expires renovates what has been eaten, and the Showerer (of benefits) is invigorated (in one form), by eating with the tongue of another, in a different form the restrainer (of) all consumes the forest trees." (Wilson translation). According to obscure language of this rc (mantra), the fire that travels from purification is made in five stages:

- Two-fold generated.
- Devours triple food.
- Renovates the food when year expires.
- The Showerer is invigorated by eating with the tongue of another.
- The restrainer consumes the forest trees.

The language of this rc (mantra) owes its obtuse meaning to the fact that it operates on so many levels. It is very possible that the "tongues of Agni" is figurative language for the flames of a fire or kindling. The phrase operates on many levels. The manner in which this phrase can be applied can be seen in a rc (mantra) found in the First Mandala, RV 140.2. According to the translation of Ralph Griffith, this rc (mantra) reads:

> Child of a double birth he grasps at triple food, in the year's course what he hath swallowed grows anew.

> He, by another's mouth and tongue a noble Bull, with other, as an elephant, consumes the trees.

Now granted, Griffith's translation is notorious for being among the most antiquated and inaccurate. Still, this rc (mantra) shows there are five elements to the powers of purification in Agni: (1) a two-fold birth, (2) devouring "triple food," (3) the food rejuvenates when the year expires,

(4) the Showerer (i.e., the Bull) is invigorated by eating with the tongue of another, and (5) the restrainer consumes the forest trees.

Agni is the Presiding Deity of this Sukta. This rc (mantra) can be found in Sukta 140 and this Sukta is notable in that it can be interpreted many ways and in many contexts. The flexibility of this Sukta demonstrates not only how rich the level of interpretation can take in interpreting the Veda, but also how the meaning remains relatively uniform despite the malleability of its meaning.

First Method: The Ritualistic Meaning of RV 1.140.2

This brings us to the first level of meaning — Sacrifice. This method of purification is grounded in a strictly ritualistic level, the meaning employed by Sayana of RV 1.140.2, the purification of fire at the sacrificial altar progresses in this manner:

Two-fold generated	Agni, the Sun, is kindled by rubbing two sticks
Devours triple food	The sacrificial altar consumes three different offerings: grhta, butter and Soma
Renovates the food when year expires	The ministrant recovers the oblation from the ladle
The Showerer is invigorated by eating with the tongue of another	The sacrificial fire is built with the offerings
The restrainer consumes the forest trees.	The sacrificial fire consumes, thereby purifying, the offerings

Second Method: Astronomical Meaning of RV 1.140.2

There is another level of meaning at work. There is an astronomical interpretation. The astronomical aspect of the Vedic dharma in many ways hold more currency than others. This aspect ties in the importance of the place and timing of the Sacrifice, which were calibrated by the ascertainment of astronomical phenomena, such as equinoxes and solstices, against the larger purview of the fulness and pervasion of the Vedic dharma.

Two-fold generated	Change (Agni) represents the unity of heaven and earth, the sun and the moon
Devours triple food	Change (Agni) pervades the earth, mid-earth, and atmosphere
Renovates the food when year expires	The Winter Solstice (Mahavrata), the beginning of the new calendar year
The Showerer is invigorated by eating with the tongue of another	The Vernal Equinox, that portion of the calendar year when regeneration is in progress
The restrainer consumes the forest trees.	The Summer Solstice, the warmest portion of the calendar year

There is yet another level of meaning. In this interpretation it has an alchemical meaning. If the astronomical meaning looked towards the macrocosmic fulness of the Vedic dharma, the alchemical meaning shifts to the microcosm, to ascertain the subtle basis of matter. The wonderful paradox in this change of perspective is that the farther one digs into the subtle basis of matter, the more the microcosm reflects and resembles the macrocosm.

Third Method: Alchemical Meaning of RV 1.140.2

Alchemy has been defined as "the art of liberating parts of the cosmos from temporal existence to achieve Salvation." (Kalyanaraman, *Indian Alchemy Soma in the Veda* (2004), p. xviii.) Switching gears, the yoga of Patanjali provides, among other things, several ways to disengage from the workings of the material world, and, deep in meditation, move towards samadhi, the ultimate unification with the Absolute Self. One such practice is *samyama*, the combined exercise of dharana, concentration, Dhyana, meditation, and samadhi. One such exercise is samyama over the five elements. In the science of alchemy, the progression of the elements were accomplished in three stages:

Elements	Alchemical Process
Earth to Water	Digestion
Water to Air	Distillation
Air to Fire	Calcination

As a result of this exercise of *samyama*, the worshiper becomes master over the elements. Having intensely concentrated on the essence of physical matter, the worshiper breaks free from the physical confines of the material world. (YS, 3.45.) This is exactly the process exercised by legitimate doctors of the alchemical arts practiced in the Middle Ages. It is another process extrapolated in RV 1.140.2. The alchemical layer of meaning progress is summarized in this chart:

Two-fold generated	Agni representing the unity of heaven and earth, the sun and the moon
Devours triple food	Refers to the triple Alchemical Process. Stage One: Finding, grinding, and distilling an herb or metal in a vessel with spirits. Stage Two: Burning the product through calcination, producing a purified rasa. Stage Three: Further distillation of the purified rasa to a powder (bhasma).
Renovates the food when year expires	Refers to the powder (bhasma) which possesses the purifying powers.
The Showerer is invigorated by eating with the tongue of another	Refers to the purifying powers of the powder (bhasma), which is to invigorate the human body, confer siddhis, immorality, or to transmute base metals to gold.
The restrainer con-sumes the forest trees.	Refers to the powder (bhasma) of rasa, the ultimate object of the alchemical process, and the mechanical alchemical process at the furnace through the process of Fire.

Triplets abound in the alchemical process. The "triple food" could refer to the progression of the elements in the alchemical fire. The triple nature of this method of purification also implicates the Three-Dimensional Universe.

The Vedic alchemist, the cousin of the Vedic astrologer, appreciates the role of Fire in the alchemical process. The Fire of the alchemical process is Agni, the Sun. Fire is a necessary element to alchemical process. Fire is used in the alchemical process to find the Philosopher's Stone. The ultimate characteristic of Agni, the Sun, the Fire of Change, is Fire itself, and fire is used in the alchemy sciences in the progression towards spiritual renewal, which is culminated in the Philosopher's Stone itself. In Western alchemical traditions, the elements are symbolized as aspects of triangles: Fire, an upward triangle, air, an upward triangle with a line through it, water a downward triangle, and earth a downward triangle with a line through it. In Western traditions, the combination of these symbols resulted in the Seal of Solomon, symbolic of the combination of all elements in a holistic unity and the Philosopher's Stone.

Similarly, RV 3.20.2 states Agni, the Sun, the Fire of Change, has three tongues. Sayana interprets this rc (mantra) as referring to the flame of fire originating from the three altars, the Grhapatya, Ahavaniya, and Daksinagni. This rc (mantra) also indicates that the three tongues emerge from their three abodes — the Grhapatya, Ahavaniya, and Daksinagni — upon which is placed three viands — *ghrta*, butter and Purification (Soma) — which create the three forms — *pavaka*, *pavama*, and *suci*. It thus becomes apparent that the Tongues of Agni is more than the flame of a fire. The tongue of Agni, the Sun, the Fire of Change, is active catalyst of the fire of change in creation, the dynamic force of evolution. The evolution of Agni, the Sun, the Fire of Change, produces three forms of creation in *pavaka*, Pavaka is the purifying agent, which produces the pavamana, an epithet for the purifying essence of Soma. Afterwards, suci, the highest state of purification, is reached. In later Vedic traditions, this composite of the triple nature of purification is represented in the Sri Yantra, a symbolic focal point to foster mental and spiritual purification. For the Nakshatras the five-fold nature of purification is the domain of Ajikapada as the dispenser of Protection, through the astral offices of the asterism P. Bhadrapada and zodiacal houses of Kumba (Aquarius) and Mina (Pisces).

Fourth Method: The Transcendental Power of Purification

There is another, ultimate, interpretation of RV 1.140.2. This process speaks simply of the purification process itself. The process of purification is accomplished in five stages. The number is significant. Five is the number of the dimension prior to liberation at the Seven-Dimensional Universe. The process is summarized in the following chart:

Two-fold generated	Polar opposites are united
Devours triple food	The internal dynamics of spiritual clarity (grhta) and inner purity (Soma) begin to operate
Renovates the food when year expires	Mental and Spiritual regeneration, the product of these internal dynamics, is received by the worshiper
The Showerer is invigorated by eating with the tongue of another	Mental and Spiritual strength arrives to the worshiper
The restrainer consumes the forest trees.	The worshiper is mentally and spiritually born again, twice-born, casting away the previous self

This level of meaning has been discussed a little earlier. The "trees" represent the presence of distracting thoughts and mental impressions. Just as an individual cannot see the "forest for the trees," the purifying fires of Agni clears the unrestrained, untrained thoughts, and allow the self-realization of the worshiper. As so many things in the Vedas, the similes used have their material, every-day correlate. While a forest fire is a terrible terrestrial, physical, fire, whenever Agni "burns the trees," the mind is clear, the unnecessary, irrelevant thoughts are cleared, and what remains after the conflagration is the clear, crystalline mind of self-realization, enlightenment, awareness. One may use whatever adjective one wishes; the fire of Agni is the fire of purification.

Fifth Method: Consumption of the Trees and Rebirth

As anyone living in the State of California can readily attest, or, indeed, anywhere in the contemporary world plagued by Climate Change, the passing of every summer sees the number, intensity, and extent of forest fires increase. The fire seasons are lasting longer and become more and more intense and destructive. While there are many man-made causes for this phenomenon, some of the causes are purely changes in atmospheric conditions. The world-wide increasing intensity and destruction of fires underscore Change and Transformation at work. All the Change and Transformation we witness in the weather conditions is yet another manifestation of the Lunar house of Agni at work. As to the forest fires in California, one explanation which is receiving more and more currency is the change in forest management. In the last seventy years State and federal forest management underwent a policy change. Time was that the respective departments of forest management would hold "controlled burns" of forest and grass lands. Before the introduction of human habitation, fires would occasionally take place; the sturdier vegetation and trees would survive, and the weaker, more vulnerable would burn. Now, however, without these intermittent, controlled fires, when a fire does occur, the effect is devastating, taking strong and weak vegetation alike. With the presence of intermittent, controlled fires, the forest as a whole would thrive. These controlled fires stimulated the germination of seeds for other trees. In this way, the purification by fire assists the regeneration of life.

This is how the fifth method of purification works. The object is completely consumed by fire, reduced to its basic elements, and reconstituted. Plato compared mortal humans to a plant, whose roots reached to Heaven. The Plant was sprinkled with celestial waters, "a divine semen, which enters the head." Water, with fire, is symbolic of the process of purification, and just as water is sprinkled to purify the subject, so must a fire take place to clear the dry, dead brush, and rejuvenate the forest and allow the forest to grow taller, stronger and in a more healthy manner.

Ajikapada dispenses protection. Other Nakshatras dispense protection. In addition to the named dispensers of protection, the AtharvaVeda gives the names of other dispensers of protections who so dispense their spiritual endowment of protection through the radiances of other Nakshatras:

- Generally, Agni, through the agency of the lunar mansion of Krittika, is aligned with the Vasus, who act through the lunar mansion of Dhanistha, to drive away the enemies which inhabit in all directions. (AV, 19.18.1.)

- Vayu, through the agency of the lunar mansion of Svasti (Srati), drives away the enemies from the Mid-World (the firmament) from the power bestowed from the Nakshatra of Svasti (Srati). (AV, 19.18.2.)

- Soma, through the auspices of the lunar mansion of Mrgashirsha, aligns with Rudra through the lunar mansion of Ardra, to drive away those enemies arriving from the Southern direction. (AV, 19.18.3.)

- Varuna through the asterism of Shatabhisha, aligns with the Adityas to drive away the enemies who arrive at any direction. (AV, 19.18.4.) This is not a reference to Aditi, representative of the lunar mansion of Punavasu. The Vedic astrologer knows the Adityas are the collective representative of the Houses of the Zodiac. (Murthy, *Vedic View of the Earth* (1997).)

- The Waters, Apas, act in conjunction with the plants in the lower world, and act through its lunar mansion in Purva Ashada, to drive away those enemies from that lower world. (AV, 19.18.6.)

- The Seven Rishis, the Vedic astronomical code-word for the Big Dipper (RV, 3.7.2), located at the lunar mansions of Krittika, Rohini and Mrgashirsha, and aligned with the zodiacal house of Vrsabha (Taurus), drives away enemies from the Northern Direction. (AV, 19.18.7.)

- Indra, though the lunar mansion at Jyestra, with the eternal assistance from the Maruts, drive away the enemies from their respective directions. (AV, 19.18.8.)

- Prajapati, through the lunar mansion of Rohini, has regenerative properties, and those properties, in conjunction with the spiritual endowments which are otherwise dispensed through Rohini, the give-and-take of *yajna*, drive away the enemies from the "fixed" region, *druva*. (AV 19.18.9.) *Druva* is another name for the Pole Star. (*https://en.wikipedia.org/wiki/Dhruva*.) This power of protection is significant due to the inherent powers for guidance, spiritual and otherwise, associated with the Pole Star.

- Brhaspati, through the powers of the Nakshatra Pushya, in alignment with the lunar mansion of Uttara Ashada, through the Visvedevas, and other powers, drive away the enemies from the upward regions. (AV, 19.18.10.)

The next two Nakshatras dispense protection, in ever more nuanced qualities. The dispensation of Uttara Bhadrapada is made in conjunction with zodiacal house of Mina (Pisces) and planetary sphere of Jupiter, whereas the protection of Revati is made in conjunction with the zodiacal houses of Kumba (Aquarius) and Mina (Pisces) and planetary sphere of Mars.

In his Capacity of Ruling The Uttara Bhadrapada Asterism, the Lunar House of Ahir Budhyana Dispenses, and the Worshiper Learns, the Spiritual Endowment of *Susarma* (Protection.)

Ahir Budhyana is a serpent God, belonging to the depths of the sea and one of Rudras. (*https://en.wikipedia.org/wiki/List_of_Nakshatras.*) Ahir Budhyana dispenses *susarma*, or providing refuge or protection. The Lunar house of Rudra, the presiding deity of the planet Jupiter, provides assistance in this dispensation. Indra is an incarnation of the fire of Agni, the Sun. The Vedic astrologer knows Ahir Budhyana as the dispenser of Protection, through the astral offices of the asterism Uttara Bhadrapada and zodiacal house of Mina (Pisces). Ahir Budhyana is a serpent. Vrtra is a serpent. Vrtra, if not only evil represents the very antithesis of everything the Vedic dharma represents. Ahir Budhyana's allegiance to Rudra indicates a somewhat malevolent character. This is how Ahir Budhyana should be considered. In the vast spectrum of Good versus Evil Ahir Budhyana represents the middle, the bridge between the veil cast by Vrtra and the brightness which is the inner essence of the Vedic dharma. This Ahir Budhyana does through the protect which is dispensed to the worshiper through the power of the Uttara Bhadrapada asterism.

The next Nakshatra, Revati, provides protection as well, also through the planetary influence of Mars.

In his Capacity of Ruling the Revati Asterism, the Lunar house of Pusan Dispenses, and the Worshiper Learns, the Spiritual Endowment of *Bhaga* (Enjoyment).

Pusan administers the Vedic Principle of Direction and Pathways, *dishah*. The Vedic astrologer knows Pusan as dispensing *Bhaga*, or Enjoyment. We encountered *Bhaga* once before as a Vedic force. As an operating principle *Bhaga* carries the same meaning. *Bhaga* is not just about having a good time but includes a cluster of qualities, all of which apply here as well.

Pusan is related to Savitr and Surya, the Lunar houses of the Sun. The Lunar House of Pusan thus dispenses *Bhaga* as a manifestation of the Fire of Agni in the firmament, and also through the asterism of Revati in conjunction with the zodiacal house of Mina (Pisces). According to the Vishnu Purana (6.5.) there are six aspects to *Bhaga*:

- Dominion.
- Might.
- Glory.
- Splendor.
- Wisdom.
- Dispassion.

The Lunar House of Pusan, with the power of the Hasta asterism, dispenses *Bhaga*, and aligns with other Vedic Forces to dispense other spiritual endowments:

- The Lunar House of Pusan aligns with the Lunar House of Soma, the Moon, through the power of the asterism of Mrgashirsha, to create all Creatures. (RV 2.40.5.)

After bestowing duration to the life of humans, Savitr conducts the remains of the worshiper's worshiper's mortal coil, upon which, in alignment, guidance, and protection of the Lunar House of Pusan (AGS 4.4.7.), the smoke of the cremated body moves upwards to the heavenly world (RV 10.17.4). The alignment is not limited to the disposition of the worshiper's body. Also through the power of the asterism of Hasta,

- The Lunar House of Pusan aligns with the wealth obtained from Agni, the Sun (RV 1.12.1), to dispense that wealth to the worshiper. (RV 1.89.6.)
- The Lunar House of Pusan aligns with the combined powers of food, Agni, the Sun to operate to eradicate and forgive sin. (RV 1.106.4.)
- The Lunar House of Pusan dispenses Bhaga through the planetary sphere of Mars, under Rudra's oversight.

The Lunar House of Pusan is not the only Lunar house dispensing Bhaga. The next asterism explains.

In his Capacity of Ruling the Asvini Asterism, the Lunar house of Asvins Dispenses, and the Worshiper Learns, the Spiritual Endowment of *Bhaga* (Enjoyment.)

The Asvins. The Twins represent the duality present in the Vedic dharma and are frequently associates for Indra. They too dispense the qualities of *Bhaga*, but though the asterism of Asvini, and through the zodiacal house of Mesa (Aries), in conjunction with assistance from Indriani, Indra's consort, the presiding deity of Venus.

The Asvins, the twin horsemen, are often associated with their healing abilities. (RV 1.112.8, 15; 1.116.10, 15, 16; 1.117.9, 13, 17, 18; 1.118.6-8; 5.74.5; 5.68.6; 5.71.5; 10.39.3, 4, 8; 10.40.8.) Because they are two they represent the principle of duality in the world. In this duality:

- The Asvins expel sin, give benefits, grant dwellings, the Knower of many things and fulfills desires. (RV 1.158.1.)
- They produce "wealth," (RV 1.158.2) the generic word of wealth here meaning granting a higher state of consciousness and awareness, mental and spiritual.
- Asvins are *Vrsaa*, the Showerer of benefits. (RV 1.173.2; 1.181.8.)
- The divine aspect of duality, the Asvins are one of the Vedic forces comprised in the Principle of Regeneration. (RV 1.181.6; 6.47.7; 8.76.1, 4; 10.106.2, 3.)

The foregoing qualities are summarized in the First Mandala, where it states that the Asvins perform the following functions (RV 1.158.1, 2):

- The Asvins expel and expiate sins. Many Hatha Yogic texts state that proper practice of pranayama destroys sins.
- The Asvins dispense spiritual endowments. Many passages of the Vedas indicate how Indra, the presiding Lunar house over Jupiter and dispenses Happiness through the power of Jyestra, acts in unison with the Asvins, who dispense Bhaga through Asvini and come to Indra's assistance. The attribute of the Asvins is indispensable to the maintenance and support of Indra. Indra, acting in unison with the Asvins, causes the waters to ascend

upwards to the mind (RV 1.32.8), a reference of the surge of the kundalini Sakti up the susumna.

- The Asvins grant dwellings. In the symbolic language of the Veda, "dwelling" is symbolic of the human body. As the personification of pranayama, this rc signifies the bodily benefits that pranayama confers.
- The Asvins know all things. The waters, once it arrives to the mind, enables the mind to create and know all forms. (AV 15.3.)
- The Asvins fulfill desires.
- The Asvins produce wealth. This is not material wealth. It is spiritual wealth. There are many such words for wealth. Here, the particular synonym for wealth has the alternate meaning of "brilliance," symbolic for the light of consciousness.
- The Asvins guide the worshiper along the northern path of the gods. (RV 1.184.6; 3.58.5.)

Theirs is not a gross, material duality. The gross manifestation of duality appears in the material world. The Asvins represent the subtle form of duality, which is in reality a unity, two aspects of a single force, such as Siva and Sakti, Ying and Yang, etc. It is what is called Divine Duad.

The Asvins represent the power, function and benefits of *pranayama*. Possessing the dual nature of duality, they represent the Vital Airs of prana and apana. Prana and apana are not the equivalent of the simple act of breathing in and out. The Vital Air is the subtle internal ventilation which is constantly in motion. *Puraka* and *recaka* is a mechanical process represented in Vayu. The Asvins represent the benefits of the practice of pranayama. The function of pranayama is to condition the mind to tolerate higher levels of consciousness for prolonged periods of time. The perfection of pranayama sustains the mind and maintains a healthy condition. Thus, the Asvins supply the concentration and intensity of mind (*gharma*) needed for the soul to follow, sustain, and incorporate the energy of Agni, the Sun, to tolerate higher states of mental awareness. (RV 1.180.4.) They represent the mind's Higher Consciousness, which is referred to in the Rg Veda as *brhat*, or "vast."

These qualities of the Asvins are significant. The Asvins are responsible for any movement that may occur while traveling the path to *Rta*, the inner essence of the Vedic dharma. (RV 8.22.7.) Without their intervention travel on this path cannot occur.

According to Sayana, Self-Realization is the knowledge gained through pranayama. The Asvins represent this Self-Realization achieved through the process by pranayama.

- The Asvins sustain the vitality of all living creatures and sustain and quench the digestive fire. (RV 1.116.8; 1.157.5.)
- Thus yogis and the learned practice pranayama the create and kindle the digestive fire in order to achieve Self-Realization. (RV 1.181.9.)

The Asvins are instrumental in regulating the intensity of *gharma*, the internal heat created the worshiper who has gained Self-Realization through *Tapas*, intense spiritual practice. The Asvins are associated with the practices of *Tapas*:

- The consistent practice of *Tapas*, the intense and sustained mental meditation and religious austerities increases the mental strength, concentration, and acuity of mind. (RV 1.164.26.)
- The Asvins are uniquely equipped with *Tapas* and the illumination of Knowledge. (RV1.112.1.)
- The Asvins furnish (RV 1.112.7) and harness, temper (RV 1.119.6), the intensity of *Tapas* with Agni, the Sun. The process of Agni, the Sun, can at times be overbearing and uncontrollable. The intensity of the experience of Self-Realization must be measured to avoid complete breakdown.
- The Asvins regulate the *Tapas* generated by Agni, the Sun. (RV 8.73.3.)

The Asvins perform their actions with the power of the asterism Asvini. Classically, Asvini had always been considered the "first" Nakshatra. So why is it in the bottom of this list of asterisms? Millennia and millennia have passed since the time the Rg Veda was first revealed. It is the consensus of most scholars who have analyzed the astronomical coordinates and data and doctrinal references far deeper than offered by the Vedic astrologer that the positions of the stars relative to the observers on earth has changed to such a degree that Krittika was considered the first Nakshatra. And so is it treated by the Vedic astrologer.

In his Capacity of Ruling the Bharani Asterism, the Lunar house of Yama Dispenses, and the Worshiper Learns, the Spiritual Endowment of Spiritual Riches.

Yama is a god of death, the south direction, and the underworld. (*https://en.wik-ipedia.org/wiki/Yama*.) The Vedic astrologer however knows Yama as the provider of spiritual riches. This is what the Vedic astrologer means when he says, "spiritual riches." It is an often-misunderstood phraseology in the Veda, those references to "property, riches, treasures," and the like. The frequent Code-Word for these spiritual riches is translated from the Sanskrit root, vrs/, which is translates as the Bull. Thus, Yama dispenses these gifts through the zodiacal house of Mesa (Aries). This spiritual endowment is also made through the power of the asterism Bharani and through the Vedic force of Indriani, Indra's consort, the presiding deity of Venus. It seems oddly fitting that the worshiper would be endowed with these gifts on death, many times the real end of the spiritual journey.

The worshiper's soul passage to heaven is a three-step process. (Merh, *Yama, The Glorious Lord of the Other World*, (2006), p. 134.)

- Upon death, Yama escorts the worshiper's soul first to the highest heaven. (RV 10.14.1, 2.)
- Yama then sends the worshiper's soul to the Region of the Eternal Light. (RV 9.113.7.) The Region of the Eternal Light is Svar, that region which in the beginning of this chapter was translated in so many words.
- After arriving at the Svar, the worshiper's final destination is in the *sukrta loka* (RV 10.85.24), the true "heaven" in the Rg Veda. And heaven indeed it is. *Sukrta* is literally the "Home of Rta," the inner essence of the Vedic dharma. On receiving grace or salvation it is here that the worshiper's soul is reposed.

From an astronomical viewpoint, once liberated the worshiper's soul occupies a divine region called "Vaikuntha." "Vaikuntha" is that space beyond the material universe which is free from those physical processes which initiate the repeated cycles of the creation and annihilation of the material world, evolving in repeated cycles again and again and again.

(http://Wikipedia.org, @ Vaikuntha.) Vaikuntha is a manifestation of Indra, and in this manifestation the Lunar house of Indra unlocks the upper levels of the Vedic dharma. The specific powers and manifestations of Indra Vaikuntha are spelled out in Suktas 47 and 48 of the Tenth Mandala of the Rg Veda. In these rcs (mantras), Indra Vaikuntha was revealed with theses powers:

- Indra Vaikuntha is the Lord of the *go* and *gobhir*, the "herds of light in the sky," and possesses the powers of the Right-Handed discrimination. (RV 10.47.1.) We learned early in this book how important this right-handed movement was. It regulates the oscillating movements of the cosmos in the Vedic dharma. It is one half of the movement of Saman. It is one-half of the subtle process that regulates prana, the Vital Life Force.
- Waves of light which shine over the four oceans are the spiritual endowments of Indra Vaikuntha. (RV 10.47.2.) The "four oceans" (*ca/tuHsamudraM*) are the four levels of the Word (*Vak*, the physical manifestation of sound; second with *paravak*, third with *para*, and fourth with *turiya*), discussed earlier in this book.
- These energies and spiritual endowments conquer the forces of evil the worshiper must contend with in the spiritual journey. (RV 10.47.3.)
- With the powers of Indra Vaikuntha the worshiper wins the riches of the vast Vedic dharma and the spiritual capabilities of the worshiper are increased. (RV 10.47.4.)
- Indra Vaikuntha is endowed and dispenses to the worshiper the spiritual endowments of the Horses (*vaa/jam*). (RV 10.47.5.)
- The worshiper seeks the powers of discrimination from Indra Vaikuntha which are used in the spiritual journey. (RV 10.47.7.)
- Indra Vaikuntha is the Supreme Lord of spiritual endowments. These endowments are given to the worshiper for use in the spiritual journey. (RV 10.48.1)
- Indra Vaikuntha released the rays of light which were held by the demon Ahi. (RV 10.48.2.) Ahi can be seen as an alter ego for Vrtra, the concealer of the inner essence of the Vedic dharma.

- Ahi was destroyed with the weapon manufactured by Tvastr. (RV 10.48.3.)
- The strength of Indra Vaikuntha is comparable to the Sun. (RV 10.48.4.)
- The real strength of Indra Vaikuntha is the concentrated beams of light, energy and knowledge, all of which bestow Bliss to the worshiper for the spiritual journey. (RV 10.48.5.)
- These spiritual endowments are given when the worshiper surrenders to Indra Vaikuntha. (RV 10.48.9.)

All this is contrasted to *mahasamadhi*, the simple death of the worshiper whose soul has not yet found liberation. In this situation, the four dogs of Yama, which escorts the unliberated soul of the Vedic astrologer to the heavens beyond. (RV 1.161.13; 1.105.11; 4.57.5; 10.14.11; 10.63.10; 10.84. 4; AV 4.20.7; 8.1.9; 18.2.12; SPB 13.5.8; TA 6.3.2.) Tilak identifies the four dogs of Yama as the Dog Star, Canus Major and Minor which stand guard at the Milky Way, "Path of Aryaman," which is itself located at the Gates of Heaven. (Tilak, *Orion or the Antiquities of the Vedas*, p. 110.)

Day and night play a part in the travel of the soul to the Northern and Southern Paths. (B.U. 6.2.16; C.U, 10.5.3.) The gods are etymologically connected to and associated with "day," as they arrive at their deified status as a result of the eight-day rite (PVB 22.11.1), or the fifteen day rite (PVB 23.6.2), and they became gods in the first place by entering heaven, *div*. (SPB 11.1.6.8; TB 2.3.8.2.) The word for demon, *asura*, the antithesis of divinity, is derived from *a + surya*, or "not light." Darkness, or rather, the absence of light, is associated with evil.

- The King of the demons is *Asita* ("Black.") (SPB 13.4.3.11.)
- After the creation of the demons there was only darkness. (SBP 11.1.6.8.)

The "Day" thus becomes the Northern Path, the Path of the Gods, and "Night" becomes the Southern Path, the Path of the Forefathers and transmigration. The soul reaches liberation and release when it travels northward in the path of the gods where there is light (TS 1.1.7), and it is condemned to be reborn again and again and transmigrate when it traverses the paths of the forefathers. Thus, Yama, Death, is admonished to go on its own path so that the worshiper may travel along the path of the gods unmolested. (RV 10.18.1, 3.)

Day thus becomes the Northern Path and night becomes the Southern Path. The soul reaches liberation and release when it travels northward in the path of the gods where there is light (TS 1.1.7) and is condemned to be reborn again and again when it traverses the paths of the forefathers. Thus, Yama, Death, is admonished to go on the path other than the path of the gods so that the worshiper may travel there unmolested. (RV 10.18.1.) His attention thereby diverted, while Death, Yama, is traversing along the path of the forefathers, the worshiper may enjoy a life full of progeny and bliss (RV 10.18.3), with spiritual riches, pure and free of sin. (RV 10.81.2.) This conclusion became established Upanishadic doctrine in later Upanishads.

The spiritual endowment dispensed by Yama are the spiritual riches. Yama dispenses these spiritual endowments — the spiritual riches on the worshiper — when in alignment with the house of Indra. Indra, through the power of the asterism of Jyestra and in conjunction with the zodiacal house of Vrscika (Scorpio), Indra dispenses Happiness to the worshiper. The Lunar house of Indra dispenses Happiness through another astronomical member — Sirius the Dog Stars. Sirius is consists of a pair of stars, Sirius A and Sirius B. These are the very same guardians of the worshiper's soul in its travel to heaven.

In the Vedic dharma, the Dog stars are named *Shuna* and *Sira*. *Shuna*, Sirius A, is considerably brighter than Sirius B, *Sira*, and was highly regarded by the ancient Vedic Rishiis, and is held in high regard by the Vedic astrologer. The reason is that the Dog stars and in particular Sirius A, *Shuna*, were — and are still — considered to be the Guardians of the Path to the Gods. In the Vedic dharma, that path is the Northern Path, the *devayana*, the path to liberation.

You may legitimately ask, Dear Reader, what this has to do with Indra, who dispenses Happiness through the power of the asterism of Jyestra. Everything. *Shuna*, as most words in the Rg Veda, has a variety of meanings. Monier Williams defines *Shuna* as

- Associated with canines, dogs.
- Auspicious.

- Happiness.

Shuna, Sirius A, is associated with a host Lunar houses. *Shuna* is associated with:

- The Lunar house of Indra, the presiding deity of Jupiter, dispenser of Happiness through the power of the asterism of Jyestra and in conjunction with the zodiacal house of Vrscika (Scorpio). (RV 3.30.22; 3.31.22; 2.32.17; 3.34.11; 3.36.11; 3.38.10; 3.29.9; 3.43.8; 3.48.5; 3.39.5; 3.50.5; 6.16.4; 10.89.18; 10.104.11; 10.160.5.)
- The Lunar house of Agni, the Sun, dispenser of the secrets of yajna and divine response, through the power of the asterism of Krittika and the zodiacal houses of Mesa (Aries) and Vrsabha (Taurus). (RV 4.3.11.)
- The Lunar house of Varuna, who dispenses Greatness through the power of the asterism of Shatabhisha and the zodiacal house of Kumba (Aquarius). (RV 10.126.7.)
- The Lunar house of Mitra, who dispenses Response, through the power of the asterism of Anuradha and in conjunction with the zodiacal house of Vrscika (Scorpio). (RV 10.126.7.)
- The Lunar house of Aryaman, who dispenses Good Works through the power of the asterism of Uttara Phalguna and the zodiacal houses of Simha (Leo) and Kanya (Virgo). (RV 10.126.7.)

That *Shuna*, Sirius A, also means the Guardian of the Northern Path, *devayana*, adds an additional layer of meaning which serves to instruct the worshiper during the spiritual search. Again, the iconic battle with Vrtra contributes to the worshiper's spiritual journey. In an amazing series of Suktas, in overcoming Vrtra the Lunar house of Indra recovers spiritual riches which had been concealed and have far-reaching implications to the maintenance of the Vedic dharma. The Suktas which follow define, literally to the item, what are those "spiritual riches." Those "(spiritual) riches" are:

- As the Lord of Existence (*saltpatish*) as a result of the death of Vrtra Indra creates the preconditions for life in the Vedic dharma. (RV 3.34.9.)
- The Waters, the subtle, essential nature of the Vedic dharma, which were held by Vrtra. (RV 3.30.9; 3.31.16; 3.33.12.)
- Releasing the Waters which were held by Vrtra. (RV 3.32.6, 18; 3.33.13; 3.34.2; 1.100.6, 18; 2.21.4.)
- The *disha*, the networks of subtle energy crisscrossing Time-Space, which were held by Vrtra. (RV 3.30.12; 3.31.18.)
- The purifying powers of the Waters which were held by Vrtra. (RV 3.31.20.)

These acts occurred early in the creation of the Vedic dharma. The death of Vrtra had implications which enabled Indra to set up the subtle basis of the Vedic dharma. As the Vedic astrologer explained early in this book, the killing of Vrtra spurred the initial separation of "What was not" into "What was" (RV 6.24.5), even before the indiscriminate mass of matter started coagulating into Rta, Satya and the other elementals blocks of the Vedic dharma. (RV 10.129.1.) This is what is meant when it is revealed in the most general manner that Indra created the Vedic dharma in "days of old." (RV 3.38.5.) Having created the subtle basis of the Vedic dharma, Indra shaped the levels of existence.

- The lunar house of Indra wins the domain of Heaven and Earth which was held captive by Vrtra. (RV 3.30.5, 9; 3.32.8, 10.)
- The lunar house of Indra wins the Svar which was held by Vrtra. (RV 3.34.4.)
- As a result of conquering Vrtra, the lunar house of Indra took control of the secrets of Heaven and Earth and united the two to create the three existential levels of Earth, Mid-World and Heaven. (RV 3.38.3.)

Indra then set about creating the gross objects of the sky.

- As a result of the lunar house of Indra conquering Vrtra, he was able to separate light from darkness. (RV 3.39.7.)

- The lunar house of Indra wins the Sun (*surya*) which was held by Vrtra. (RV 3.34.9.)
- The lunar house of Indra lays claim to the Earth (*pRthivii/M*) which was held by Vrtra. (RV 3.34.8; 3.44.3.)
- The lunar house of Indra lays claim to the Heaven (*dyaa/m*) which was held by Vrtra. (RV 3.34.8; 3.44.3.)
- The lunar house of Indra wins the Mid-World (*anta/rikSam*) which was held by Vrtra. (RV 3.34.10.)

At this stage on a very rudimentary level the lunar house of Indra is allowed to create the general structure of the Vedic dharma. Conquering Vrtra also allowed Indra to create the Stellar population. The Veda describes the manner in which light was created. Brilliant white radiance pervaded Vayra, Indra's weapon, which enabled Indra to find Soma, which was released by resplendent pressing stones, and thereupon released the light of the *go* or the *gobhir*, the "herds of light." (RV 3.44.5.) This is the meaning of the lunar house of Indra "releasing" the light which was concealed by Vrtra. Vrtra's death then released specific types of light.

- The light, generally, was released which was held by Vrtra. (RV 3.30.19; 3.31.9.)
- The lunar house of Indra creates the light present in the Vedic dharma which forms the basis of the worshiper's bliss and the bliss of all sentient persons. (RV 3.34.4.)
- The lunar house of Indra creates the light of *ghrta* which was held by Vrtra. (RV 3.31.10.)
- The lunar house of Indra creates the Light of the Cows, *go* or the *gobhir*, the "herds of light" which was held by Vrtra. (RV 3.30.10, 20; 3.31.5, 11; 3.34.3.)

Having created the Stellar population the lunar house of Indra set about to work on the worshiper and other sentient beings. The key element are the "Impulsions." "Impulsions" are defined as the presence, movement and force of consciousness of knowledge and thoughts of sentient beings.

- The horses (Strength, and the power of knowledge) which were held by Vrtra. (RV 3.30.2, 6, 20; 3.34.9; 3.35.1 – 5.)
- The lunar house of Indra releases the power of impulsions in the vastness of the Vedic dharma which were held by Vrtra. (RV 3.30.11.)
- The lunar house of Indra creates the impulsions in all sentient beings, including the worshiper, which were held by Vrtra. (RV 3.34.5.)
- In creating the impulsions in all sentient beings, the lunar house of Indra, as a result of the death of Vrtra, creates the words in the worshiper's speech (*vi/vaaco/*), which were held by Vrtra. (RV 3.34.10.)

"Impulsions" is a quasi-symbolic term. "Impulsions" are the medium through which the thoughts, feelings, and desires of the worshiper and all other sentient being make their presence in the mind. When Vrtra was overtaken by Indra the worshiper and sentient beings gained their thoughts. The thoughts of the worshiper and sentient beings are symbolized in different ways by the Veda. "Impulsions" are frequently described symbolically in watery terms.

- The lunar house of Indra releases the Rivers, symbol of the flow of Consciousness, which were held by Vrtra. (RV 3.33.1, 4, 6, 8, 10, 12.)
- The lunar house of Indra releases the Ocean, symbol of higher Consciousness, which was held by Vrtra. (RV 3.32.16; 3.33.2, 3.)
- The lunar house of Indra yokes, restrains, the thoughts of the sentient beings and worshiper which while held by Vrtra were uncontrolled and unrestrained. (RV 3.35.4.)

From this point, the killing of Vrtra allows for the worshiper's spiritual development and education.

- The lunar house of Indra allowed the possibility of spiritual increase in the worshiper, which had been restrained by Vrtra. (RV 3.34.1.)

- The lunar house of Indra won the inner secrets of *yajna*, Sacrifice, which were held by Vrtra. (RV 3.30.15; 3.32.12; 3.34.2.)
- The lunar house of Indra guides the worshiper during the spiritual journey along the "path of Indra," which in this context would be the *devayana*, or Northern Path. (RV 3.30.15.)
- With the passing of Vrtra, the lunar house of Indra spreads the light of *yajna* throughout the expanse of the Vedic dharma. (RV 3.39.8.)
- As a result of these spiritual riches the lunar house of Indra won happiness for the worshiper and sentient beings as a result of Vrtra dying. (RV 3.30.18.)

These and others are the "spiritual riches" dispensed by the lunar house of Yama. The greatest endowment of the lunar house of Yama is the Vedic dharma itself, at a time when the worshiper needs those spiritual riches the most. What better representation of the Vedic dharma other than Speech, the Word, Vak, itself. Vak is the over-arching representation of Vedic dharma, the natural order (Rta).

- The Vedic dharma begins at Vaikhari, the underlying basis of material existence present in the Two-Dimensional Universe, where the worshiper experiences the insane tug and pull of maya.
- The worshiper begins to break free of the chains of maya, the worshiper begins to live and experience in the material world reflected in the Three-Dimensional Universe.
- Through meditation the worshiper discovers the subtle basis of the material world in the Five-Dimensional Universe.
- Through intense worship, ritual and meditation (*Tapas*) the worshiper, if lucky, transcends and is teleported to liberation in the Seven-Dimensional Universe.

This entry represents the worshiper's final destination.

Life is a journey, and every journey has a destination. In the Vedic world, that final destination is the seven-dimensional universe, call it Heaven, the translucent realm of divinity, of light, the world of the gods, nirvana, the Atman, whatever you want. It is the original source of the worshiper's soul, and when the worshiper's soul arrives at the door of the seven-dimensional universe, it returns to the place where it once began its journey. It is here that the worshiper's soul belongs. When the brahmanas speak of re-integrating the body to Prajapati. This is coded language to signify re-uniting with the Vedic dharma, the natural order (*Rta*). When it was said in the very beginning that enlightenment and understanding obtained from the natural order (*Rta*), this is the full import. The Vedic worshiper is to know and understand the dharma which surrounds and implement the vital forces and rhythms in its life. In much later times, the Dante in his Divine Comedy will describe this arrival as the soul joining with the love that moves the stars. The Vedic astrologer understands very well what Dante meant to say. That most ancient wisdom is locked in the stars, and the Vedic astrologer identifies that wisdom in the Nakshatras. This is what the Vedic astrologer seeks to discover and what the worshiper seeks to implement. When the worshiper taps into that wisdom when traveling the *devyama*, the Path of the Gods, the worshiper is one with the love that moves the cosmos. This is what is meant when the worshiper strives to incorporate the wisdom of the Vedic dharma and live in balance with that wisdom. It is at that point that the journey is over, at least for the moment. If there are no more lessons to learn, the soul is liberated and dwells for eternity with the Absolute Self, at peace. If not, the worshiper's soul gets ready for the next journey, and it tries again.

ABBREVIATIONS

AA	Aitatreya Aranyaka
AB	Aitatreya Brahmana
AU	Aitatreya Upanishad
AV	Atharva Veda
BB	Brhad Brahmana
BD	Brhad Devata
BJ	Brihat Jataka
Br.S.	Brhat Samhita
BPHS	Brihat Parasara Hora Sastra
BU	Brhad Aranyaka Upanishad
CU	Chandogya Upanishad
GB	Gopatha Brahmana
JB	Jaiminiya Brahmana
JUB	Jaiminiya Upanishad Brahmana
KA	Katha Aranyaka
KB	Kaustika Brahmana
KGS	Kathaka Ghyra Samhita
KS	Kathaka Samhita
MB	Mahabharata
MS	Maitrayani Samhita
Nir.	Nirukta
P	Parasaratantra
RV	Rg Veda

RVJ	Jyotisha Rig Veda
RVK	Khila Sutras of the Rg Veda
SA	Sakhaya Aranyaka
SB	Sadvimsa Brahmana
SBP	Sri Bhagavatam Purana
SK	Samkhya Karika
SPB	Satapatha Brahmana
SS	Surya Siddhanta
SSS	Sakhayana Srautasutra
SST	Sri Svacchanda Tantra
SV	Sama Veda
TA	Tattiritya Aranyaka
TB	Tattiriya Brahmana
TL	Tantraloka
TS	Tattiriya Samhita
TS	Tantrasara
VS	Vajasaneyi Samhita
Vas. S	Vasistha Samhita
Vas. Yoga	Vasistha Yoga
YS	Yoga Sutras
YV	Yajur Veda

Printed in the United States
By Bookmasters